IMAGES
of America

MACEDON

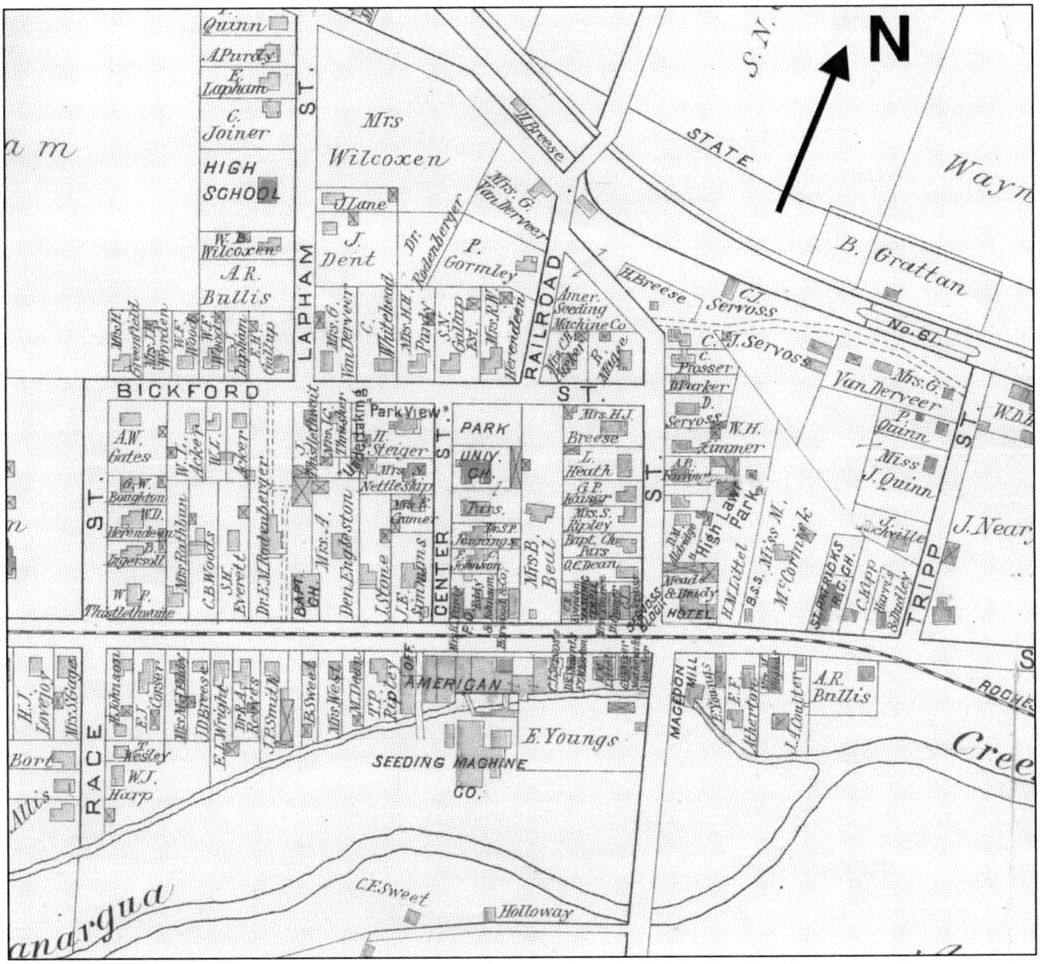

This map shows the heart of Macedon Village in 1904. Main Street runs horizontally across the page, and the Rochester, Syracuse & Eastern trolley tracks are indicated in the middle of the thoroughfare. Erie Street crosses Ganargua Creek at the bottom of the map and extends vertically across Main Street to end at Railroad Avenue, which crosses the Erie Canal. The high school indicated on Lapham Street no longer exists. Tripp Street is another geographic feature that has vanished; it was located approximately where today's State Routes 350 and 31F meet Route 31. The American Seeding Machine Company, on the south side of Main Street, was the corporate successor to the Bickford and Huffman Drill Works. Just behind its buildings is the raceway for the Macedon Mills, located at the southeast corner of Main and Erie Streets. (From the *Atlas of Wayne County*.)

ON THE COVER: Workers pose at Macedon's Bickford & Huffman Drill Works, a manufacturer of agricultural equipment. The drill works was Macedon's largest employer for many years. The photograph was taken in 1904, during the presidential campaign. Theodore Roosevelt defeated Alton B. Parker. (Courtesy of Macedon Town Historian.)

IMAGES
of America

MACEDON

Reginald W. Neale

ARCADIA
PUBLISHING

ISBN 978-0-7385-9912-0

Published by Arcadia Publishing
Charleston, South Carolina

Printed in the United States of America

Library of Congress Control Number: 2012952041

For all general information, please contact Arcadia Publishing:
Telephone 843-853-2070
Fax 843-853-0044
E-mail sales@arcadiapublishing.com
For customer service and orders:
Toll-Free 1-888-313-2665

Visit us on the Internet at www.arcadiapublishing.com

This book is dedicated to my wife, Mary Lyn Neale.

Contents

ACKNOWLEDGMENTS

This book benefited enormously from the enthusiastic cooperation of June Hamell, Macedon town historian, assistant librarian, and curator of the Bullis Collection at the Macedon Town Library; and Sally Millick, Macedon village historian and curator of the Macedon Historical Society. I owe a great debt to both of these individuals for allowing me access to historical materials, for patiently enduring my numerous requests, and for their general encouragement and consistently helpful suggestions.

I am also indebted to Hod Conant, who generously gave me permission to make digital copies of his amazing personal collection of photo postcards; to Charles Lenhart, for sharing information from his extensive files; to Marlene Zimmer LeMoyne, for allowing me to scan her late father, John Zimmer's, collection of glass plate negatives; to Margaret Hartsough, Town of Farmington historian, for contributing Macedon-related material from her files; and to Joan Moore and Jason Kuntz, both of whom reviewed drafts and made extensive comments.

I also want to acknowledge contributions from the following individuals, who shared historic items, commented on drafts, or otherwise helped to make this book possible: John Blyth, James Brundage, Helen Burgio, John Cieslinski, Roger Delyser, Peter Evans, Jim and Barbara Forshay, Rosalie Gabbert, Judy Gravino, Pete Henry, Betty Hill, Joseph Hill, Floris Lent, Martha and Jim Miller, Joan Moore, Patrick Neale, Sandy Pagano, Dr. Ed Papenfuse, Marjory Allen Perez, Bill Rider, Kathy Roberts, Jim Schmitt, Dave Taber, Barbara Wehrlin, and Judy Wellman.

While acknowledging my considerable debt to everyone listed above, I should emphasize that the accountability for any factual errors in this book rests with me alone. None of the individuals acknowledged here bear any responsibility for the accuracy of this material.

Introduction

In 1788, the end of a legal battle between New York and Massachusetts opened up the Phelps & Gorham Purchase for settlement. This huge tract ran north from the Pennsylvania border to Lake Ontario, and west from Seneca Lake to the Genesee River. Within a year, the numbered townships on the map began to acquire names and permanent settlers. The area that is now Macedon was one of those towns. It began its existence as the western half of Palmyra Township. The Town of Macedon gained its own status in 1823. The Village of Macedon received its charter in 1856 and was officially incorporated in 1876.

Macedon's pioneer settlers, like those in neighboring towns, came mostly from Massachusetts. Many of them were Quakers, members of the Society of Friends. They were attracted by cheap, fertile land and abundant waterpower. Because there were no roads, most settlers traveled to their new homes during the winter and early spring, when the frozen rivers and creeks could support the oxcarts and sleds that carried their belongings. Macedon's first recorded settlers, Webb Harwood and his wife, Hannah, came in 1799 from Adams, Massachusetts. They built a log cabin on what is now Quaker Road, a few hundred yards east of the current intersection of Quaker and O'Neil Roads. A year later, the first federal census recorded the township's population as 14 persons. Almost as soon as they had some kind of roof over their heads, pioneers chose a place to worship, elected a local government, and cooperated to fund a district school.

With few exceptions, the white settlers peacefully coexisted with the indigenous Native American population, whose footpaths became the first rudimentary roads. Macedon was a center of progressive and social activity in the 19th century. Prominent Macedonians were early supporters of such causes as the abolition of slavery, women's suffrage, and fair treatment for Native Americans. In 1847, the Liberty Party gathered at Macedon Locks and nominated Gerrit Smith for president of the United States.

The Erie Canal, built in the 1820s, had an enormous influence on the growth and history of the town. Macedon's prosperity grew as the canal and, later, the New York Central & Hudson Railroad connected it to the wider world. Grain, produce, and machinery from the Macedon area were shipped all over the country. The town's largest population centers, Macedon and Wayneport, were busy terminals on the canal. When 26 canal construction workers died in an epidemic, they were buried together in a cemetery at Wayneport. In 1918, the canal was widened, deepened, and straightened. Some locks were eliminated and others were improved, and the new lock gates were operated by electric motors instead of manually. These changes left some historic remnants of the earlier canal in the Macedon area. Wayneport was also home to an important coaling, watering, and icing station for the New York Central Railroad in the 1900s. While Macedon grew into an incorporated village, Wayneport declined and is now just a crossroads.

In the early 1900s, the Rochester, Syracuse & Eastern Electric Railroad (RS&E) gave Macedonians convenient travel connections to destinations east and west. Two trolley tracks, one for eastbound traffic and one for westbound, ran directly down Main Street. But the RS&E's business plan was overly ambitious. When sufficient commercial traffic failed to materialize and ridership declined, it went out of business in 1930. The electric substation that distributed power to the trolleys in the Macedon area has been repurposed. It can still be seen on Beebe Road west of the village.

Western New York was a manufacturing center for agricultural equipment. Macedon was home to the Bickford & Huffman Company, known locally as the Drill Works. A grain drill is a mechanical implement that plants seeds in a precise repeatable manner. The Drill Works was a major local employer, and it shipped its products to destinations all over the world. In 1903, Bickford & Huffman was acquired by the American Seeding Machine Company, which gradually moved production out of Macedon. It was eventually absorbed by the Oliver Tractor Company. Surviving specimens of the B&H Farmer's Favorite Grain and Fertilizer Drill are prized by collectors.

Macedon Academy was founded in 1841 and lasted more than 50 years. It was located in what is now the hamlet of Macedon Center, about four miles northwest of the village of Macedon. In an era when most district schools taught only up to the eighth grade, the academy's educational mission was roughly the equivalent of today's high schools. Its outstanding curriculum and reputation brought in students from a wide area. The building still stands and is today the home of the Macedon Historical Society.

Although it is impossible to mention every important early Macedon family, a few stand out. Abraham Lapham was a pioneer settler, moving to Macedon in 1795. Dr. Increase Lapham, born in Macedon, was among the first to conduct a systematic study of weather patterns. In 1870, his actions were instrumental in establishing the US Weather Bureau, which is now known as the National Weather Service. Abraham Lapham's sister Hannah was Susan B. Anthony's grandmother, and his great-grandson John Lapham Bullis became a famous soldier in southern Texas. The Bullis family has a distinguished history in Macedon, beginning with Abraham Bullis in 1791.

Many of the historical photographs in this book reflect the fact that America's transition from an agrarian economy to an industrial economy was changing the landscape. In the 20th century, commercial traffic began shifting from the canal and railroads to highways. Macedonians could easily drive to jobs in Fairport, Palmyra, or Rochester. The once close-knit community shown in many of these photographs was slowly changing. As Macedon continues to evolve, we recognize that local history is a community resource. There is renewed interest in the Erie Canal as a recreational and tourist attraction. Preservation efforts are under way at the Macedon Academy building. The Bullis Collection at the Macedon Public Library has its own climate-controlled room. This priceless collection of historical artifacts, documents, and photographs is a wonderful resource for anyone interested in local history. I hope that this book's glimpses into the past will give us a renewed appreciation for those who came before us and will remind us of how important it is to leave a record for those who follow.

One

Old Macedon's Main Street

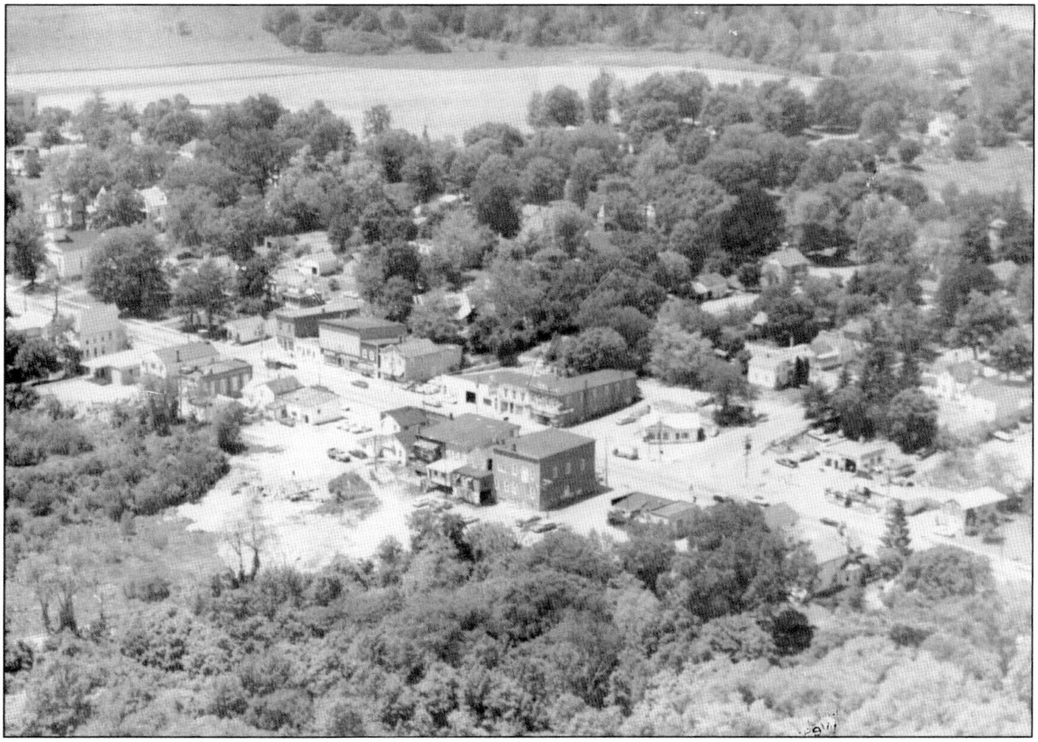

Downtown Macedon is seen from above on a summer day in the 1950s. Lapham Hill is in the background, and part of the canal is visible at the top right. This is before the Route 350 intersection was created on the east side of the village. This aerial photograph was taken by Henry DeWolf, a prolific photographer of villages and farms in upstate New York. (Courtesy of Aerial Surveys.)

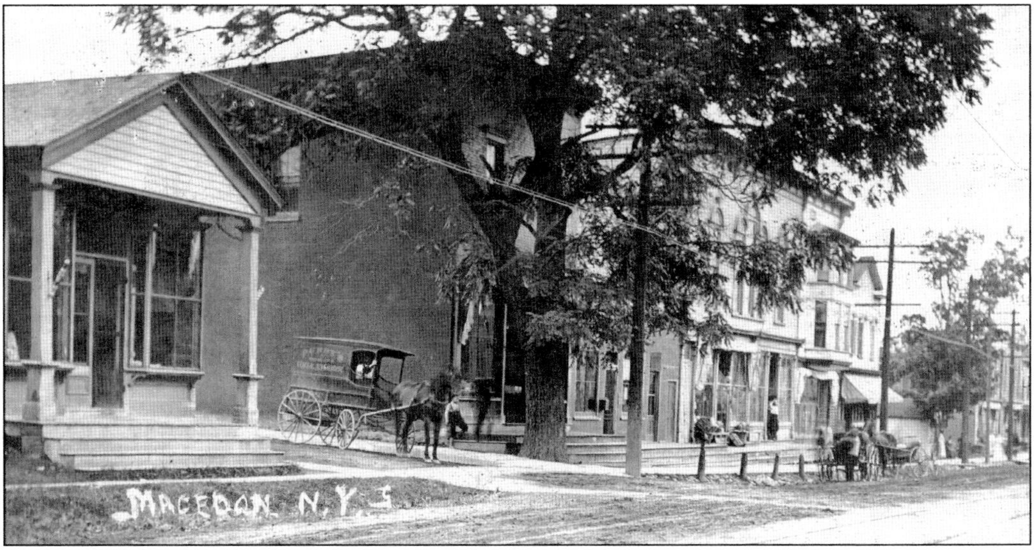

In 1890, Ira Purdy bought land on the east corner of Main and Center Streets and erected a brick building for his business. He sold groceries on the ground floor and dry goods upstairs. Here, Purdy's horse-drawn delivery wagon is coming down Center Street. The store was operated by the Purdy family until 1930. Later, it became the Market Basket grocery, operated by Harriet Crane Fluker. The building was demolished in 1973, and today the space is a parking lot. (Courtesy of Hod Conant.)

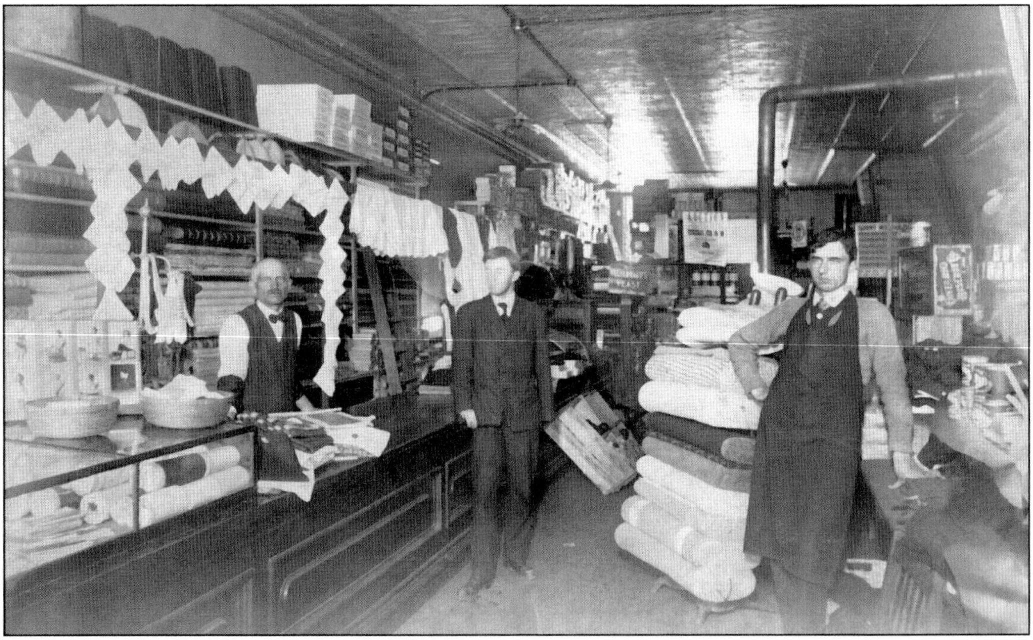

Seen inside the Purdy General Store is Allen Purdy (center), son of Ira Purdy and Hannah Hall Purdy. Allen's left sleeve hangs empty, as he lost his hand in a fireworks explosion. Also shown are L. Clayton Gascoyne (left), Allen's brother-in-law, and David H. Parker. The long counters with shelves behind them and the embossed tin ceiling are typical of stores of that period. A notice in the *Wayne County Journal* in November 1906 notes that electric lights were installed in the H.H. Purdy store and in the J. Simons barbershop. (Courtesy of Macedon Town Historian.)

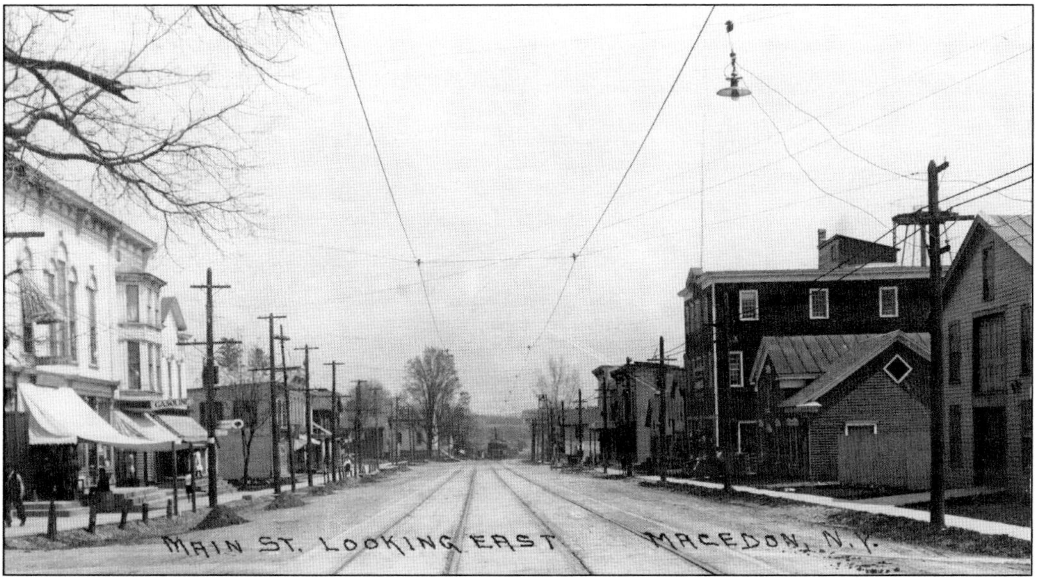

The view in this c. 1910 photograph looks straight down the trolley tracks toward Palmyra, about three miles away. The trolley route east from Macedon to Palmyra eventually became State Route 31. At the time of this photograph, the road to Palmyra for horse-drawn vehicles and automobiles followed Quaker Road, a quarter mile to the north, or Creek Road, a quarter mile to the south. Both sides of Main Street can be seen here, and a trolley is barely visible in the distance. The overhead lines provided electrical power for the trolley and for early streetlights. (Courtesy of Hod Conant.)

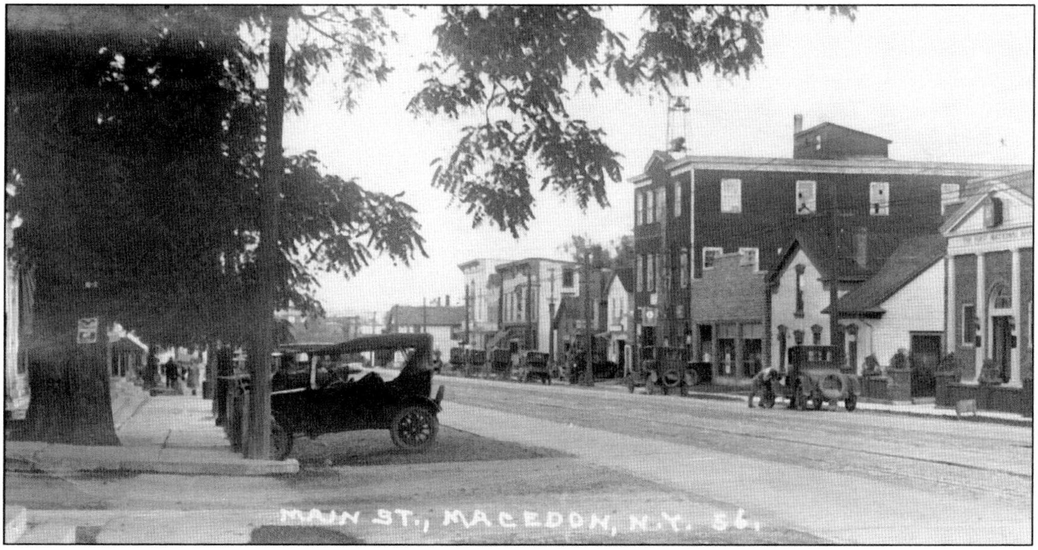

In this 1923 photo postcard, a motorist is working on his vehicle on the right. Macedon seems to have adapted to the new technology, with lots of cars, and no horse-drawn vehicles, on Main Street. At the far right is the First National Bank, which failed in 1931 during the Great Depression. That building is now the Macedon Village Hall. The giant walnut tree at the left, in front of the Purdy store, served for decades as a community bulletin board. When it was cut down around 1959, Benson Gabbert recycled some of the wood and made furniture from it. (Courtesy of Hod Conant.)

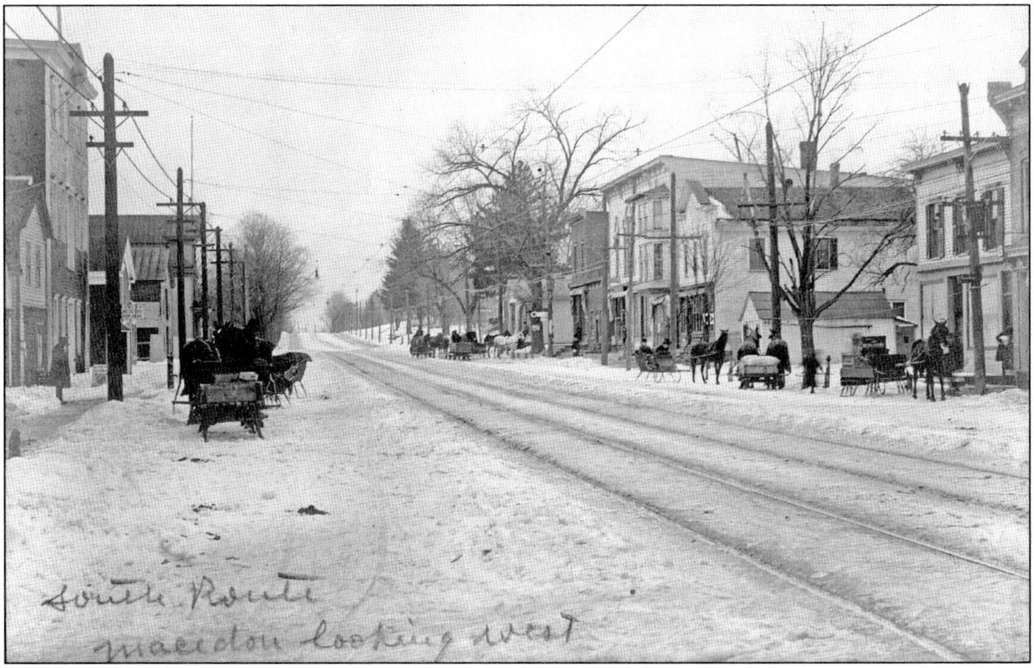

Horse-drawn sleighs and cutters are parked along Main Street in this winter scene from about 1910. A cutter is a small vehicle with runners, designed for one or two persons. A sleigh is larger and has more widely spaced runners. Although there were some automobiles at this time, they were not reliable winter transportation. (Courtesy of Macedon Town Historian.)

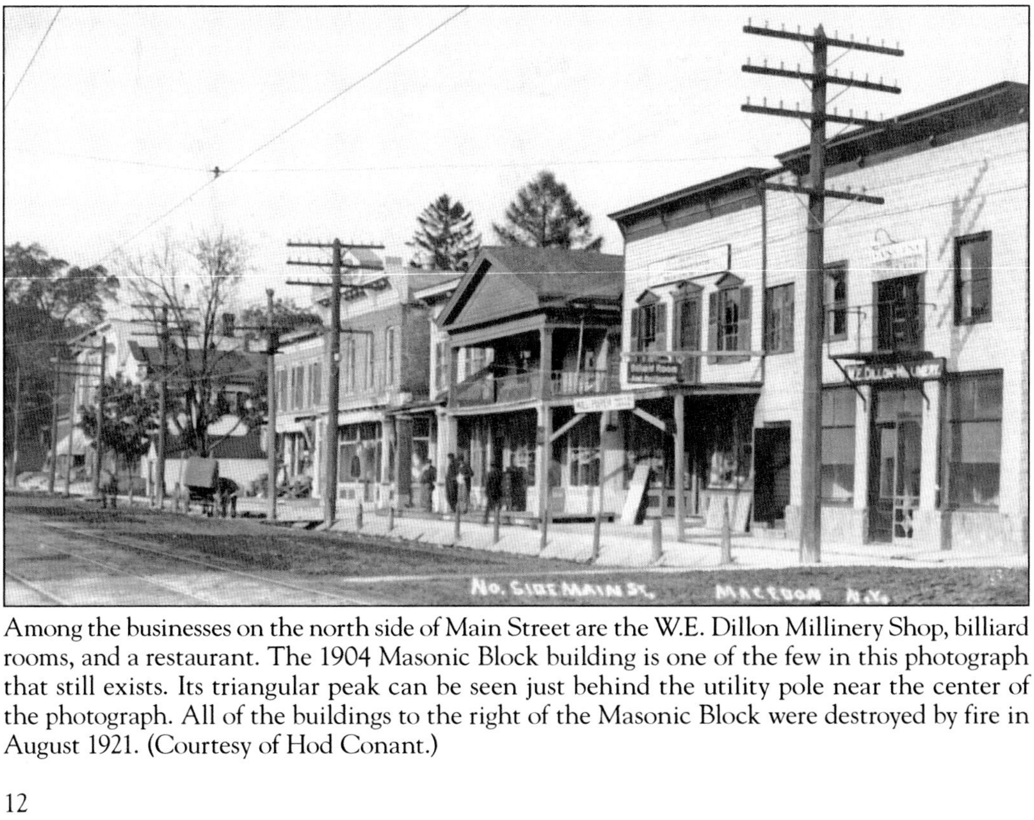

Among the businesses on the north side of Main Street are the W.E. Dillon Millinery Shop, billiard rooms, and a restaurant. The 1904 Masonic Block building is one of the few in this photograph that still exists. Its triangular peak can be seen just behind the utility pole near the center of the photograph. All of the buildings to the right of the Masonic Block were destroyed by fire in August 1921. (Courtesy of Hod Conant.)

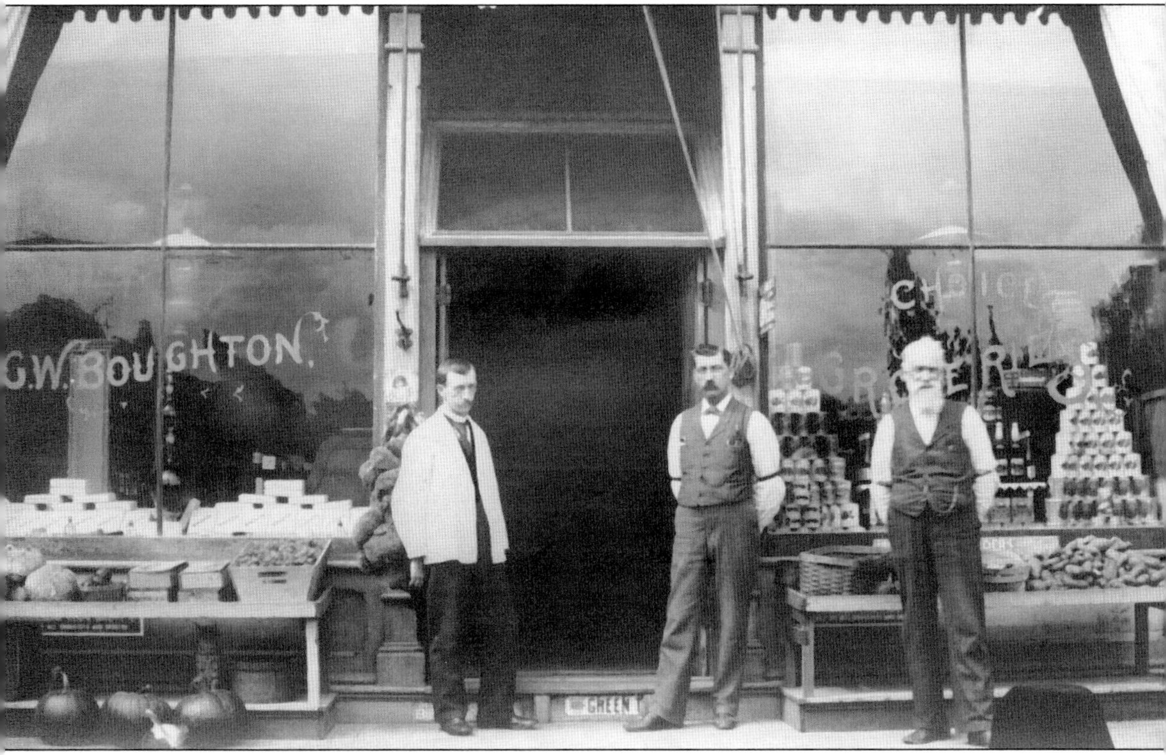

The store at 76 Main Street has been many things over the years, but its most frequent use has been as a grocery store. In 1889, the proprietor was George W. Boughton. The 1880 federal census lists his occupation as "manufacturer of patent medicines." This image is from a glass plate negative taken by Farmington resident Edwin J. Gardner. (Courtesy of Farmington Town Historian.)

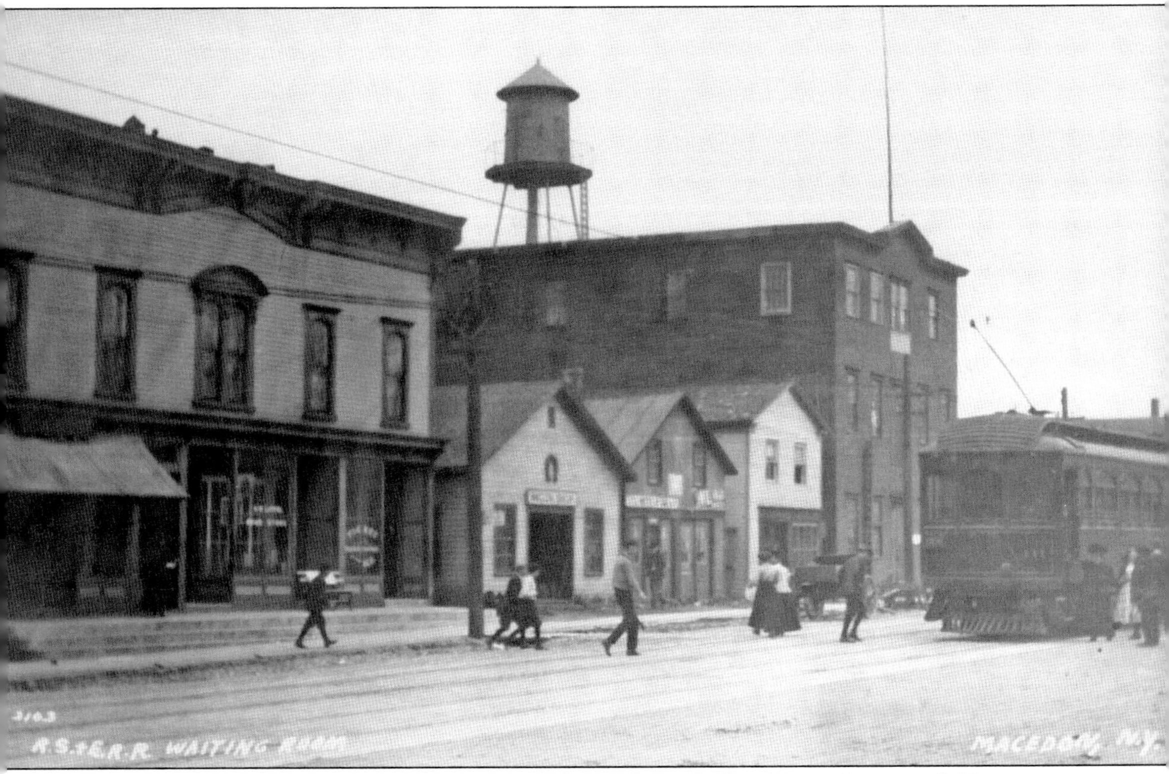

On the south side of Main Street, passengers hurry from the Rochester Syracuse & Eastern waiting room to catch the trolley. The building on the left, at 97–99 Main Street, still exists, now as an apartment building. In the early 1900s, the right side of the building housed the trolley ticket office and waiting room. In the middle of the building was Henry M. Littel's drugstore and, on the left side, Thrasher's Grocery and Butcher Shop. (Courtesy of Hod Conant.)

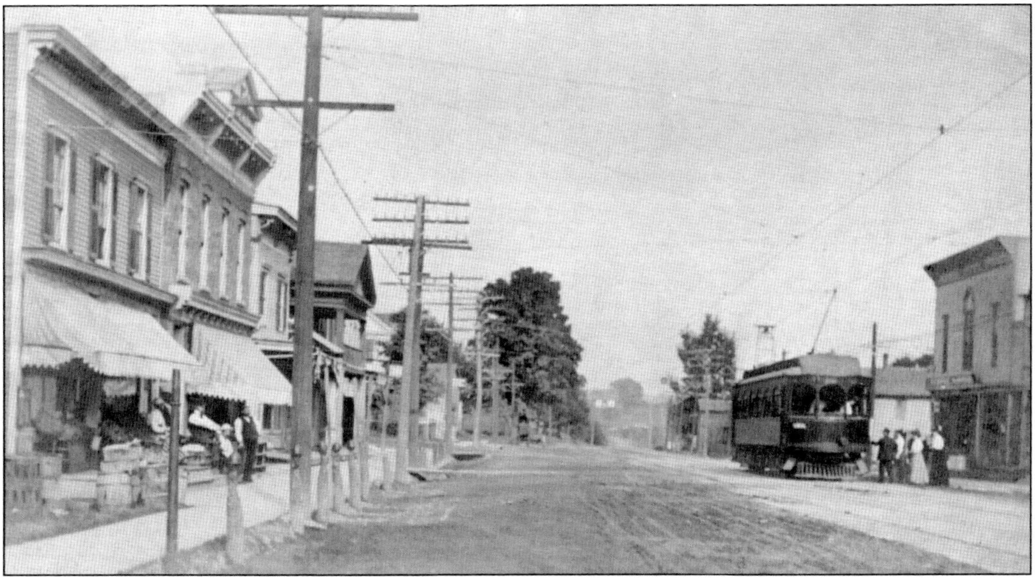

Onlookers outside of the grocery stores on the north side of Main Street watch as passengers board the trolley in front of the hardware store. The electrically powered trolley offered riders dependable, clean, and relatively inexpensive service west to Rochester and east as far as Syracuse. The view in this c. 1910 photograph is looking east toward Palmyra. (Courtesy of Hod Conant.)

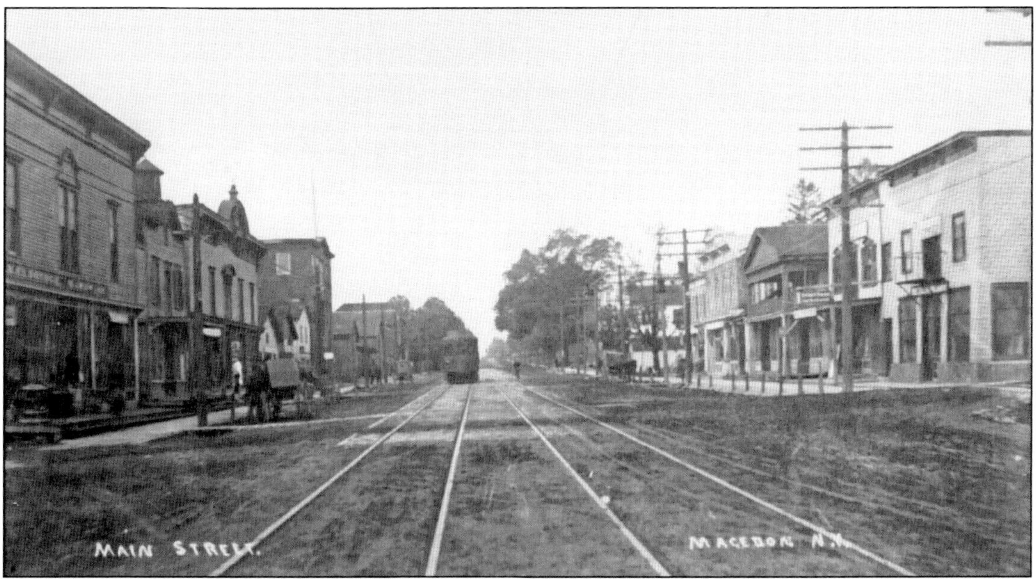

The view in this photograph of Main Street is looking west toward Egypt. On the left is the Eldredge hardware store. A trolley is visible in the distance. There are two sets of tracks, one for eastbound traffic and one for westbound. The RS&E trolley never turned a profit, and it ceased operation in 1930, a victim of the automobile's popularity and competition from trains. (Courtesy of Hod Conant.)

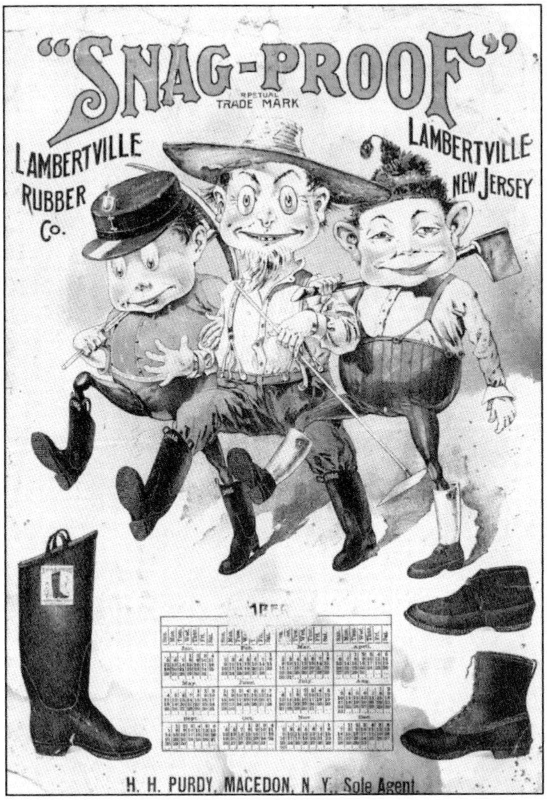

These advertisements for two Main Street stores would have been familiar to turn-of-the-century Macedon residents. The left photograph shows a promotional calendar for the H.H. Purdy Grocery and Dry Goods Store. It is an advertisement for Snag-Proof Boots, featuring the Palmer Cox Brownies. The copyrighted Brownies were enormously popular at the time. Kodak named a camera after them. The below advertisement for the H.M. Littel Drug Store is typical of patent medicine notices of the period. It features Green's Great Dyspepsia Panacea and Dr. A. Bosche's German Syrup. The Purdy store was at 74 Main Street, and the Littel store was across the street at 97 Main Street. Customized calendars and almanacs were popular ways for local merchants to advertise their goods. (Both, courtesy of the Macedon Public Library, Bullis Collection.)

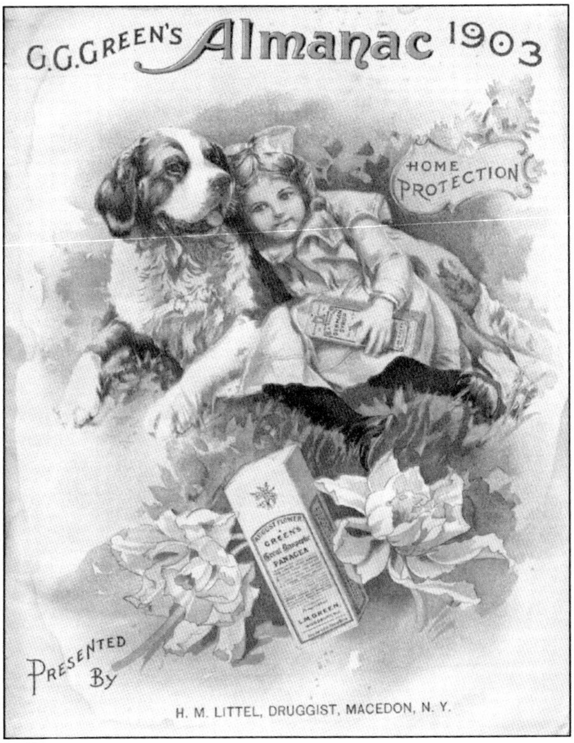

Mayme Lapham and Rudolph Kuebler stand in front of Kuebler's Merchant Tailor shop. This building once stood on the south side of Main Street, near the site of the current village hall and former bank building. (Courtesy of Macedon Town Historian.)

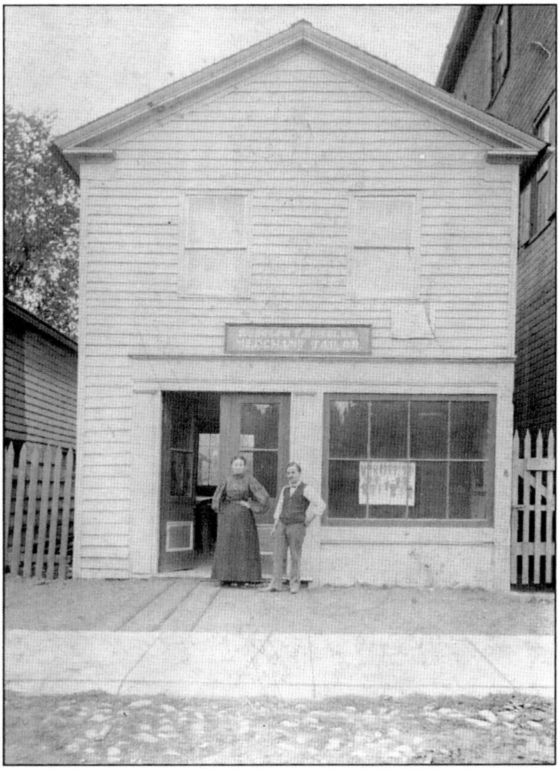

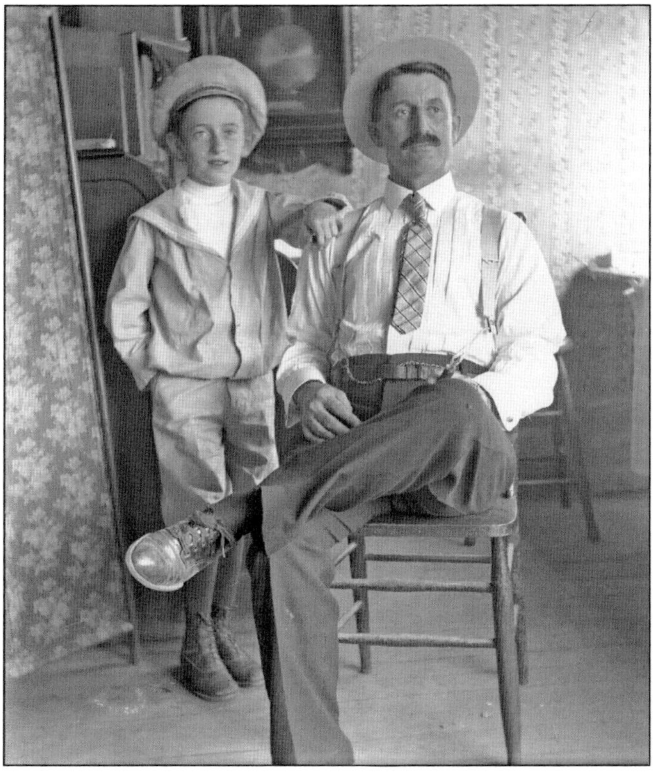

John Thrasher and his son Fremont owned Thrasher's Butcher Shop and Grocery at 97 Main Street for 45 years. In 1941–1942, Alvah Kingsley bought the building and operated a grocery store there. He sold the business to Clarence "Stub" Miller. In the mid-1970s, it became the TNT Restaurant. (Courtesy of Marlene Zimmer LeMoyne.)

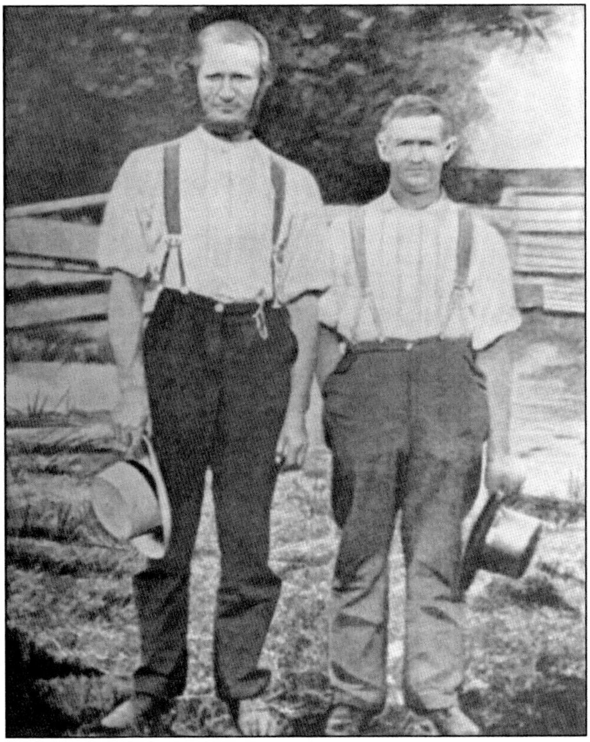

Western New York was an incubator for inventors and manufacturers of improved farm implements. Macedon was home to one of the most successful of those firms. Lyman Bickford (left) and Henry Huffman founded their company in 1842. The Bickford & Huffman Farmer's Favorite Grain Drill was credited with being one of the products that opened up the Great Plains to farmers. A grain drill is a machine for mechanically planting seed or spreading fertilizer. It is much faster and more consistent than planting by hand. (Courtesy of Macedon Town Historian.)

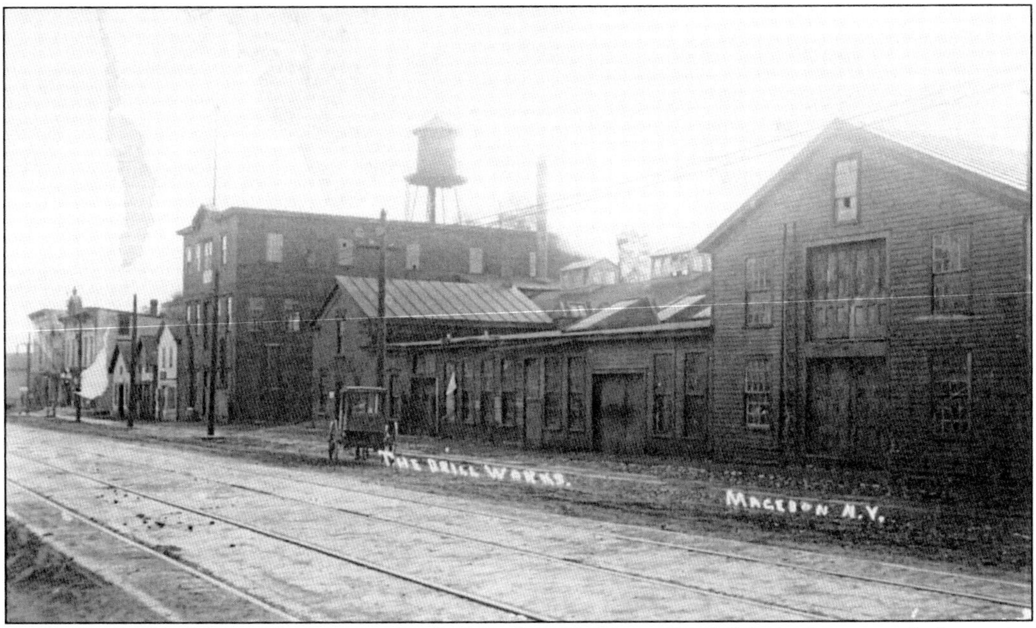

In the last half of the 19th century, the Bickford & Huffman Drill Works dominated the entire south side of Main Street, from about 71 Main Street east to old Erie Street. It had its own foundry, machine shop, and lumberyard. In 1903, the company was acquired by the American Seeding Machine Company, and manufacturing moved away from Macedon. Eventually, the firm was absorbed by the Oliver Tractor Company and then by the White Motor Company. (Courtesy of Macedon Town Historian.)

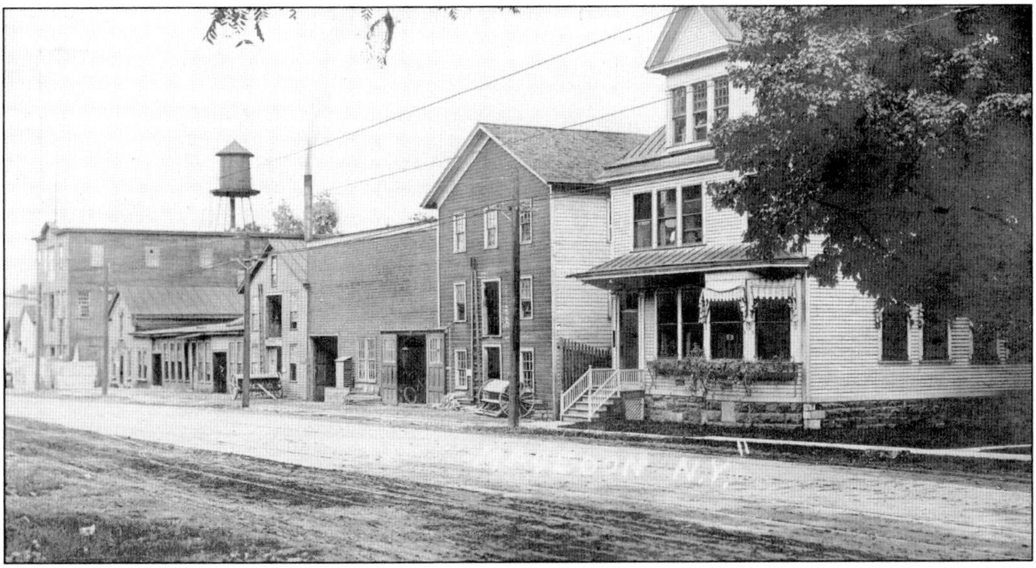

For many years, the Drill Works was Macedon's largest employer. Not until 1951, when Kordite came to Macedon, would a single business so dominate the local economy. At the height of its prosperity, the building at the right, at 71 Main Street, was the office for the Drill Works. The building is still there, and is now the home of the Gingerbread House store. This photograph was taken in 1910. (Courtesy of Hod Conant.)

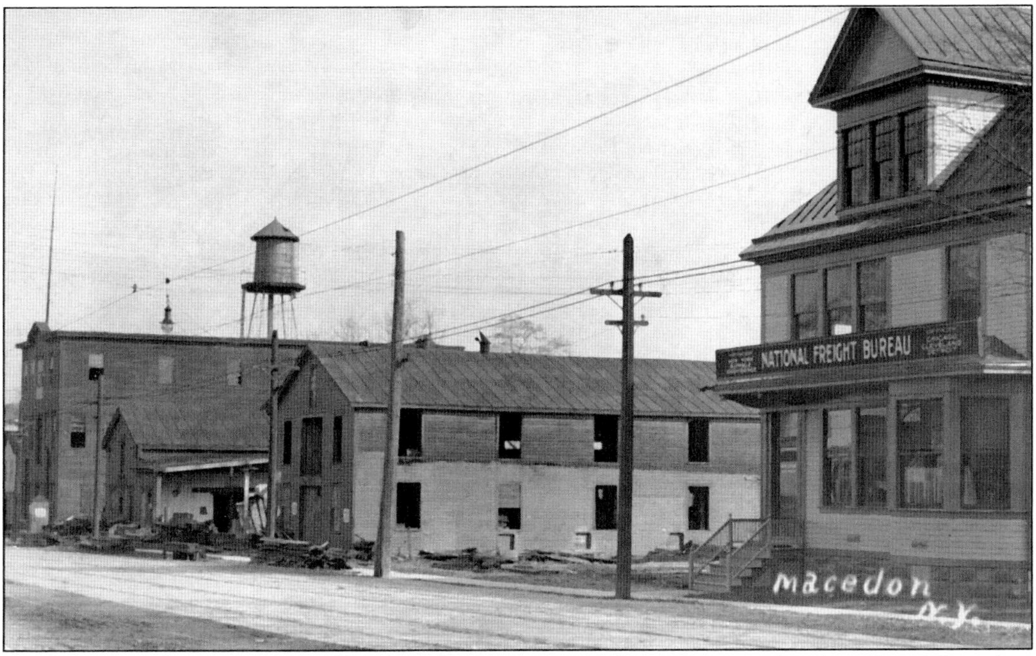

Sometime in the early 1900s, 71 Main Street was transformed into a freight office. Note that some of the earlier Drill Works buildings have been demolished, and others stand empty. The message side of this photo postcard reads: "Vina, in the building to the right is where I received my business training." (Courtesy of Hod Conant.)

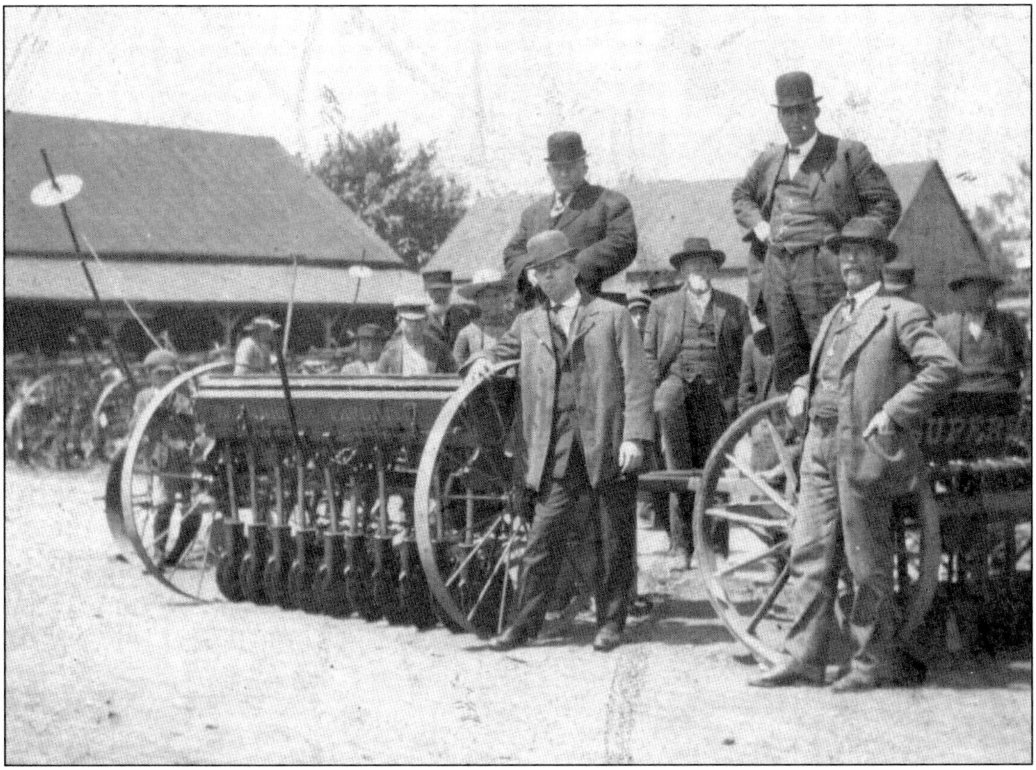

Unidentified Bickford & Huffman officials pose with an example of the company's Farmer's Favorite grain drill. It provided farmers with a mechanized device for sowing seeds in a consistent, reproducible way. Tightly controlled seeding also helped to limit the spread of weeds in cultivated fields. Today, surviving B&H grain drills are prized by collectors. (Courtesy of Macedon Town Historian.)

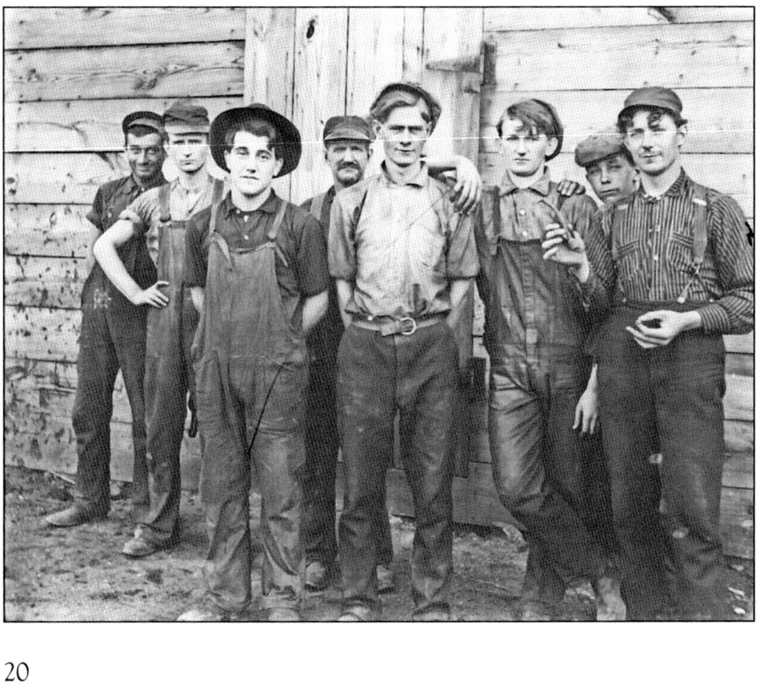

The inscription on this print from a glass plate negative calls these Bickford & Huffman workers "The Drill Works Chore Makers." Shown here are, from left to right, Fay Harrington, Dennis O'Keefe, Thomas O'Keefe, Nat Lalton, Aren Cator, Ed Hughes, Frank Clark, and Fred Kolber (foreman). (Courtesy of Marlene Zimmer LeMoyne.)

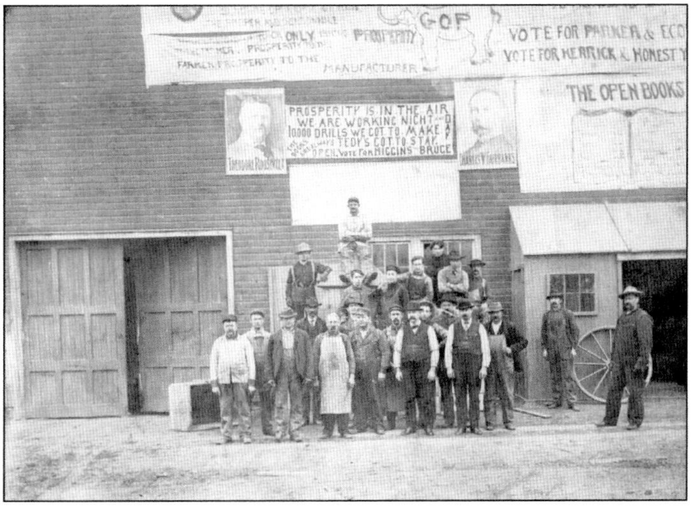

Political passions ran high in 1904 when employees of the Drill Works put up these homemade signs supporting Theodore Roosevelt for president and Charles Fairbanks for vice president. In 1901, William McKinley had been assassinated, and Vice President Roosevelt assumed the presidency. Now, TR was running in his own right. He won this election and continued to serve as president for four more years. (Courtesy of Macedon Town Historian.)

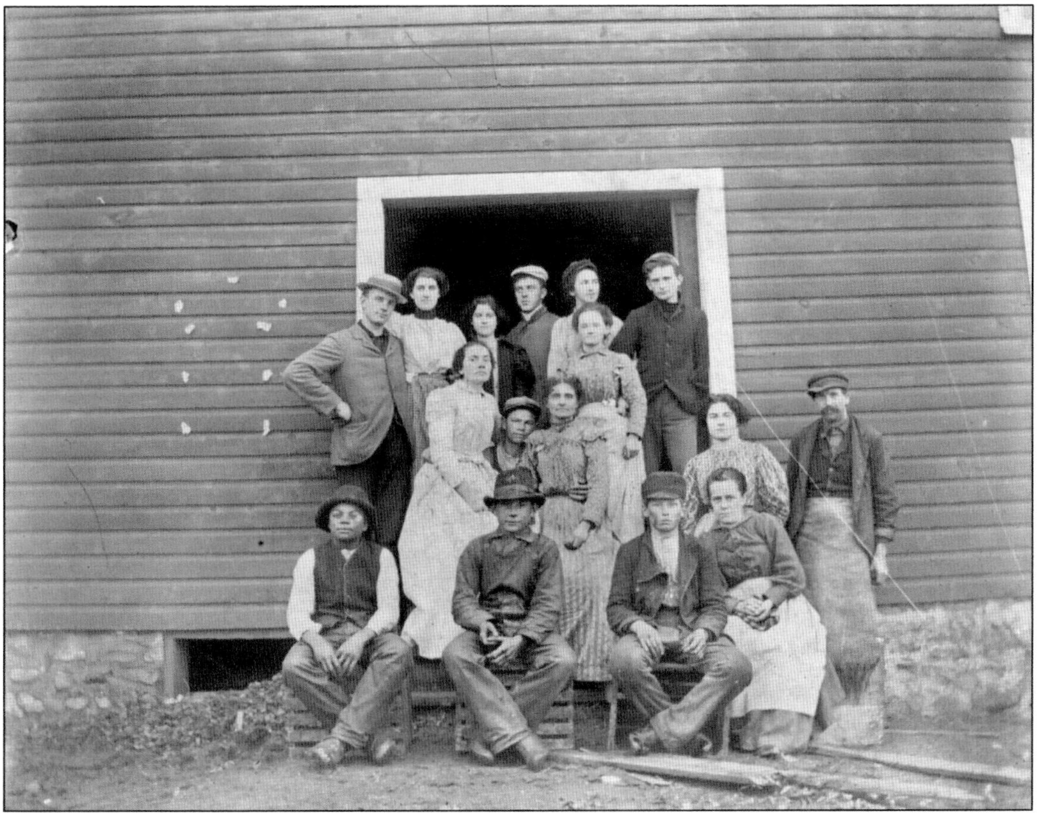

Bickford & Huffman workers pose in the late 1800s. Among those shown here are Joe Lawler, Ella Lawler, May Lauder, Dennis O'Keefe, Ralph Hall, Leon Hall, Tommy Johnson, and Johnny Moran. Although the inscription states that these are office workers, the leather apron on the man at right suggests that he works in the foundry. (Courtesy of Macedon Town Historian.)

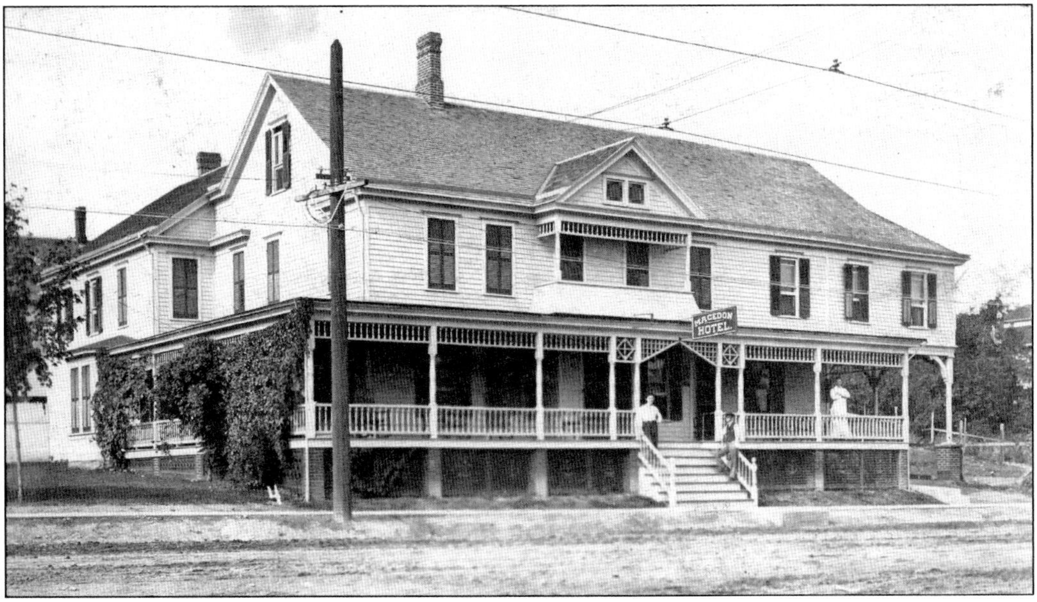

The Macedon Hotel was constructed by Henry Breese in 1884 to replace a building that had been destroyed by fire the year before. It was located on the northeast corner of Main and Erie Streets. In 1910, this structure was also destroyed by fire and was not rebuilt. In the 1930s, a gas station was located on this corner, and behind it was a miniature golf course. The trolley wires date this photograph from between 1906 and 1910. (Courtesy of Hod Conant.)

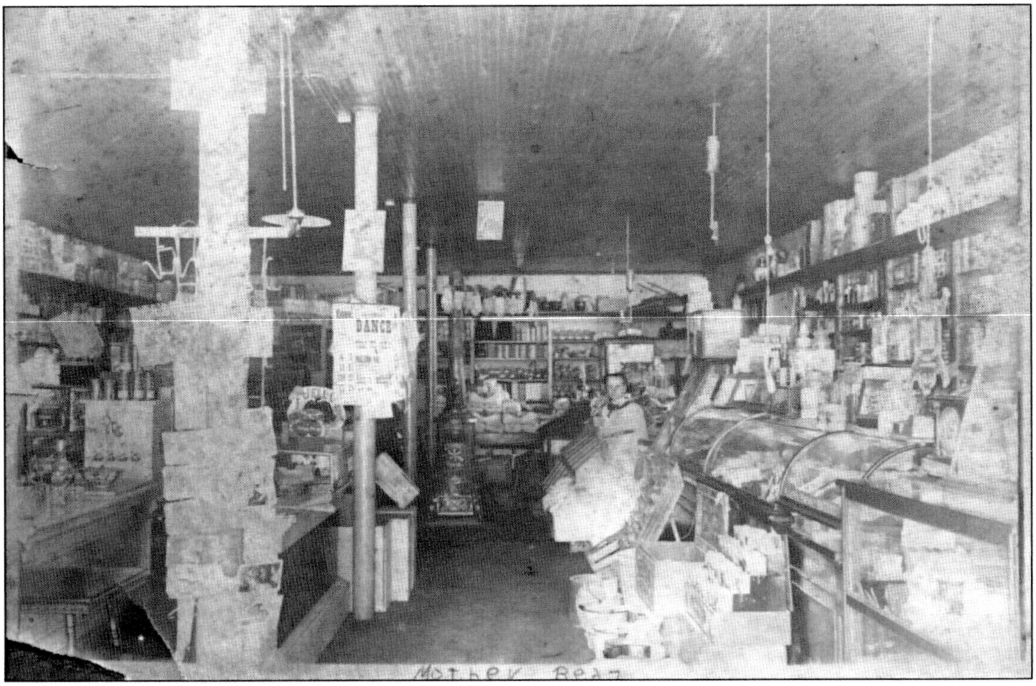

Celia Beal poses at the back of the Beal store in the Masonic Building. The calendar identifies the year as 1913. A potbellied stove at the rear provides heat. The store is crowded with glass-front display cases, the walls are covered with merchandise, and even the structural pillars are used for display. (Courtesy of Macedon Historical Society.)

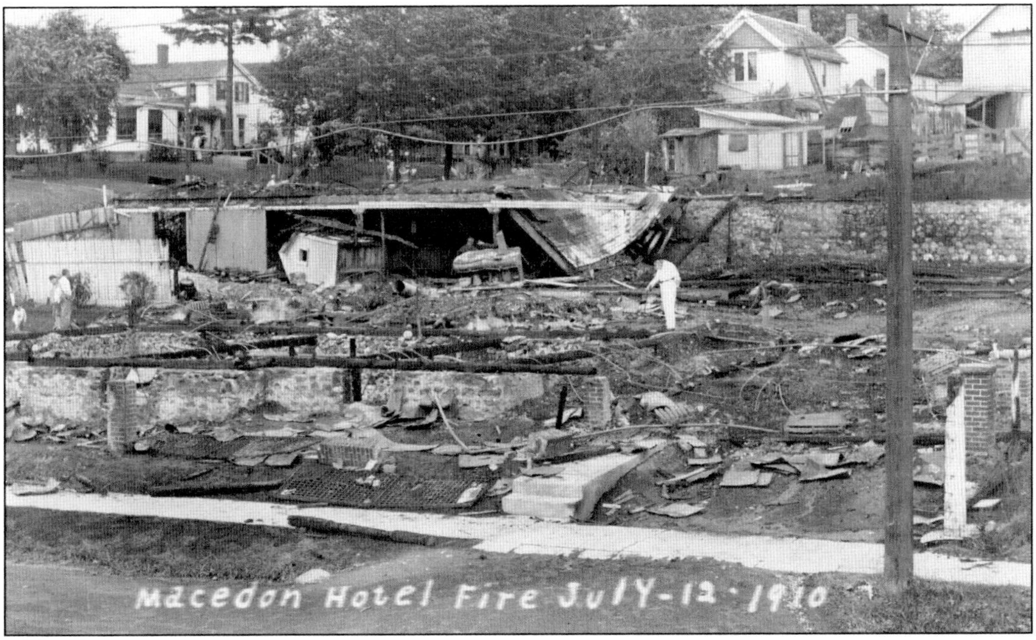

According to the message on this photo postcard, the man examining the ruins of the Macedon Hotel after the disastrous 1910 fire is Faye Herrington's father. The view is southwest toward Main Street. Building fires were a fact of life in the years before safety codes and modern firefighting equipment. (Courtesy of Hod Conant.)

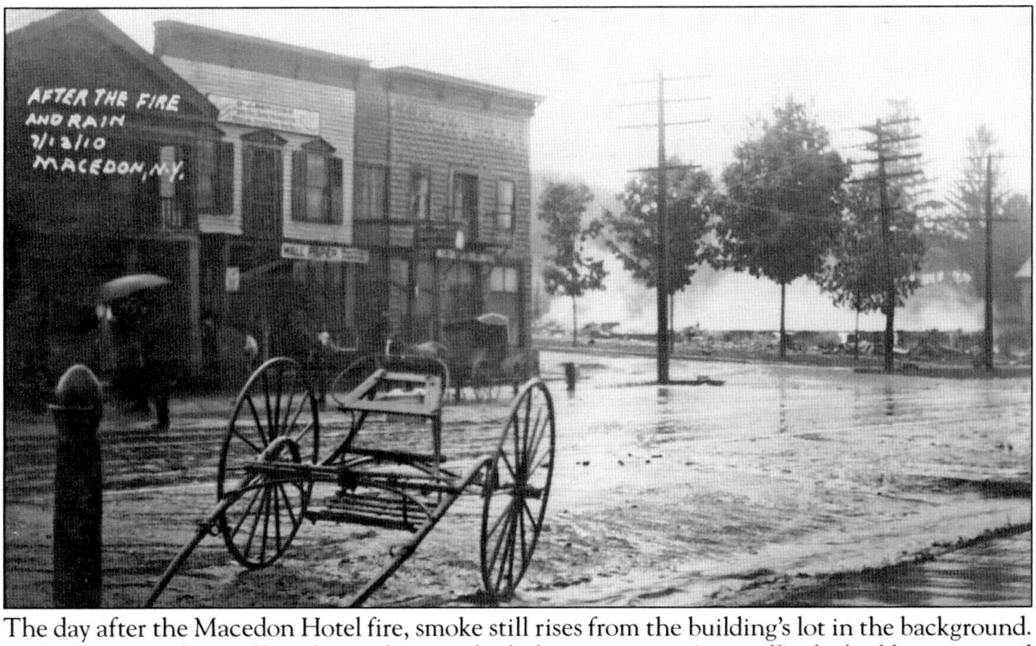

The day after the Macedon Hotel fire, smoke still rises from the building's lot in the background. In the foreground is a sulky, a horse-drawn vehicle for one person. Ironically, the buildings pictured here on the north side of Main Street were later destroyed by another fire, in 1921. Today, this site on the northwest corner of Main and Erie Streets is the home of Garden Gate Florist. (Courtesy of Hod Conant.)

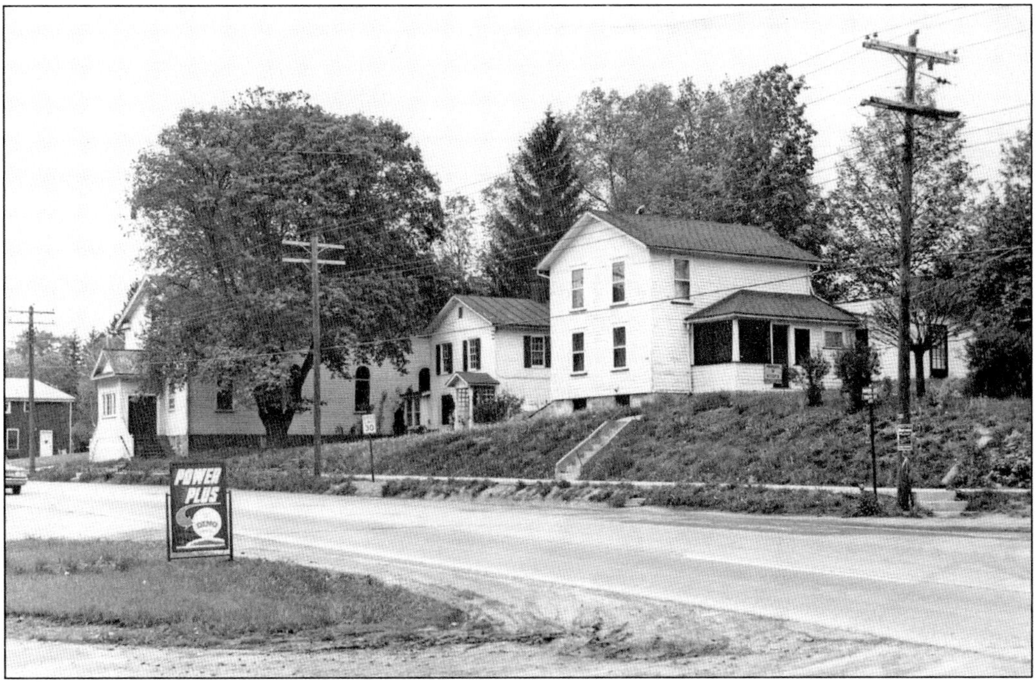

This view toward the northwest shows three buildings at the east end of Main Street that were demolished in the 1950s to make way for a new intersection with State Route 350. The buildings are, from left to right, the old St. Patrick's Catholic Church, the Gorman residence, and the Gratton residence. At the extreme left, the east side of the Blacksmith Shop Restaurant is visible. This photograph was taken sometime before 1958. (Courtesy of Macedon Town Historian.)

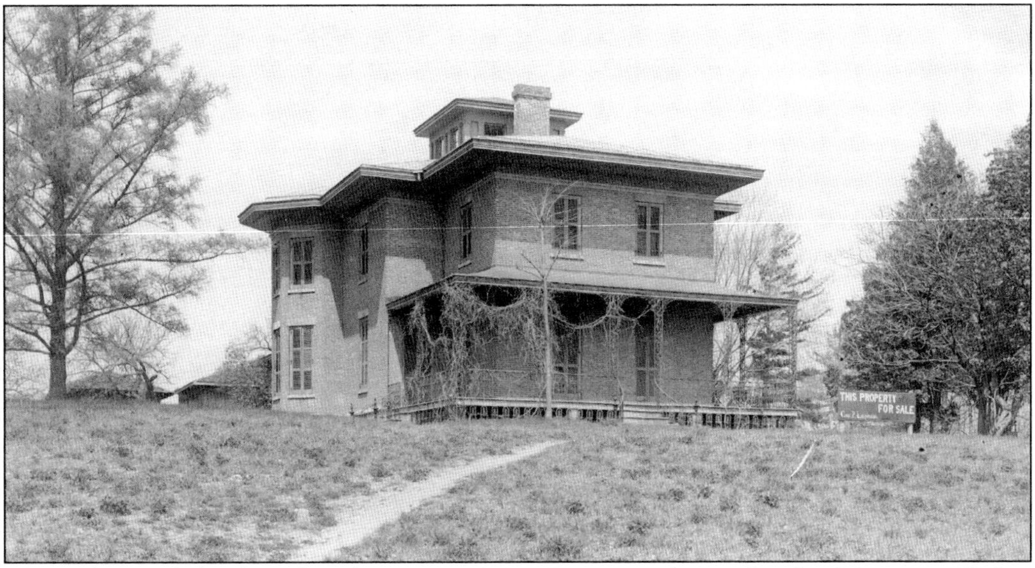

This is the stately brick Lapham house at 44 Main Street, on the north side of the street. Today, more trees cover the surrounding space. The house now includes a frame addition on the west side, but it otherwise looks much the same as it does in this photograph from the last century. The sign on the right indicates that owner George P. Lapham has put it up for sale. (Courtesy of Hod Conant.)

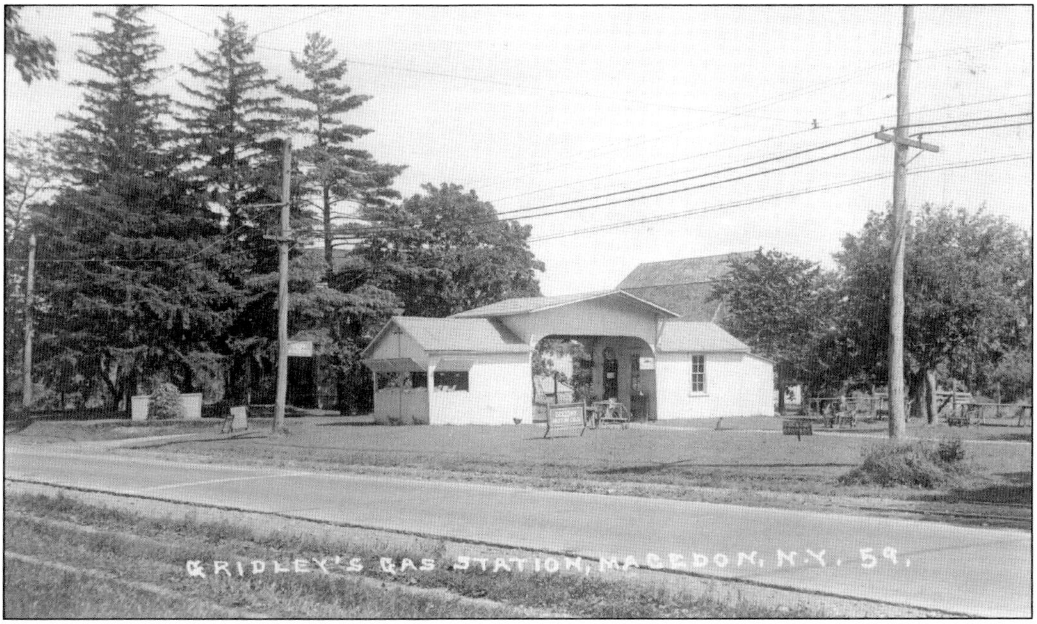

Gridley's Gas Station was located on West Main Street. The barn in the background was moved up to the side of the road and turned into a store, with a rathskeller, or bar, in the basement. Later, the store became Delyser's Tavern, a favorite Macedon eating establishment for decades. Today, it is the site of MJ's Pub & Grill. (Courtesy of Hod Conant.)

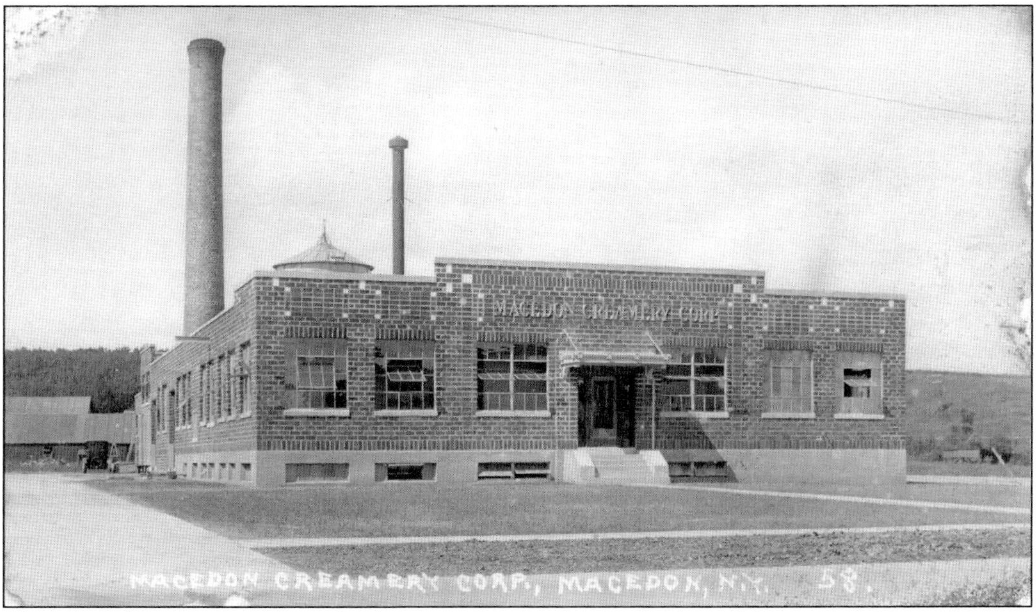

The Macedon Creamery was built in 1925, near the west edge of the present Berry Plastics plant (formerly Kordite/Huntsman/Mobil/Pliant). The front of the building faced Main Street. After the creamery ceased operations, it was reputed to have been the site of an illegal distillery during Prohibition. After that, it was used as a cannery. In 1951, the Samuels brothers bought the property. They moved the Kordite Company to this site from Victor, New York. (Courtesy of Hod Conant.)

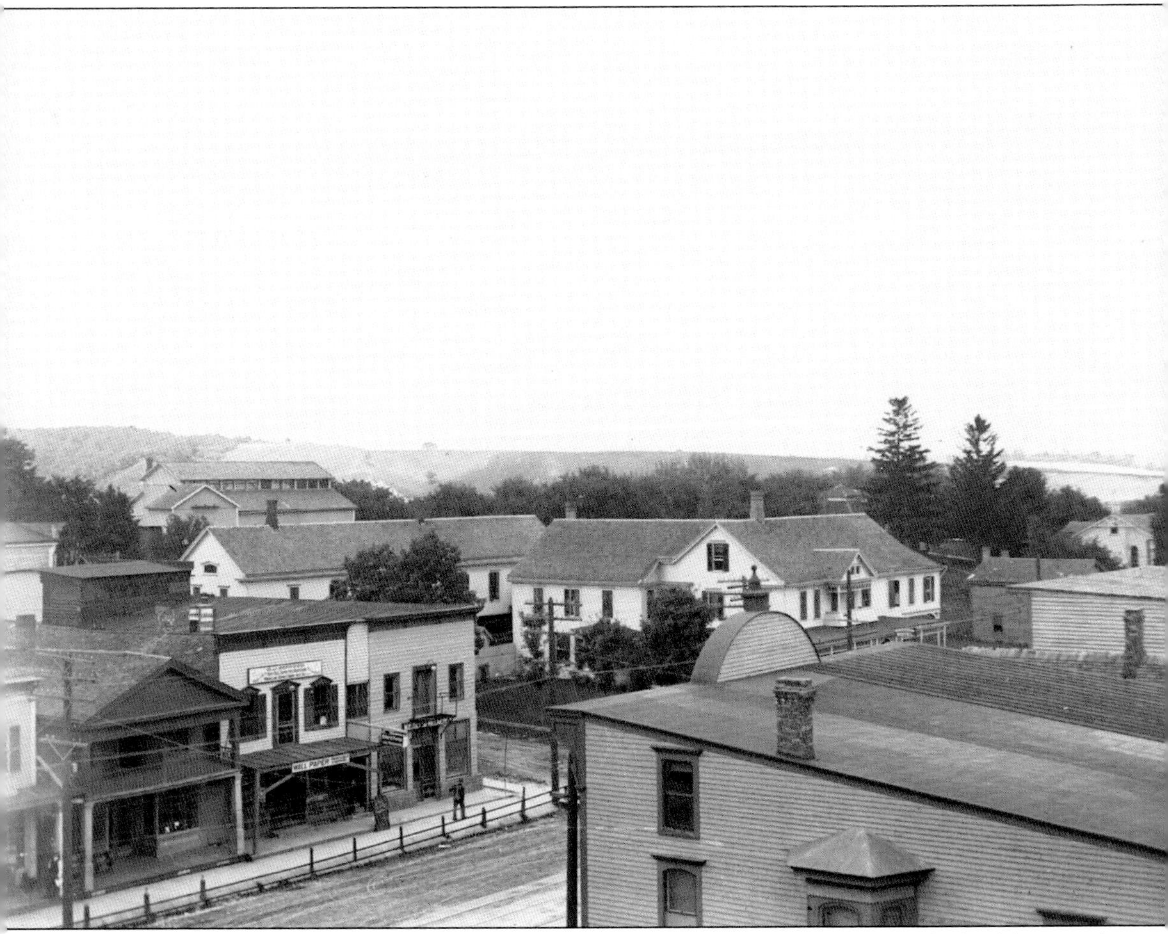

In this image from a glass plate negative, the view is toward the northeast. The building in the right foreground is 97–99 Main Street. Just beyond its rounded facade is the Macedon Hotel, prior to the 1910 fire, on the northeast corner of Main Street and Erie Street. All of the buildings at left were destroyed by a fire in the 1920s. (Courtesy of Marlene Zimmer LeMoyne.)

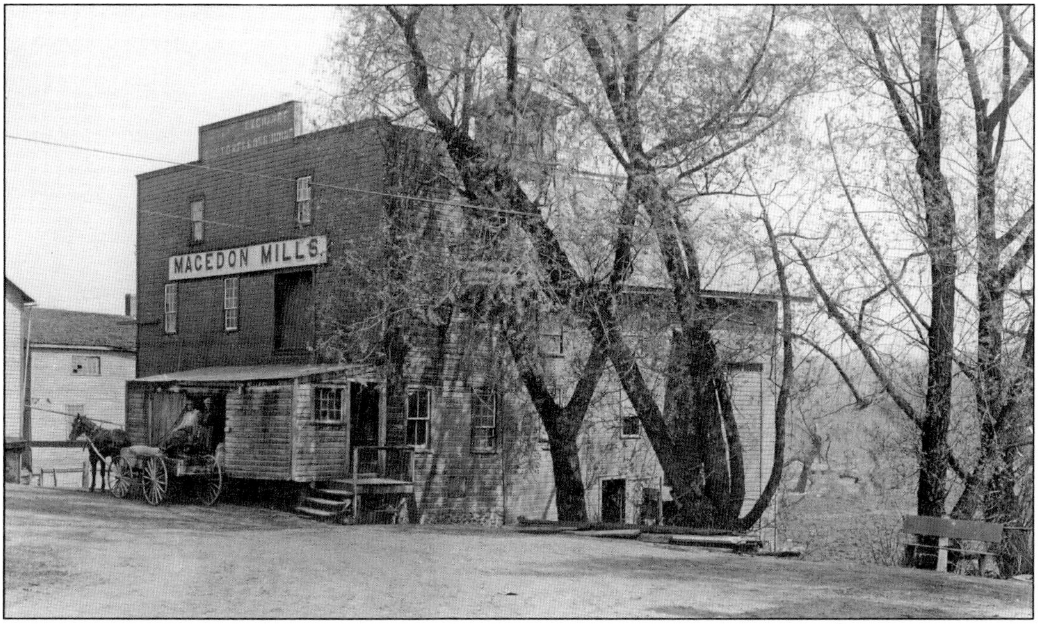

A horse-drawn wagon is ready to be loaded at Macedon Mills. The mill was near the southeast corner of Main and Erie Streets. Waterpower was provided by a dam on Ganargua Creek and a raceway from the pond to the mill. The dam and raceway were originally created as a feeder for the Erie Canal. Traces of the raceway can still be seen, parallel to Main Street and just south of Poplar and Race Streets. (Courtesy of Hod Conant.)

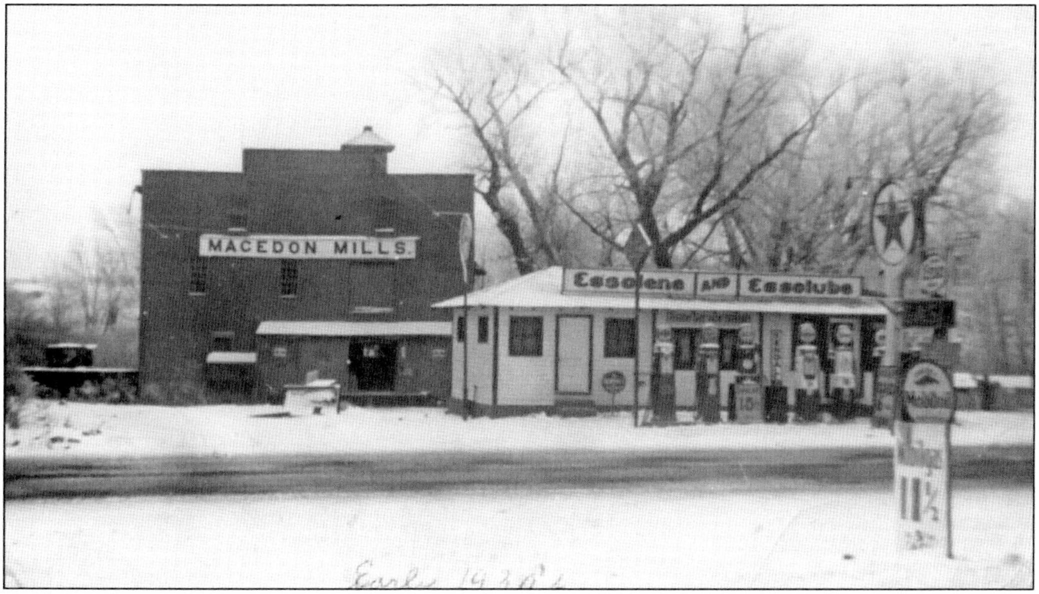

In the early 1930s, this Esso gas station stood in front of Macedon Mills, at the southeast corner of Main and Erie Streets. In the right foreground, a sign for a Mobilgas station on the opposite side of the street advertises gasoline for 11-1/2¢ per gallon. Esso and Mobil were formed from the breakup of Standard Oil in 1911. The firms would merge once again 88 years later to become ExxonMobil. Gasoline would be 30 times more expensive than in that previous era. (Courtesy of Macedon Town Historian.)

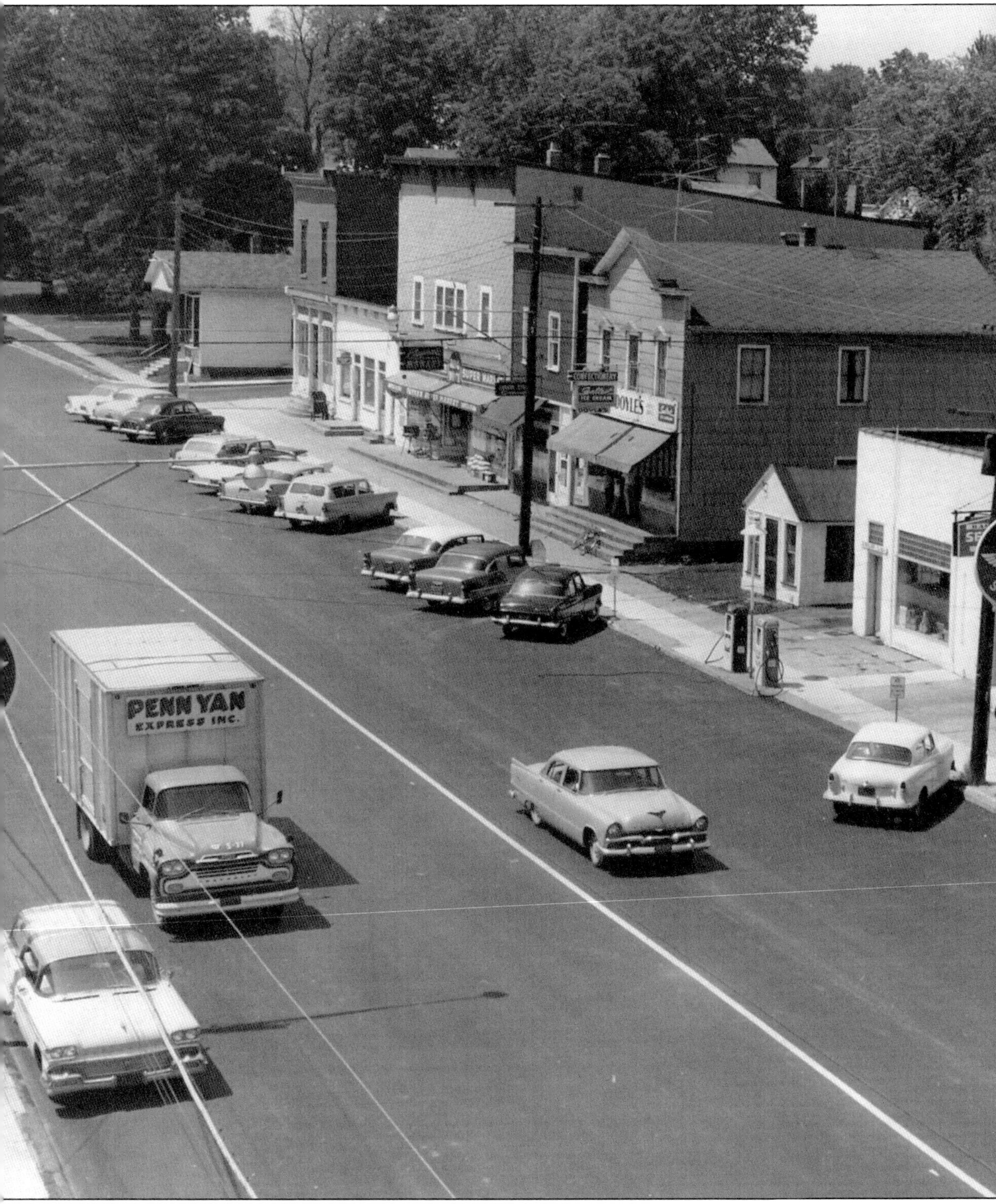

Most of these buildings on the north side of Main Street date from the early 1900s or before, and many are still standing today. In the late 1950s, when this photograph was taken, the Masonic Block building on the right, at 96 Main Street, was the home of Gravino's Grocery. Joe Gravino bought his father-in-law, Charlie Pronest's, grocery business when Gravino returned from World War II. In March 1967, he moved his business to the former Red & White store at 76 Main Street,

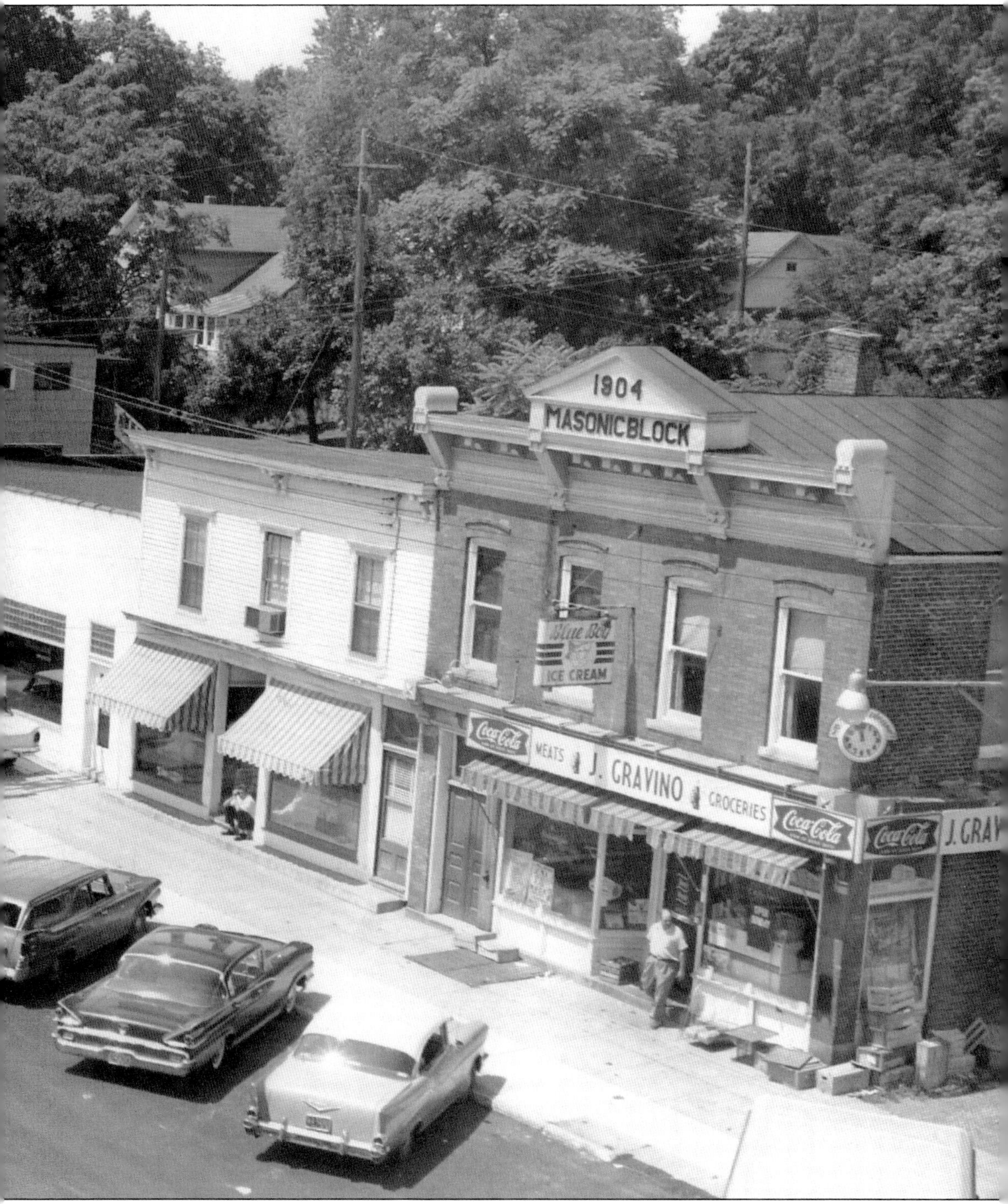

near the far end of the line of buildings. That structure had housed many other grocery stores over the decades. In the early 1900s, there were several buildings between the Masonic Block and Erie Street, beyond the photograph to the right. A fire in 1922 destroyed them all. (Courtesy of Macedon Town Historian.)

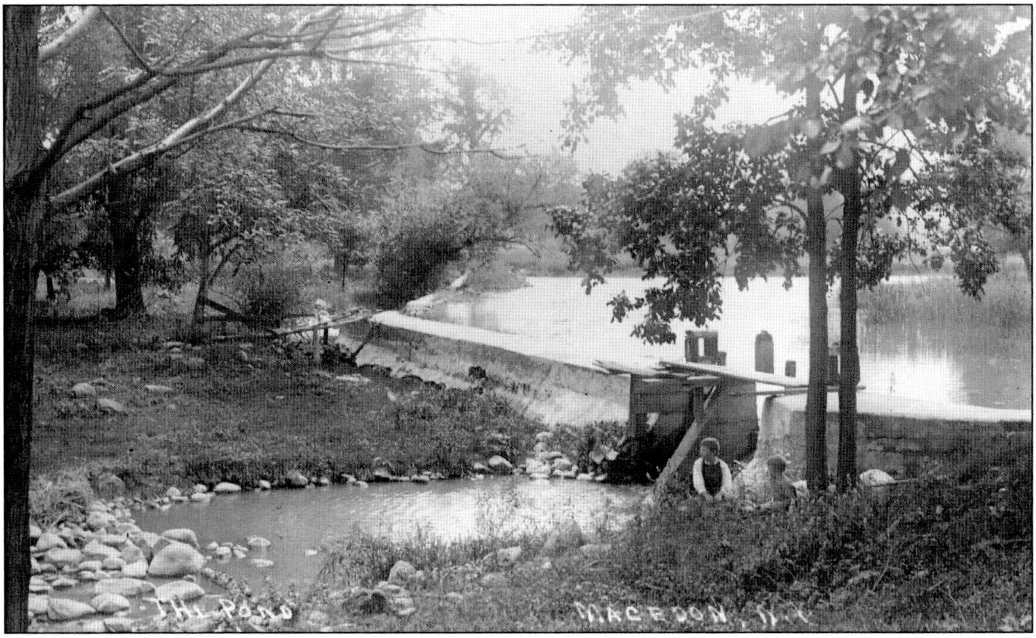

Children play near the dam that created the millpond that provided power for the Macedon Mills. Like most mills, this one depended on a dam on a local waterway to establish the difference in water level that drove the millstones that ground the grain. The pond was located on Ganargua Creek, near the foot of Poplar Street. (Courtesy of Hod Conant.)

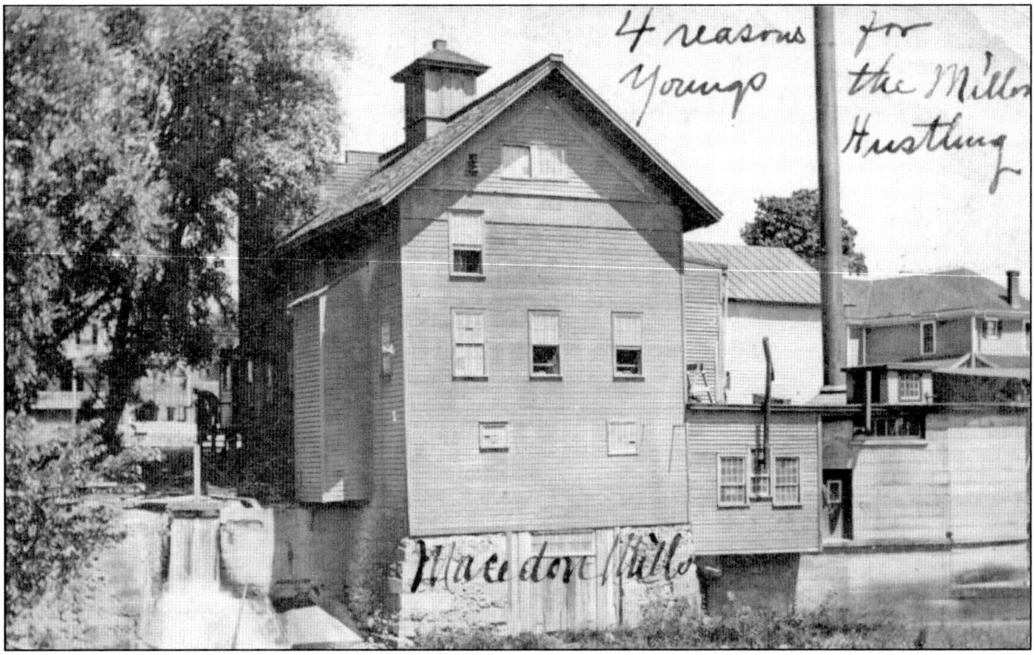

The back of Macedon Mills is seen from old Erie Street. Note the spillway at left. The Youngs family owned this mill at the turn of the century. This photo postcard is addressed to Warren Youngs, Seneca Falls, New York, and is postmarked July 11, 1905. (Courtesy of Hod Conant.)

Two

Macedonians, Their Homes, and Families

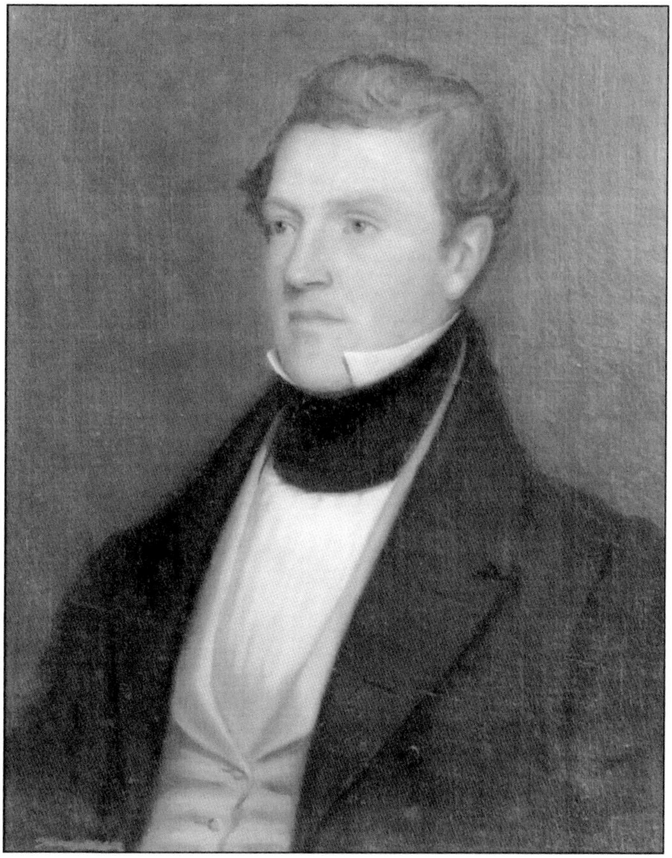

This is an undated oil portrait of Macedon settler Ichabod Briggs. He was born in 1809 in Schenectady County and died on August 1, 1893, in Macedon. The Briggs home stood on Wayneport Road, a little north of the current New York Central Railroad crossing. Briggs's 1851 diary mentions cutting wood for the railroad as it was being built through the town of Macedon. Early locomotives had wood-fired boilers and used prodigious amounts of wood. Briggs, who served as postmaster at Wayneport for 30 years, was interested in horticulture and contributed to farming publications. (Courtesy of Margaret Hartsough.)

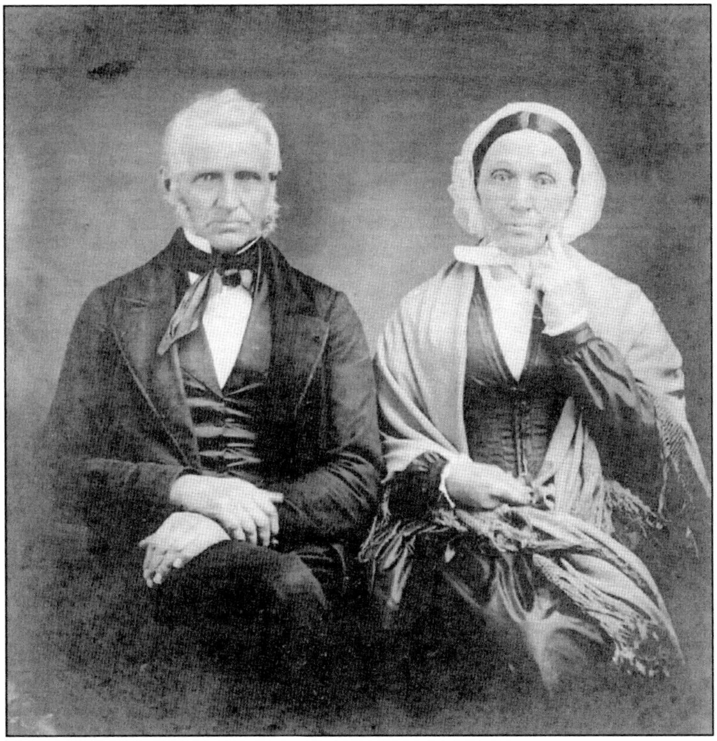

Macedon settlers Eseck and Maria Wilber bought a mill west of the village originally built by Enoch Gannett in 1801. They then moved the mill to the southeast corner of Main and Old Erie Streets. The Wilbers were Quakers and were active in the women's suffrage movement. Maria was one of the signers of the Seneca Falls Declaration of Sentiments in 1848. (Courtesy of Macedon Town Historian.)

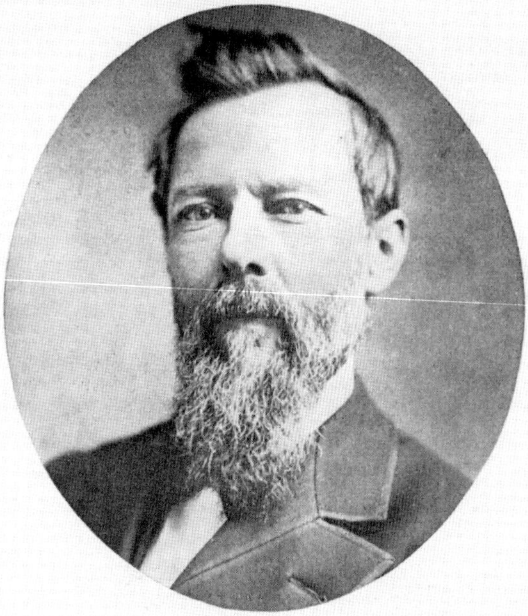

JEREMIAH THISTLETHWAITE.
Supervisor from Macedon, 1876. Died October 16, 1901, aged 76 years.

Jeremiah Thistlethwaite was born in England about 1825. He married Abigail Packard, and the family lived on Bickford Street in the village. In addition to serving as supervisor of the town of Macedon, Jeremiah was elected to the New York State Assembly in 1877. He is buried in the Macedon Village Cemetery on Cemetery Hill, off of South Erie Street. (Courtesy of Macedon Town Historian.)

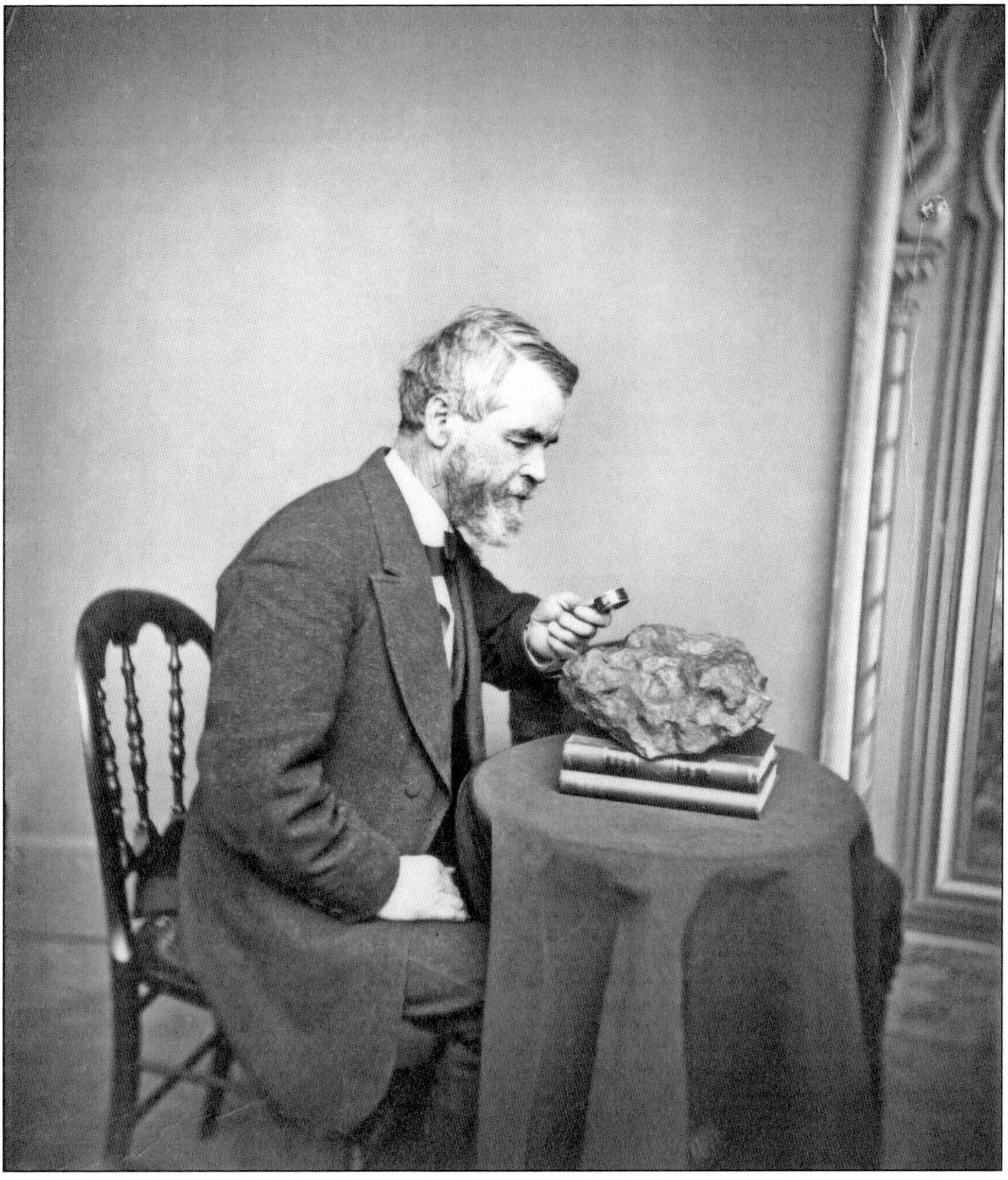

In this 1871 photograph, Macedon native Increase Allen Lapham examines a meteorite. He had moved to Wisconsin in July 1836 and became a scholar and scientist. He was one of the first to systematically study weather patterns, and is considered the father of the National Weather Service, serving as its first forecaster. He also was a respected authority on geology and paleontology. The *American Journal of Science* published his treatise on the geologic formations in the Erie Canal, written when he was only 16 years old. The University of Wisconsin has an Increase A. Lapham Professorship. (Courtesy of Wisconsin Historical Society. Image WHi-1944, used with permission.)

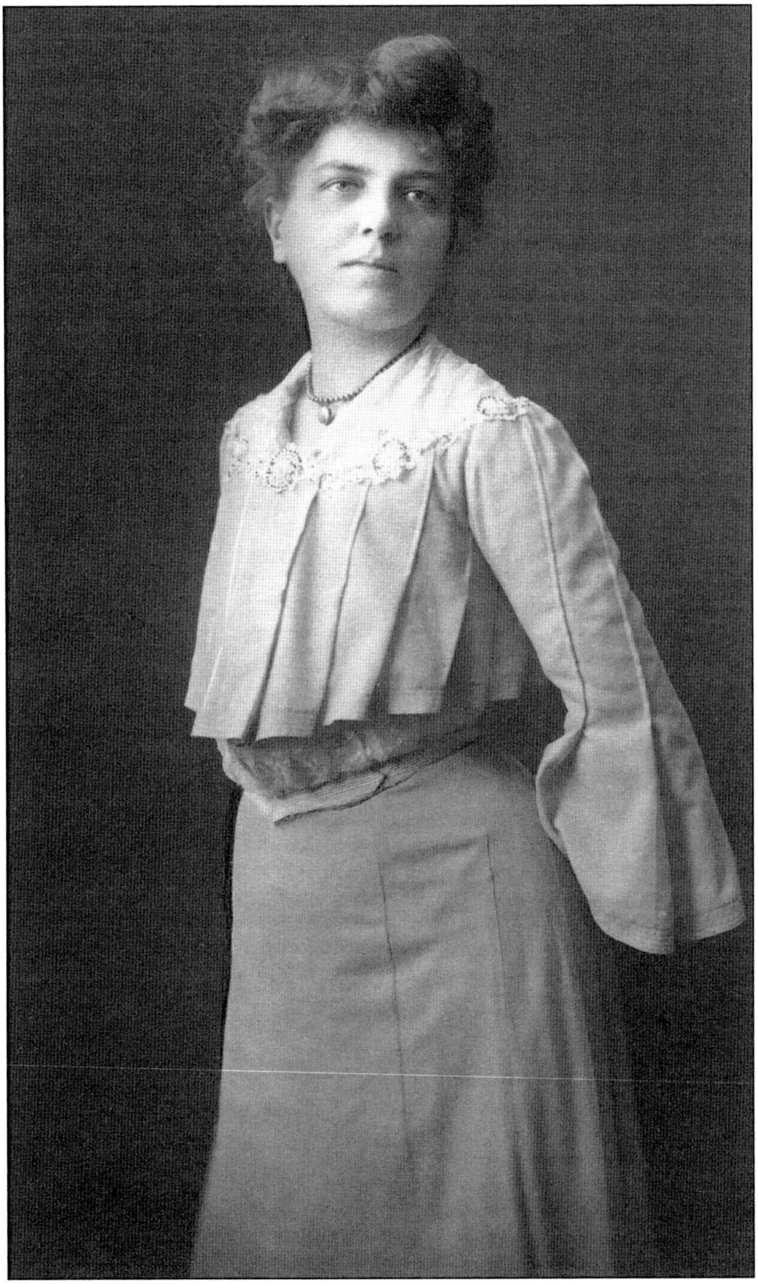

Emma Biddlecom was born in Macedon on August 13, 1862. She married Rochester businessman Fred G. Sweet. Biddlecom was a cousin of Susan B. Anthony, and served as Anthony's personal secretary during the last years of the famous suffragist's life. The two women traveled all over the country promoting women's rights. After Anthony's death, Biddlecom continued to fight for women's right to vote. With the passage of the Nineteenth Amendment to the United States Constitution in 1918 and its ratification by two-thirds of the states in 1920, women finally received the right to vote. Several states did not ratify the amendment until later. Mississippi was the last holdout, finally passing it in 1984. (Courtesy of the Department of Rare Books and Special Collections, University of Rochester Libraries.)

In 1900, Susan B. Anthony persuaded the University of Rochester that it was time to admit women to the student body. In 1901, Ella Salome Wilcoxen of Macedon was the first woman to receive a degree from the university, a bachelor of philosophy. She became a high school teacher and religious worker. (Courtesy of the Department of Rare Books & Special Collections, University of Rochester Libraries.)

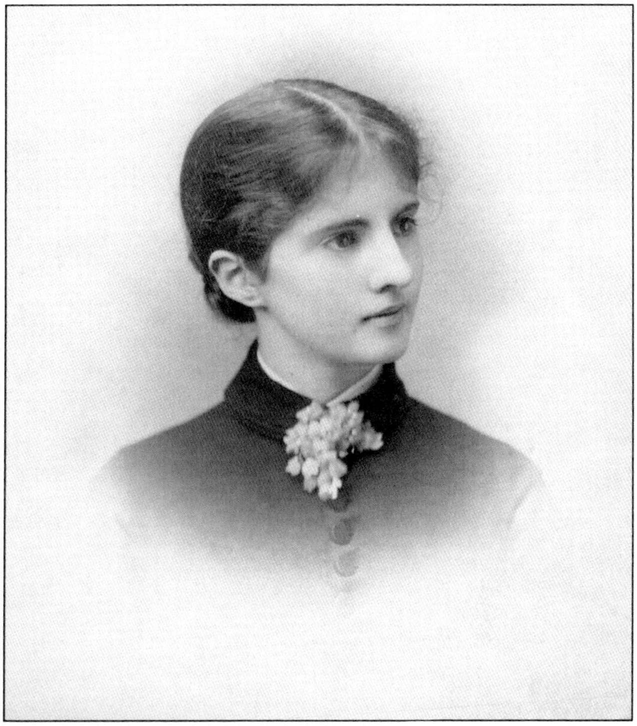

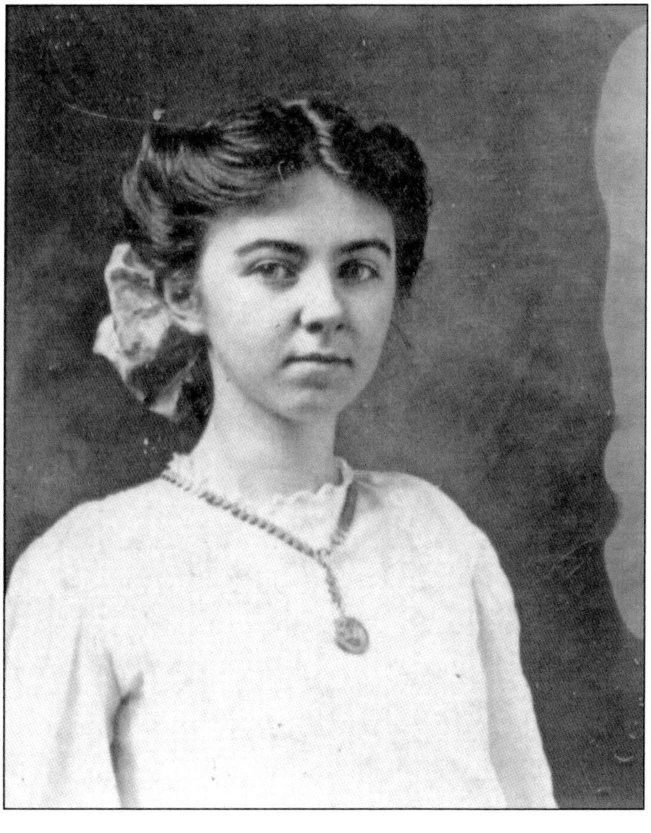

Edna Wilcoxen, Ella Wilcoxen's niece, had this photograph taken about 1908, when she was 16. Edna graduated from the old Macedon High School on School Street and then became a teacher there for the fifth and sixth grades. Later, she married Leon Plumb. She also served a term as Macedon historian. The Wilcoxen, Lapham, and Bullis families share many connections. (Courtesy of the Macedon Public Library, Bullis Collection.)

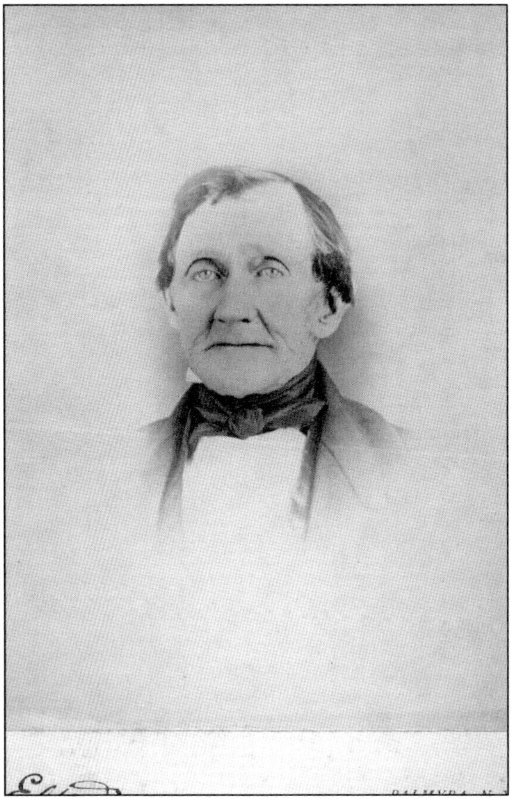

Charles H. Bullis (left) and his wife, Eleanor Carbone Bullis (below), were early residents of Macedon. Charles was a farmer. He and Eleanor were from Vermont, and their two children, Charles and Amy, were born in Manchester, Vermont. The family left the state in 1837 and took a canal boat from Troy, New York, to Macedon. Although these portraits are not dated, records show that Charles and his son, Dr. Abraham Bullis, both died in 1866, so the photographs were probably taken sometime in the 1860s. (Both, courtesy of the Macedon Public Library, Bullis Collection.)

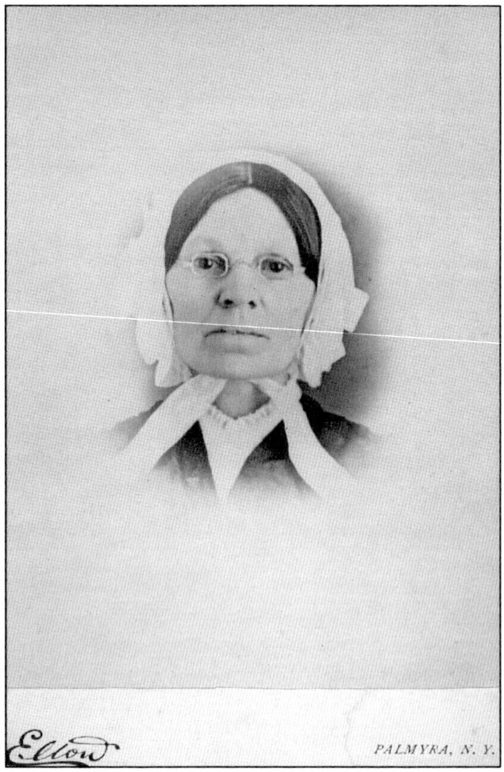

Dr. Abraham R. Bullis, son of Charles and Eleanor, was born in 1815. He graduated from Geneva Medical College in Geneva, New York, and practiced medicine in Macedon and Farmington from 1841 until his death in 1866. Abraham Bullis was one of Macedon's first physicians. He married Lydia Porter Lapham, and they had seven children. After Lydia died, he married Olive Aldrich. (Courtesy of the Macedon Public Library, Bullis Collection.)

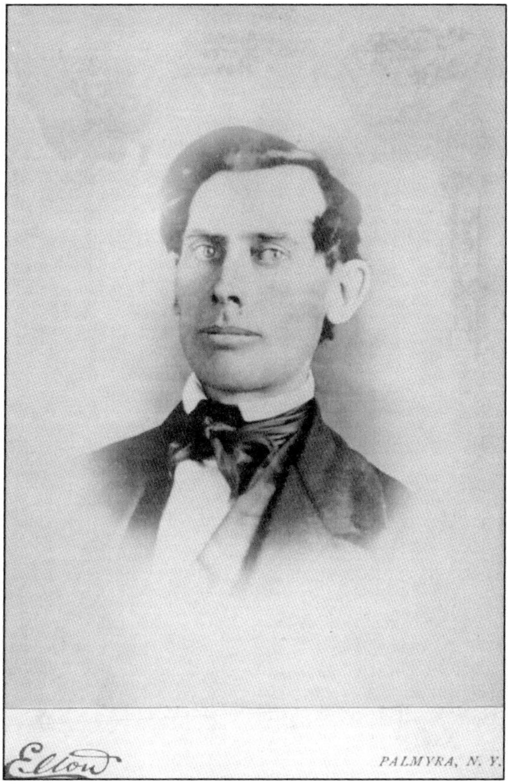

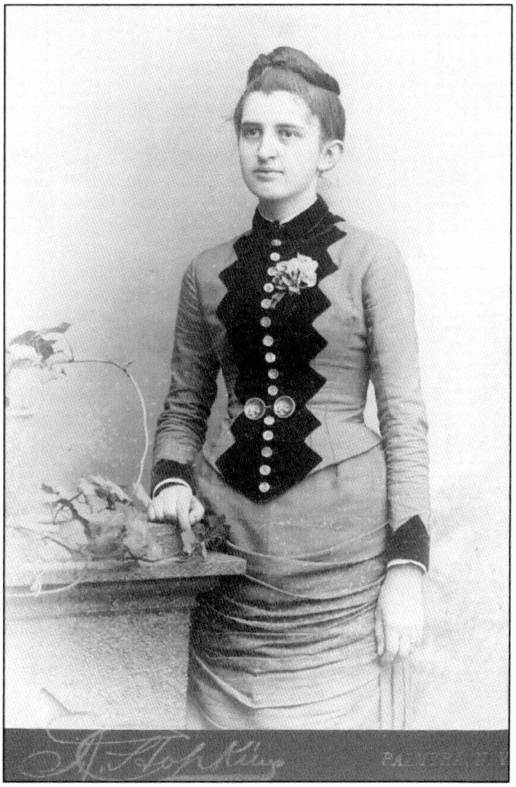

Geneva Breese was the daughter of Bickford & Huffman worker Justin Breese and his wife, Vernadia. Geneva attended Macedon Academy in 1886–1887. This photograph was taken sometime before her marriage to Randolph Knapp in 1887. (Courtesy of the Macedon Public Library, Bullis Collection.)

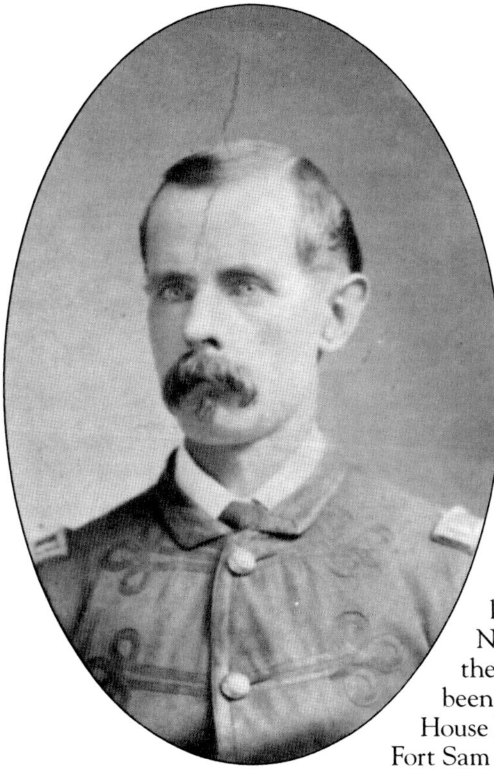

Macedon native John Lapham Bullis was the eldest of the seven children of Dr. Abraham Bullis and Lydia Porter Bullis. In the photograph at left, he is shown early in his military service. Below, he is shown wearing the insignia of a captain. Bullis had a very successful military career, retiring at the rank of brigadier general. He was given command of a special troop, officially known as the Seminole Indian Negro Scouts. Military records show that the unit distinguished itself in battle. Ironically, General Bullis is better known in San Antonio, Texas, than in Macedon, New York. At Fort Sam Houston in San Antonio, the house he built and spent his retirement in has been turned into a bed-and-breakfast, the Bullis House Inn. (Both, courtesy of John Manguso, director, Fort Sam Houston Museum.)

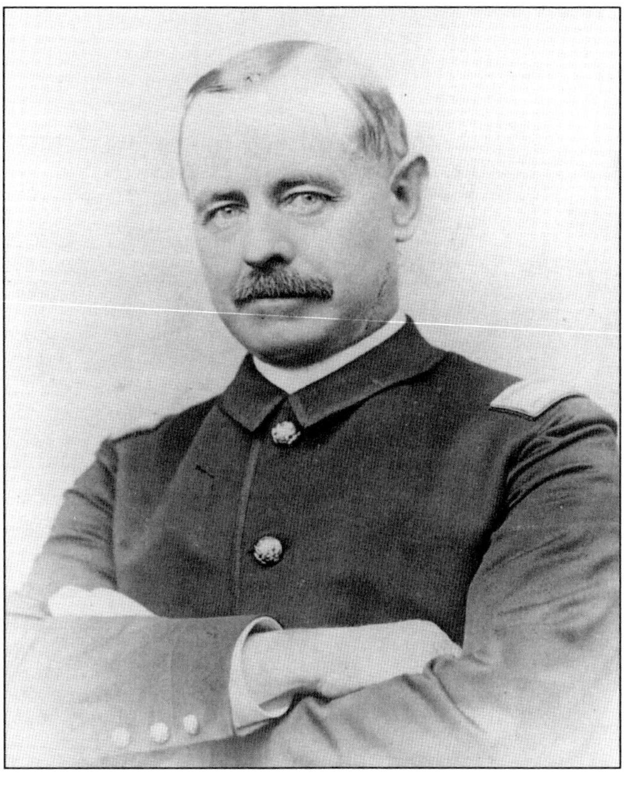

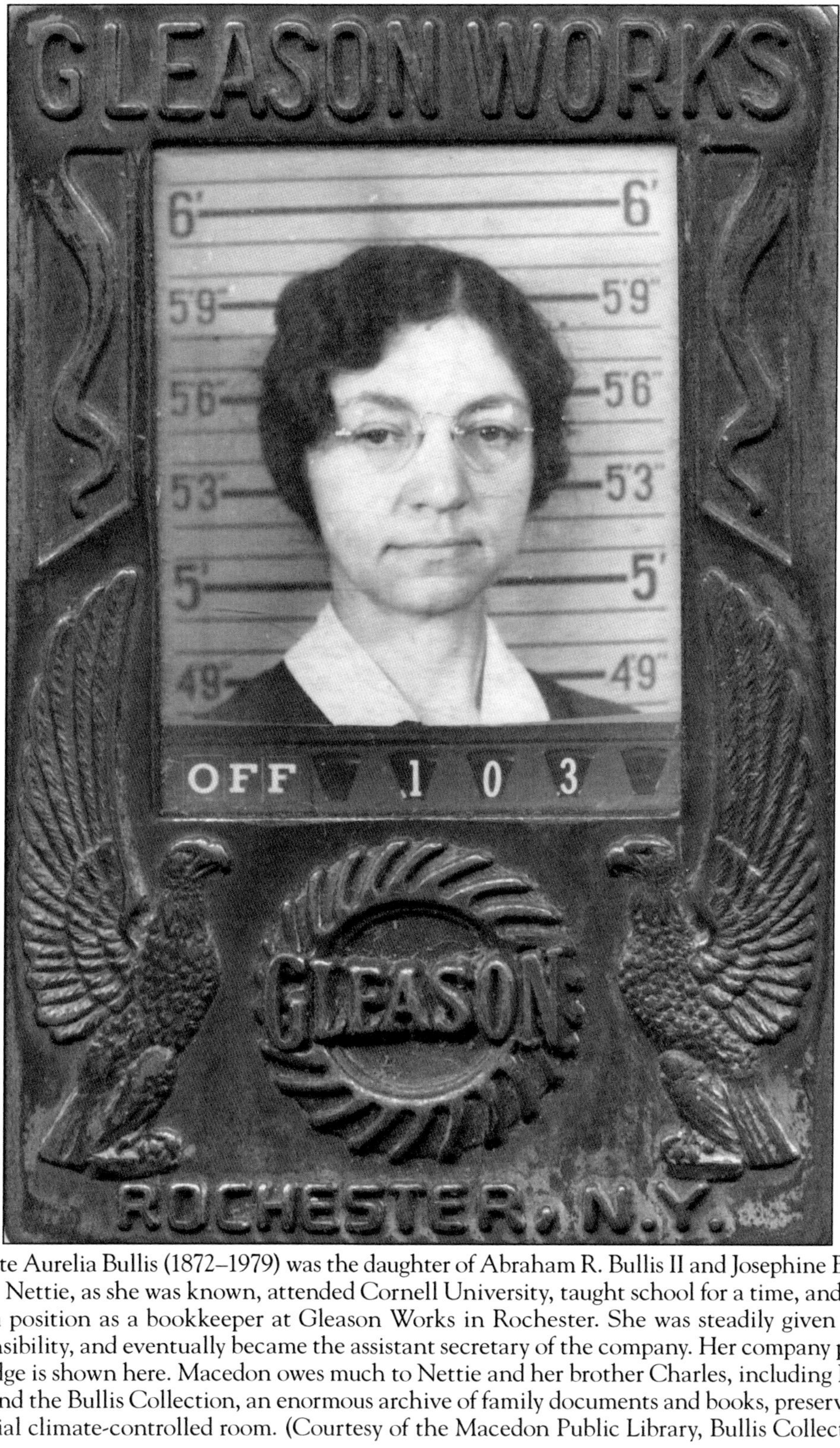

Jeanette Aurelia Bullis (1872–1979) was the daughter of Abraham R. Bullis II and Josephine Breese Bullis. Nettie, as she was known, attended Cornell University, taught school for a time, and then took a position as a bookkeeper at Gleason Works in Rochester. She was steadily given more responsibility, and eventually became the assistant secretary of the company. Her company photo ID badge is shown here. Macedon owes much to Nettie and her brother Charles, including Bullis Park and the Bullis Collection, an enormous archive of family documents and books, preserved in a special climate-controlled room. (Courtesy of the Macedon Public Library, Bullis Collection.)

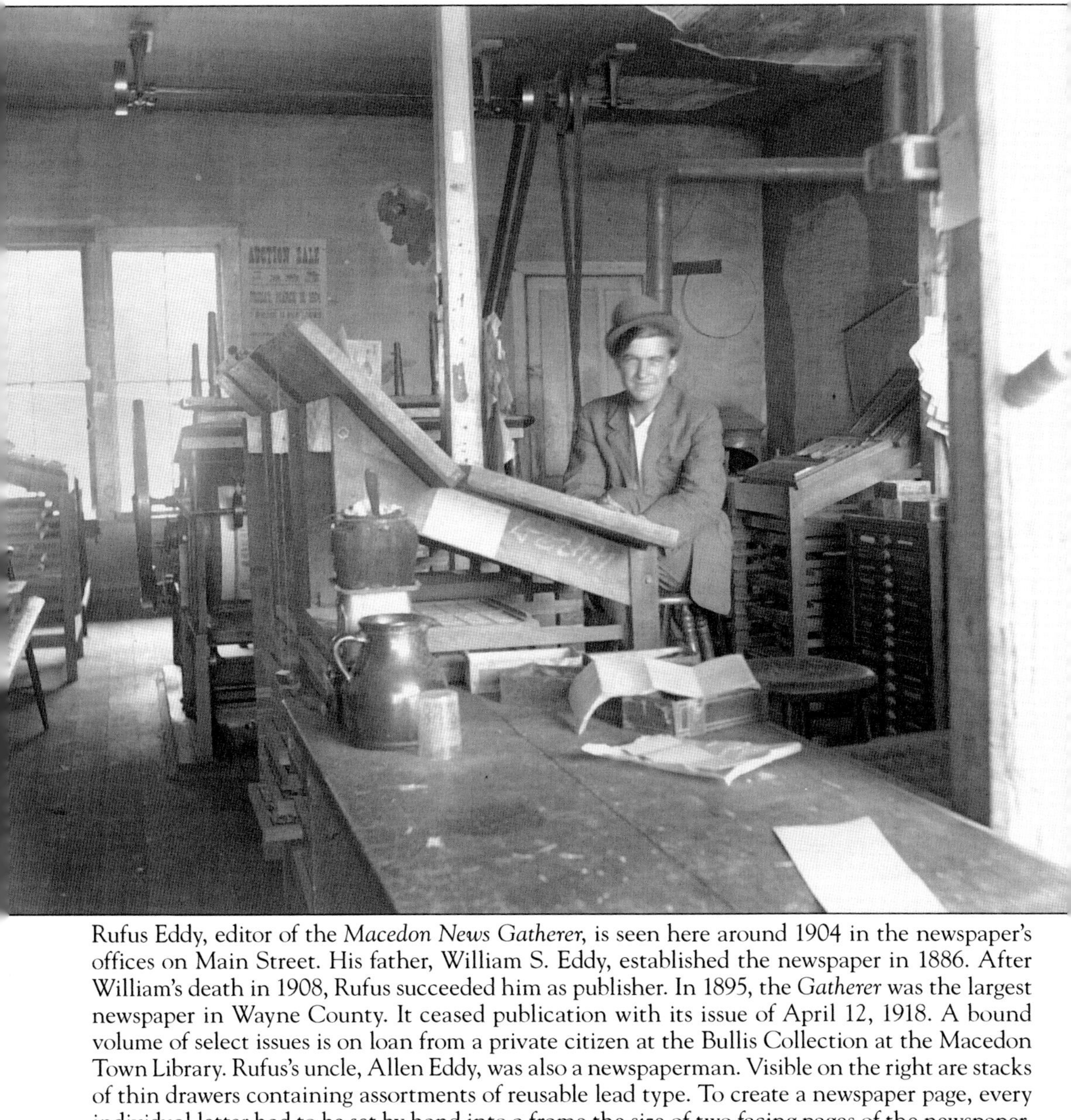

Rufus Eddy, editor of the *Macedon News Gatherer*, is seen here around 1904 in the newspaper's offices on Main Street. His father, William S. Eddy, established the newspaper in 1886. After William's death in 1908, Rufus succeeded him as publisher. In 1895, the *Gatherer* was the largest newspaper in Wayne County. It ceased publication with its issue of April 12, 1918. A bound volume of select issues is on loan from a private citizen at the Bullis Collection at the Macedon Town Library. Rufus's uncle, Allen Eddy, was also a newspaperman. Visible on the right are stacks of thin drawers containing assortments of reusable lead type. To create a newspaper page, every individual letter had to be set by hand into a frame the size of two facing pages of the newspaper. (Courtesy of Marlene Zimmer LeMoyne.)

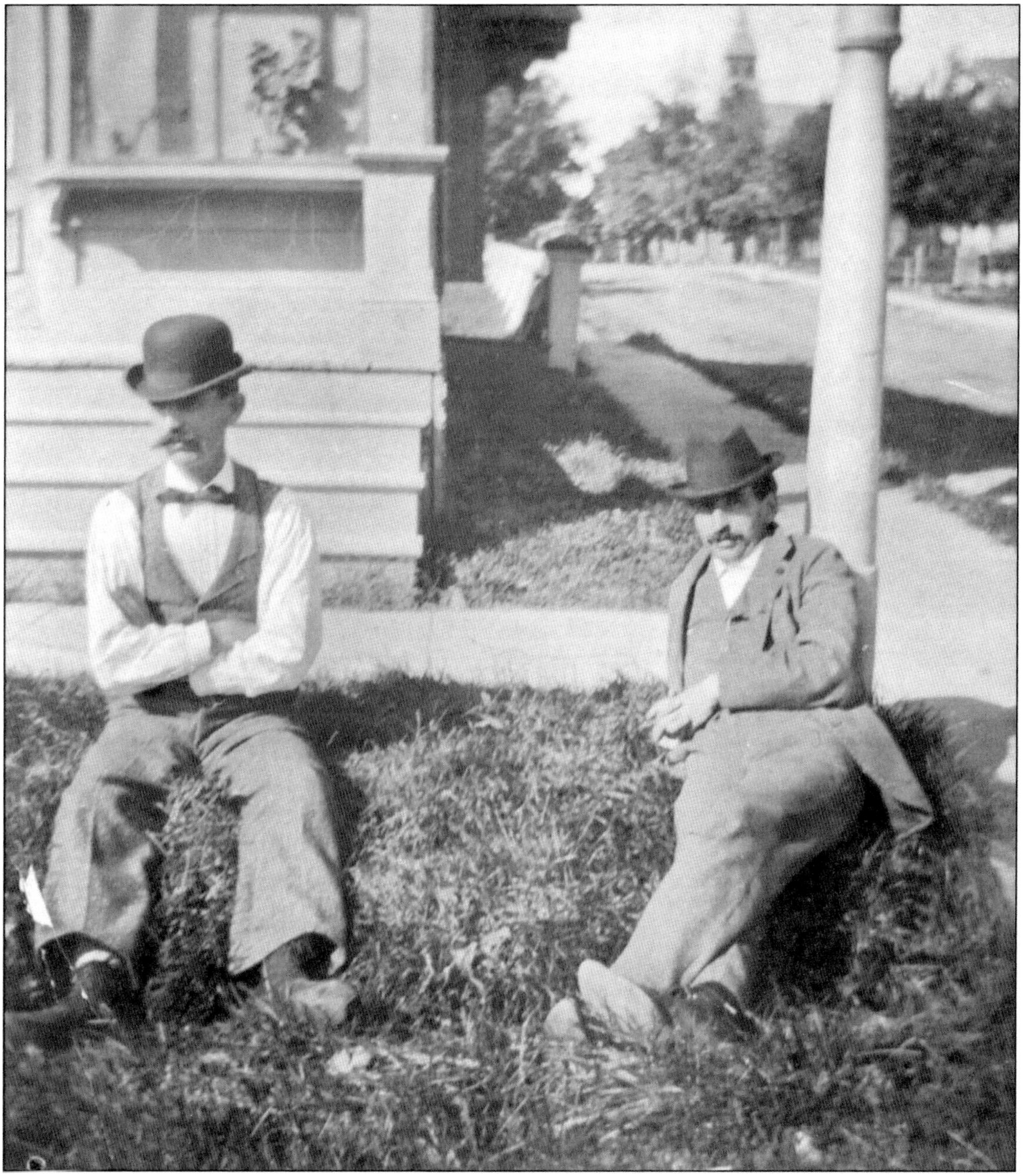

Newspaperman Will Eddy (left) and barber John Simmons take a break about 1906. Although they are captured in a casual pose, the two men are stylishly dressed. This was an era when gentlemen invariably wore a hat in public, and often a jacket and tie as well. (Courtesy of Macedon Town Historian.)

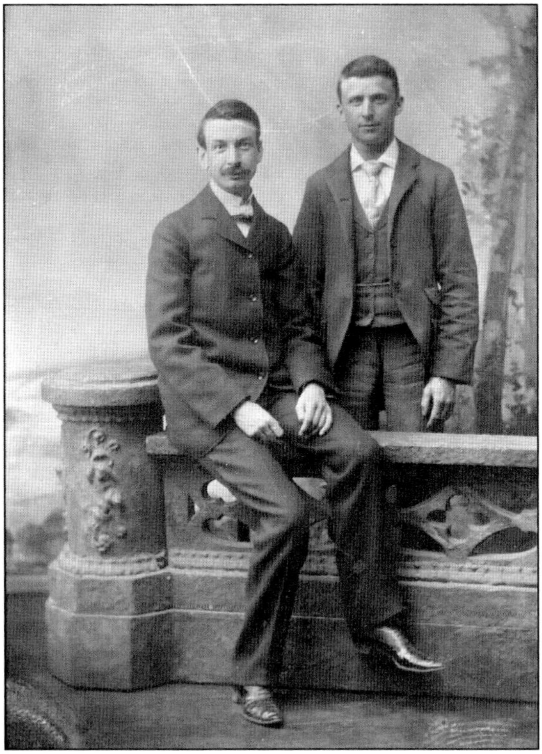

This tintype from May 1896 is a studio portrait of Macedon residents Allen Eddy (left) and George Brundage. Eddy had a distinguished newspaper career, including positions at the *Chicago Chronicle* and *Evening Herald*, the *New York Herald*, the *Syracuse Herald*, and the *Knickerbocker Press* in Albany. (Courtesy of Macedon Town Historian.)

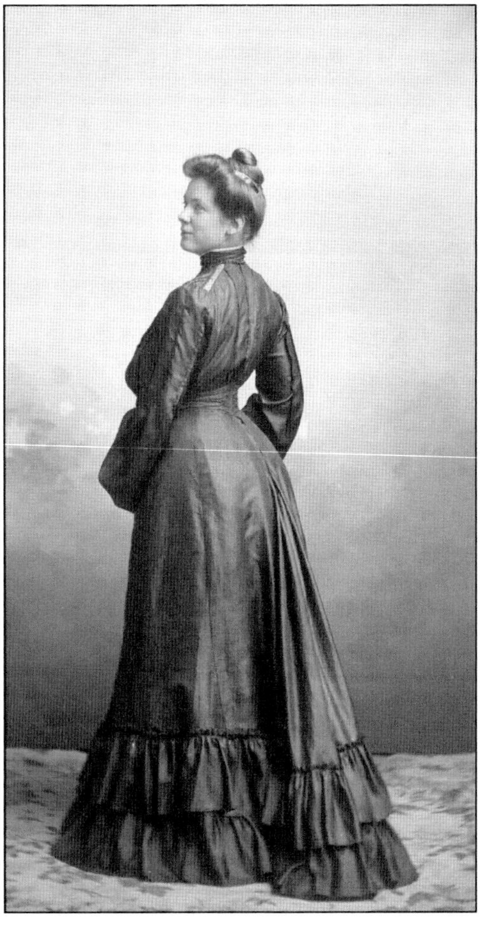

This stylish lady is Augusta Brundage, pictured about 1907 when she was 30 years old. At 46, she became the second wife of Macedon druggist Henry M. Littel. Gussie was a longtime member of the Macedon Baptist Church. The Rev. Frieda Ehrlich, who was the church's pastor for many years, roomed with the Littels until the church acquired a parsonage. (Courtesy of Macedon Town Historian.)

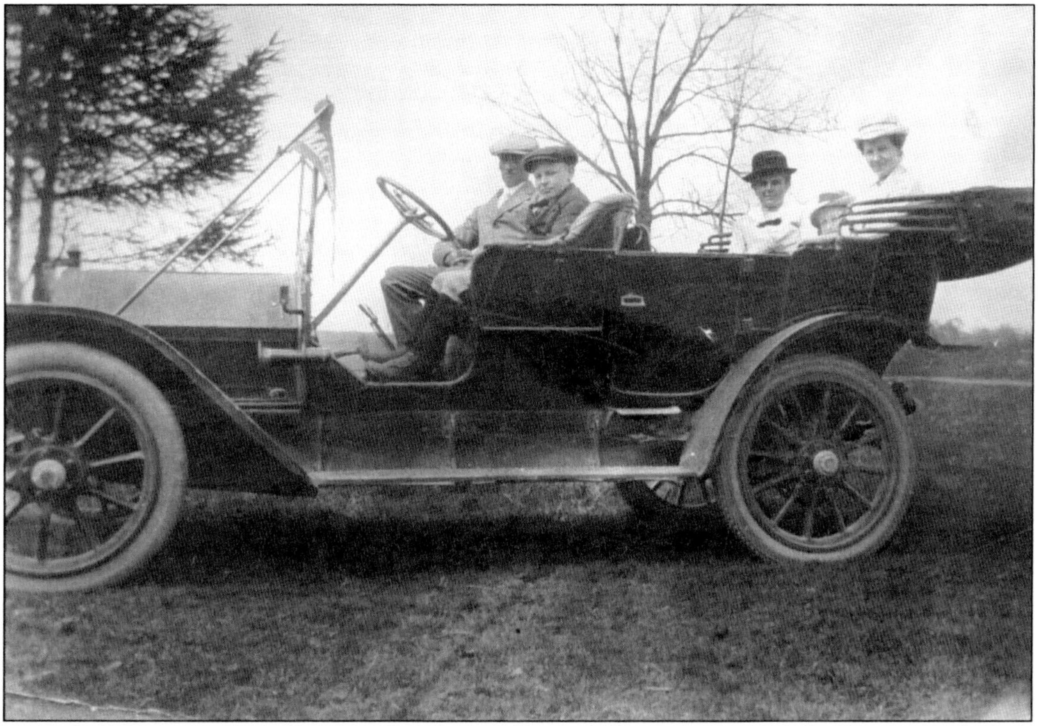

Frank Diebold and his son Ernest sit in the front seat of the family automobile around 1915. In back are Frank's wife, Emma, their son Charles (in bowler), and friend Nora Hoag. A Macedon pennant flies from the strut that holds the windshield. (Courtesy of Macedon Town Historian.)

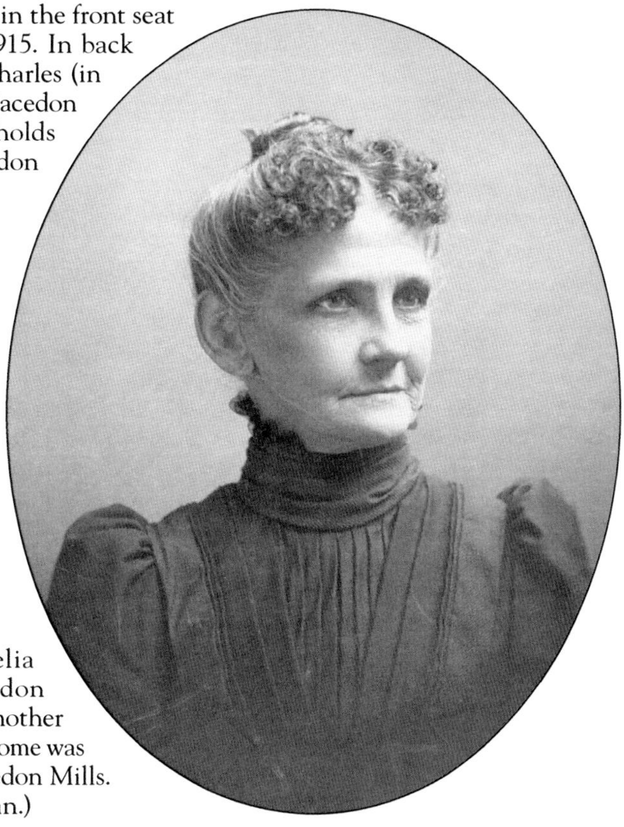

This is a studio portrait of Amelia Brundage, second wife of Macedon carpenter DeWitt C. Brundage and mother of Augusta Brundage. The Brundage home was on Main Street, just east of the Macedon Mills. (Courtesy of Macedon Town Historian.)

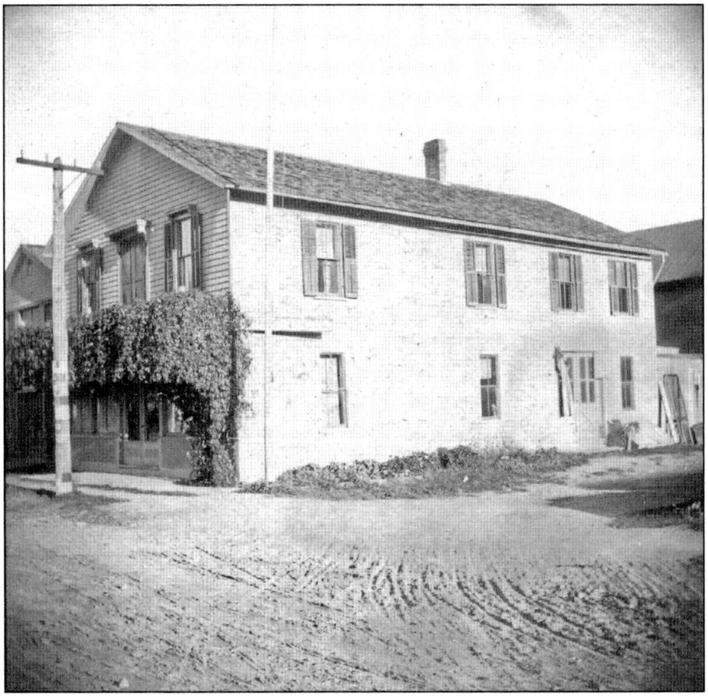

The home of DeWitt Clinton Brundage and his second wife, Amelia, is pictured here in the late 1800s. The house still stands, near the southeast corner of Main Street and old Erie Street. DeWitt and Amelia were the parents of Augusta "Gussie" Brundage Littel. (Courtesy of Macedon Town Historian.)

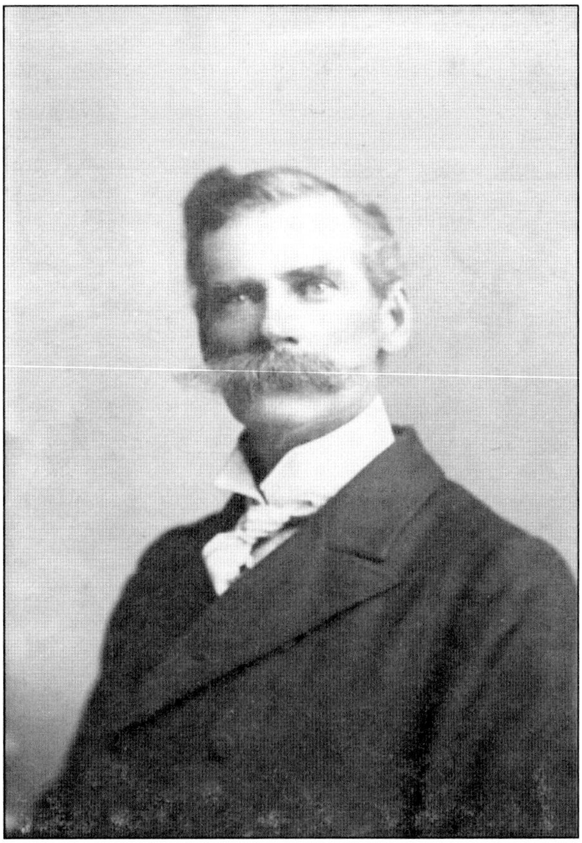

Macedon farmer Roderick McLeod sports a fierce mustache in this 1880s photograph. Roderick was born in Canada. He and his wife, Charlotte (daughter of Ichabod Briggs), raised a family in Wayneport, west of Macedon Village. Although today it is a sleepy crossroads, heavy traffic on the Erie Canal and the New York Central Railroad made turn-of-the-century Wayneport a busy commercial hub. (Courtesy of Margaret Hartsough.)

Emma Corser is 21 years old in this photograph taken about 1910. She and her sister Mayme "Mary" were dressmakers in Macedon. They and their brother Frank were living with their widowed mother, Clara, at the time of this photograph. (Courtesy of Macedon Town Historian.)

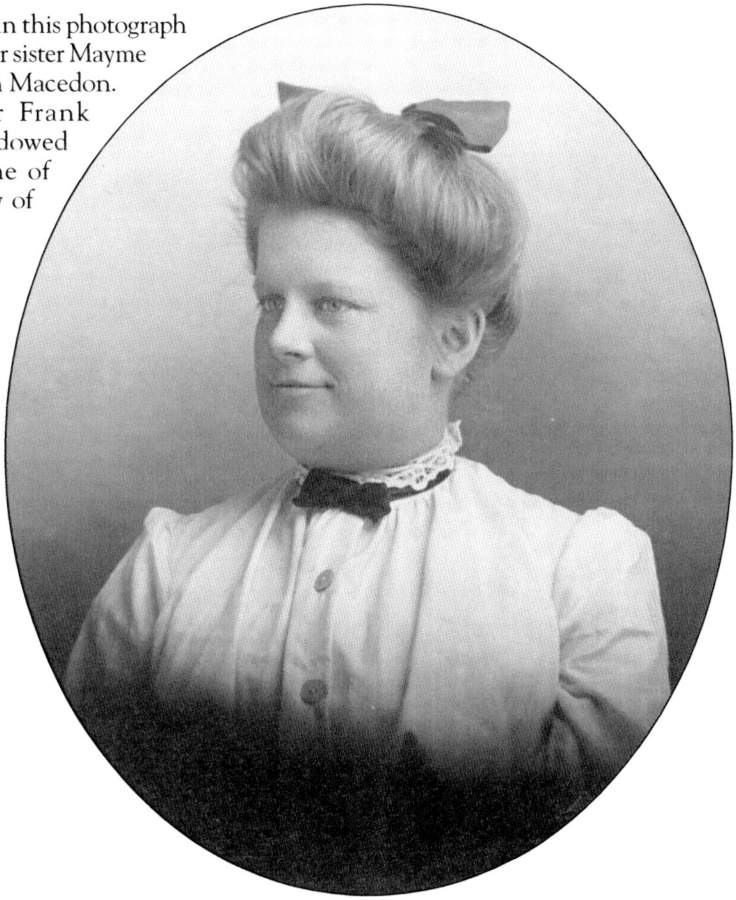

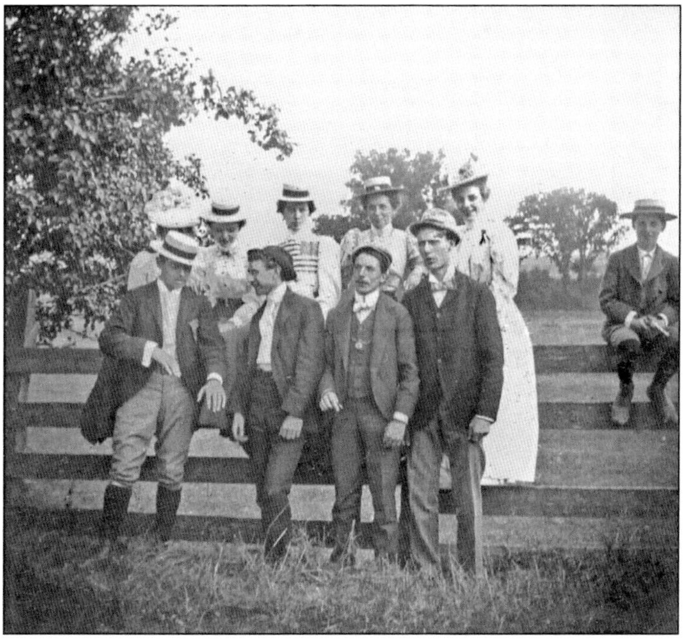

The individuals in this July 4, 1898, photograph are identified as, in no particular order, John Youngs, Evah Farrington, Carl Acker, Mabel D. Littel, Charles H. Ely, Gertrude Phetteplace, Elbert N. Ripley, Gussie Brundage, and Harriette A. Herendeen. Straw hats called skimmers were popular for both men and women. (Courtesy of Macedon Town Historian.)

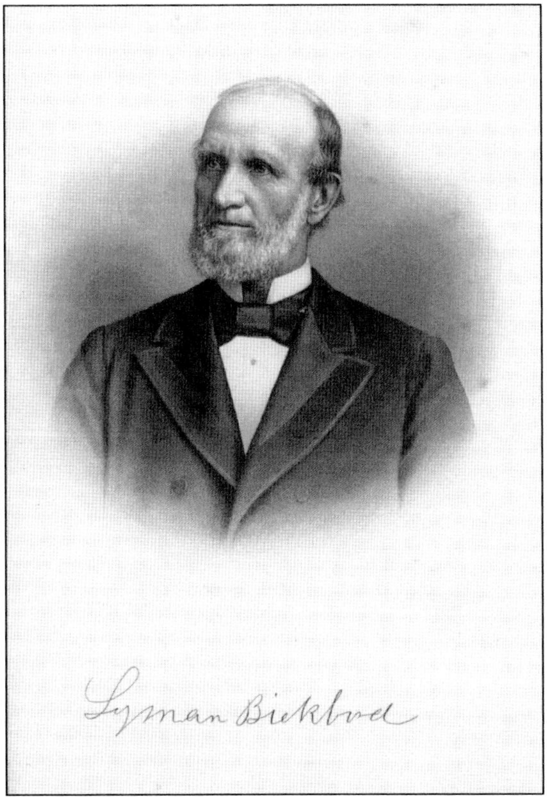

This is an engraving of Lyman Bickford, who, with his partner Henry Huffman, founded the Macedon Drill Works. The firm later became the American Seeding Machine Company. Bickford and his family lived on Bickford Street, in a house that is still a private residence. He donated land on the southeast corner of Center and Bickford Streets for a village park. (From *Landmarks of Wayne County*.)

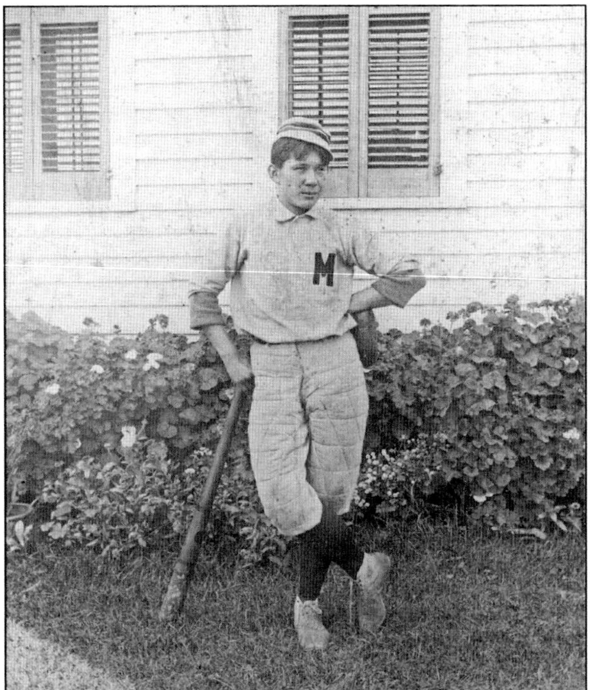

John Cook was a full-blooded Iroquois who lived with his family in Macedon for several decades. He was employed at the Drill Works and played on the Macedon baseball team when this photograph was taken about 1902. John's father, Charlie Cook, died in 1939 at the age of 85. Charlie, often called "Indian Charlie," was a renowned basket weaver whose handcrafted products can still be found locally. (Courtesy of Macedon Town Historian.)

School Street resident Ina Klock cuddles her cat as she sits outdoors in a rocking chair about 1920. Her lace-up boots, while not very convenient, were much better than the older high-button shoes, which could take as long as half an hour to fasten. (Courtesy of Macedon Town Historian.)

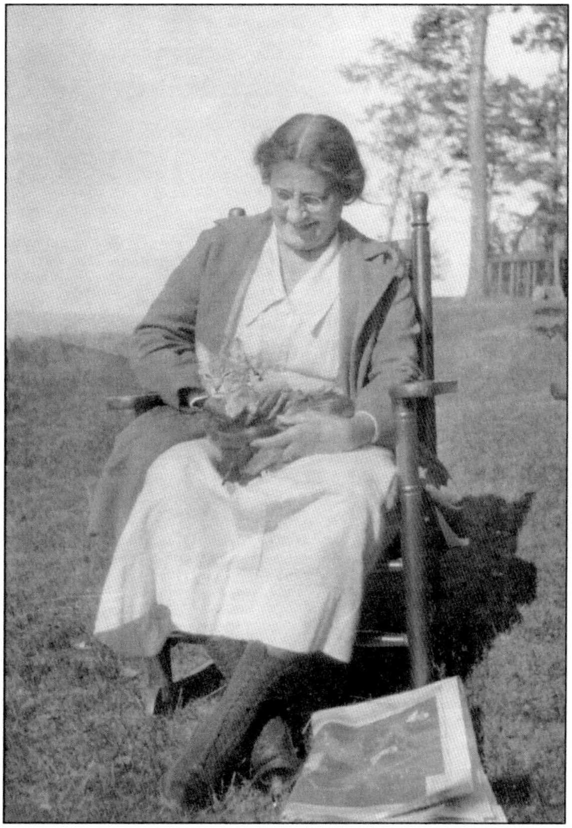

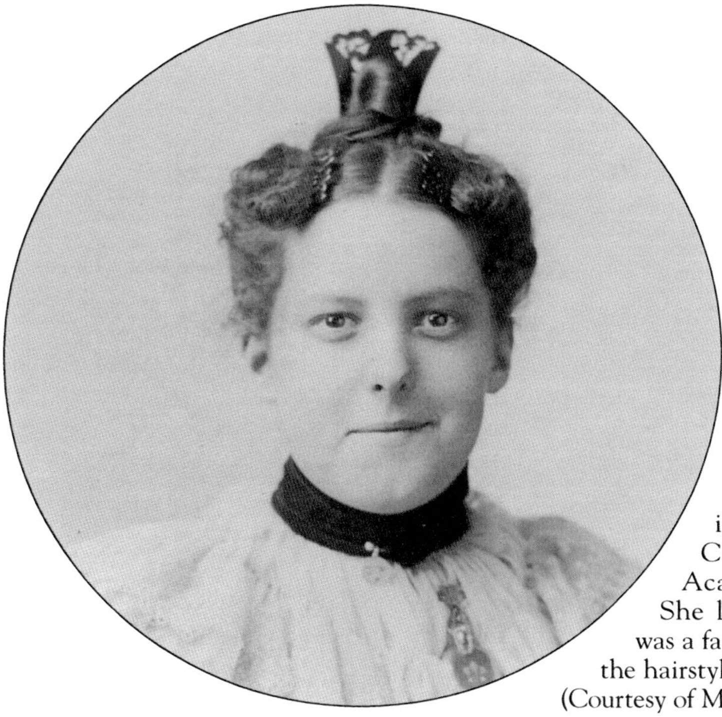

Mayme "Mary" Corser, dressmaker and seamstress, is pictured here about 1900. Corser attended Macedon Academy from 1889 to 1891. She later married Carl May. It was a fashion at the time to emulate the hairstyles of classical Greek statues. (Courtesy of Macedon Town Historian.)

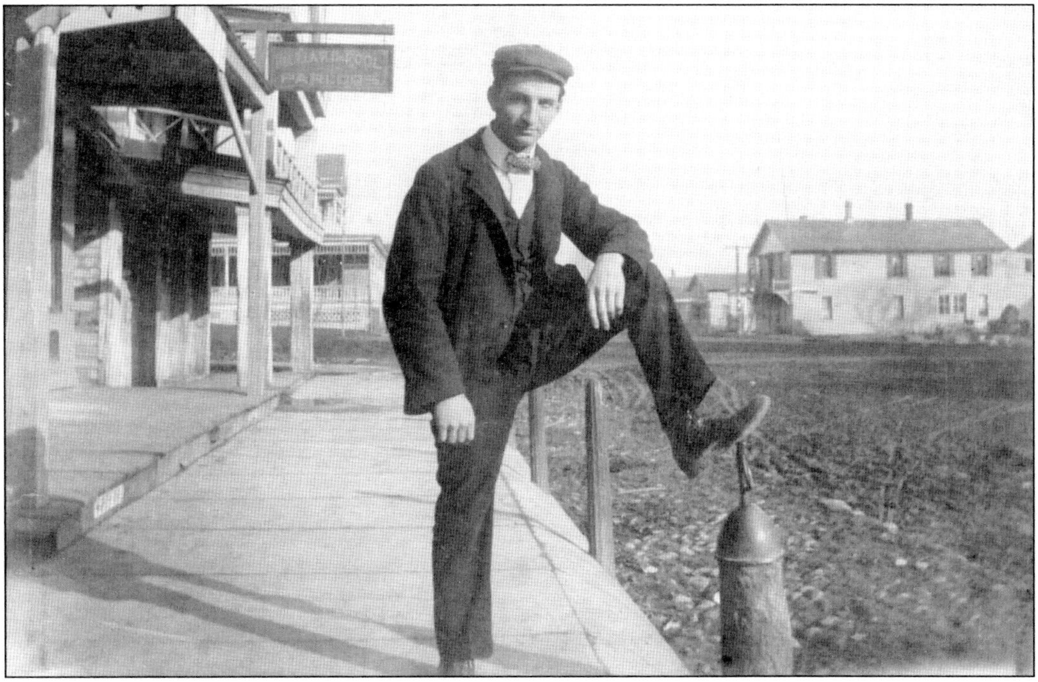

The inscription on this c. 1910 photograph identifies this gentleman as George Hoad, the first graduate of Macedon High School. George is standing on the north side of Main Street near Erie Street, in front of the billiard parlor, whose sign is visible at the top. (Courtesy of Macedon Town Historian.)

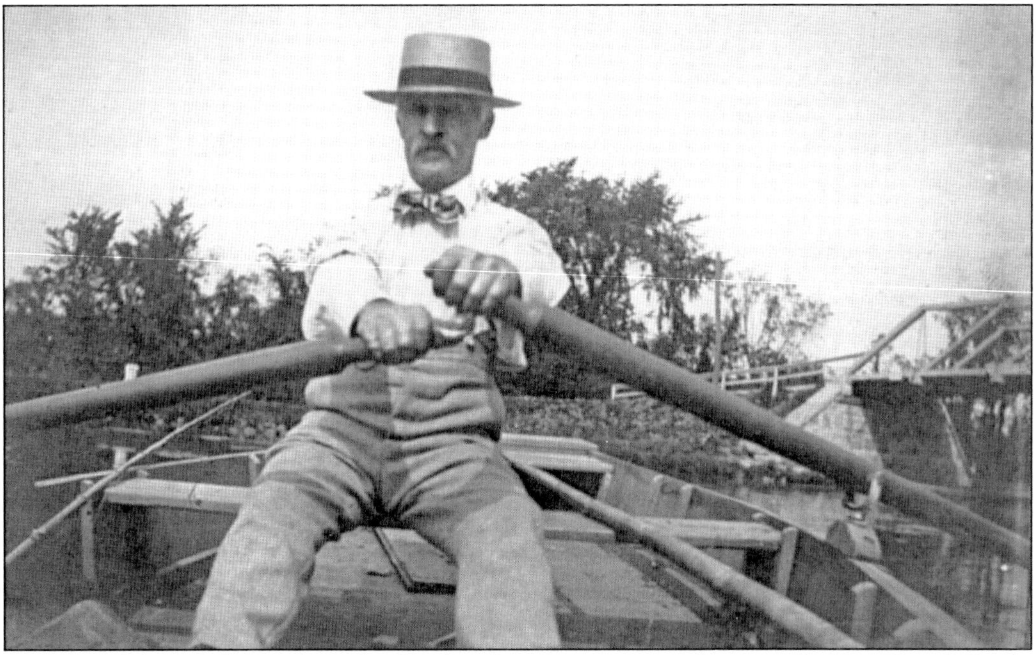

Grocer and dry goods merchant Ira Purdy takes a spin in a rowboat on the Erie Canal. Purdy had a store on the canal, and another on Main Street in Macedon. The fishing pole beside him suggests that he is out for some angling. (Courtesy of Macedon Town Historian.)

This photographic greeting card shows Macedon peddler Orville Hewitt in his buggy on the south side of Main Street around 1890. The inscription reads, "With best wishes for a very Merry Christmas, from 'Orv' Hewitt." The sign on the building at left says "Market." (Courtesy of Macedon Town Historian.)

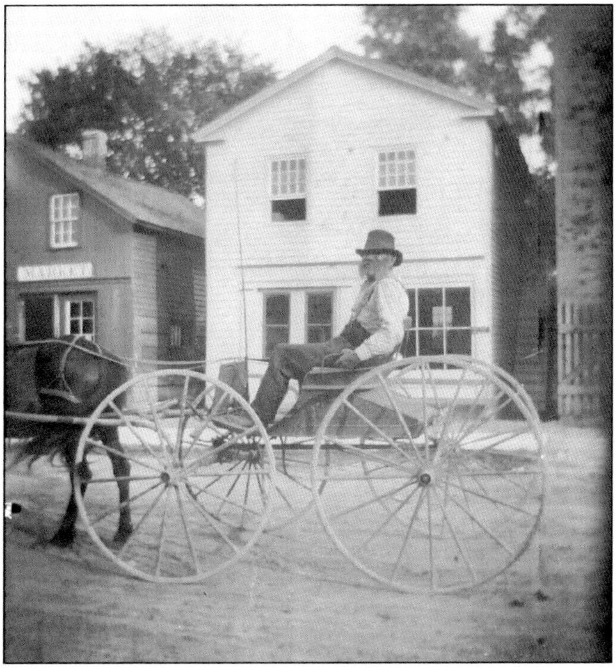

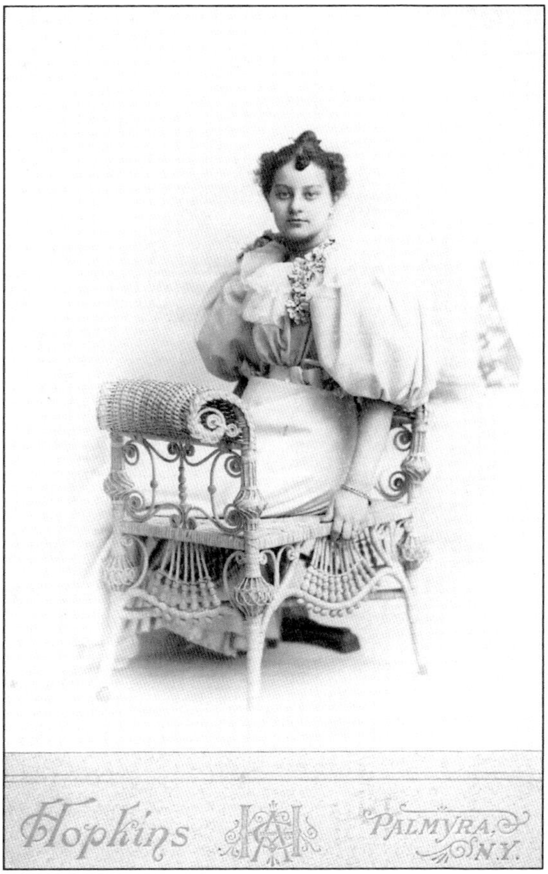

Effie Booth, daughter of hotelkeeper Edson Booth, poses for this photograph in 1896 at age 17. Elaborate wicker seats like the one seen here were fashionable at the time and were often used as props in studio portraits. (Courtesy of Macedon Town Historian.)

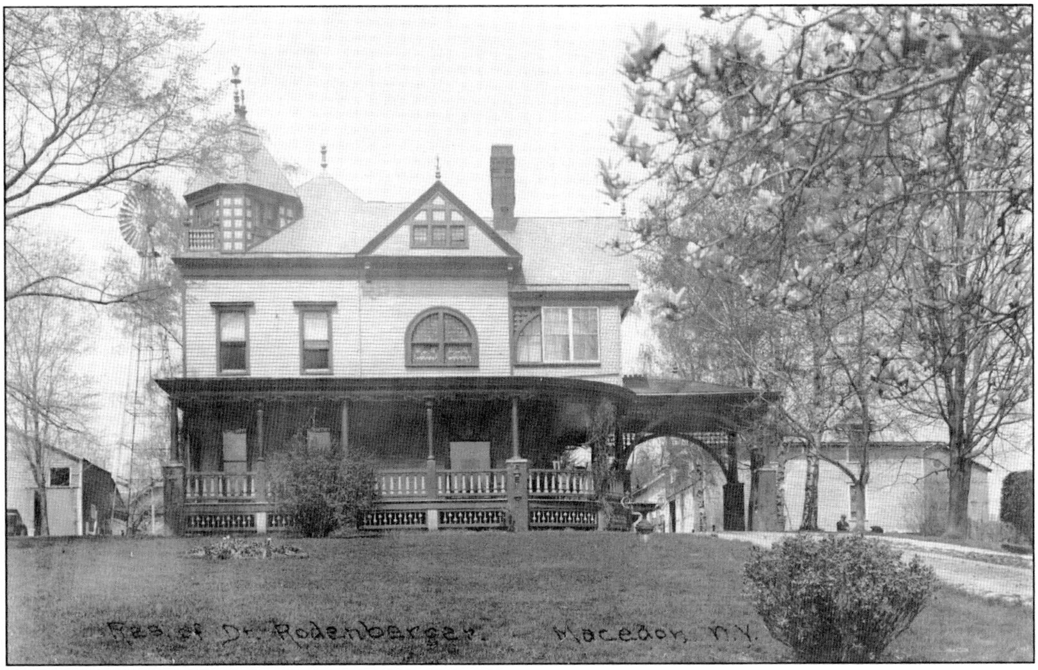

This house at 56 Main Street is locally known as the Bickford House, although Lyman Bickford, cofounder of the Bickford & Huffman Drill Works, lived more than a block away, on the west corner of Bickford and Center Streets. It was Bickford's partner Henry Huffman who actually built this house. In the undated photograph above, a windmill stands in the yard on the left. The below image, from a photo postcard, shows the building about 1912, during a period in its history when it was operated as the Kirk Home Sanitarium by Dr. E.M. Rodenberger. (Above, courtesy of Jason Kuntz; below, courtesy of Hod Conant.)

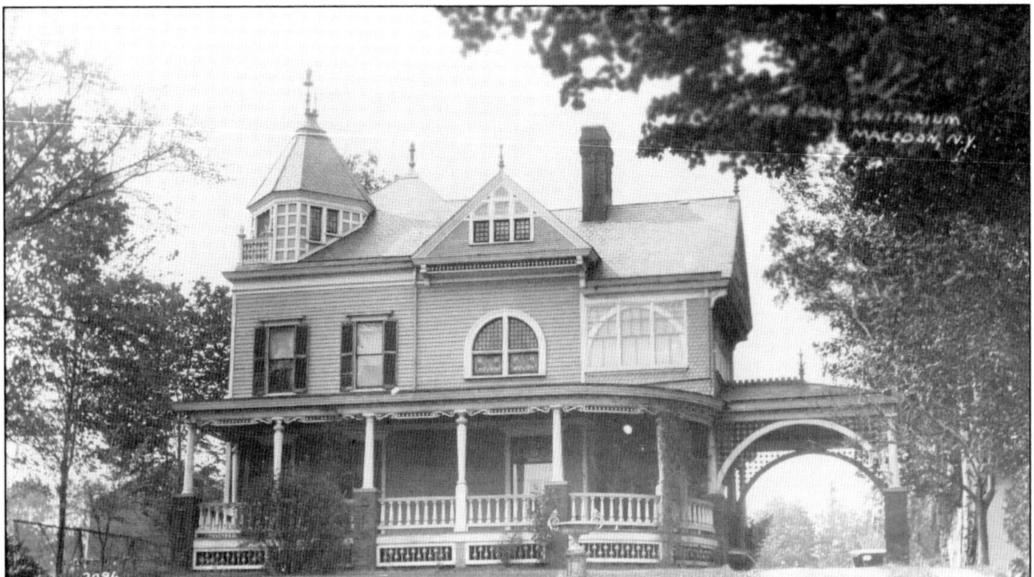

This house at 2195 State Route 350 is seen here when it was the home of Myron and Alice Hoag and their family. Myron was a successful farmer and former teacher. His great-grandfather Benjamin Hoag was a pioneer settler of Macedon. (Courtesy of Margaret Hartsough.)

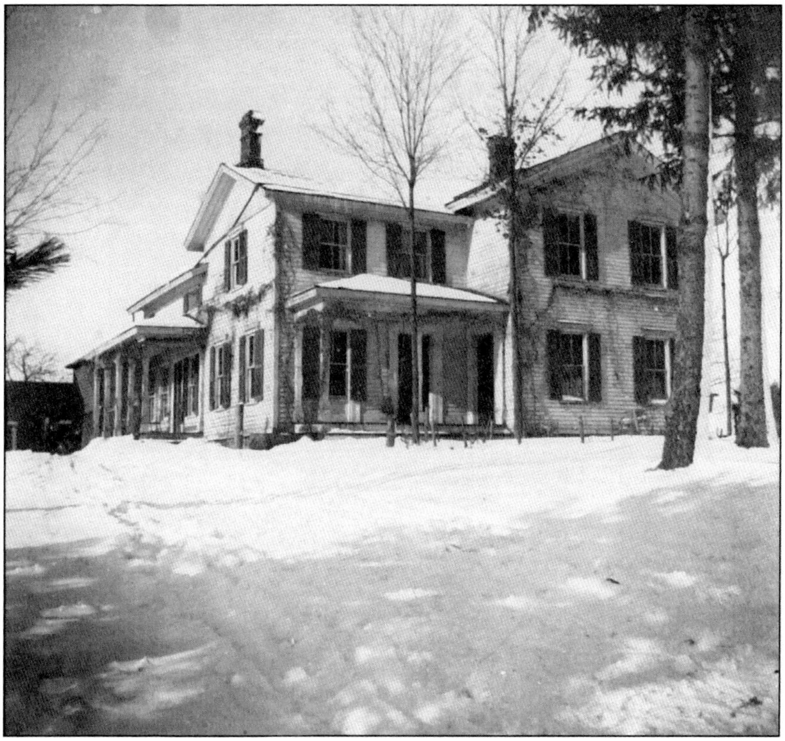

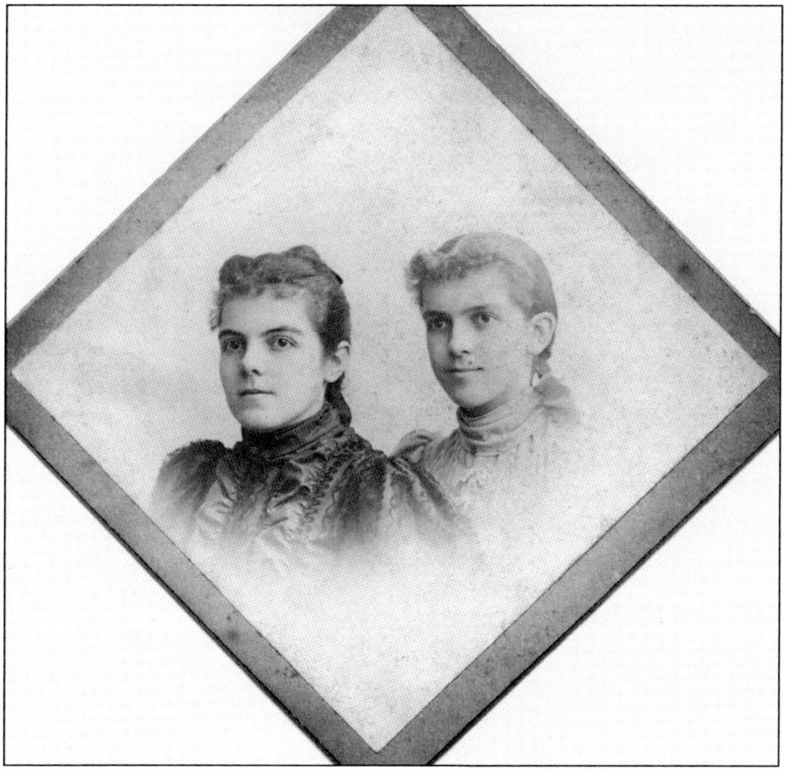

This 1895 photograph shows Myron and Alice Hoag's daughters, Nora (left) and Marion. Nora was 26 at the time of the photograph, and Marion, 16. (Courtesy of Margaret Hartsough.)

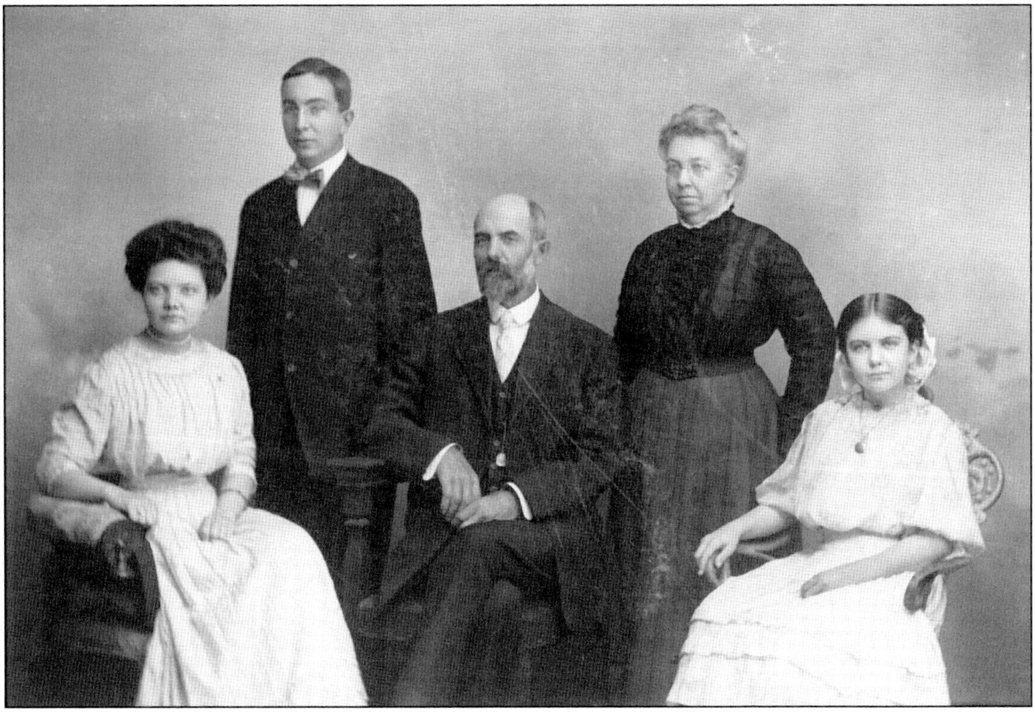

This portrait of the Blyth family was taken about 1910. Shown here are, from left to right, daughter Bessie Blyth Sanford, son Ray J. Blyth, father Edson J. Blyth, mother Ada Gilbert Blyth, and daughter Hazel Blyth Jeffrey. Edson owned the Cragg's Roller Mill, near the Macedon/Walworth border. (Courtesy of Macedon Town Historian.)

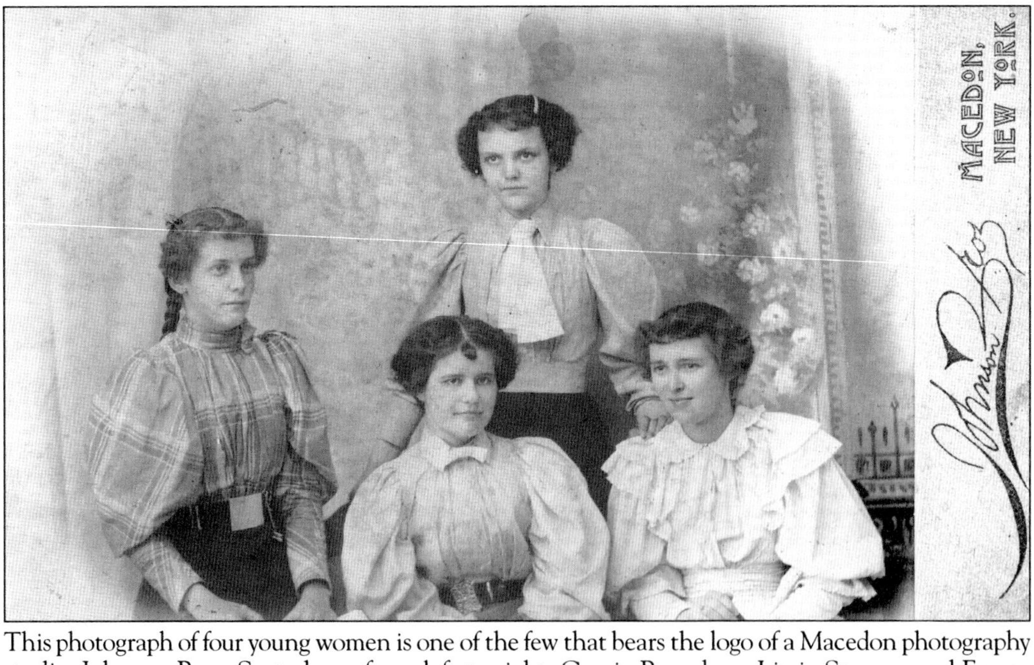

This photograph of four young women is one of the few that bears the logo of a Macedon photography studio, Johnson Bros. Seated are, from left to right, Gussie Brundage, Lizzie Storms, and Emma Cramer. Mabel Littel is standing at rear. (Courtesy of Macedon Town Historian.)

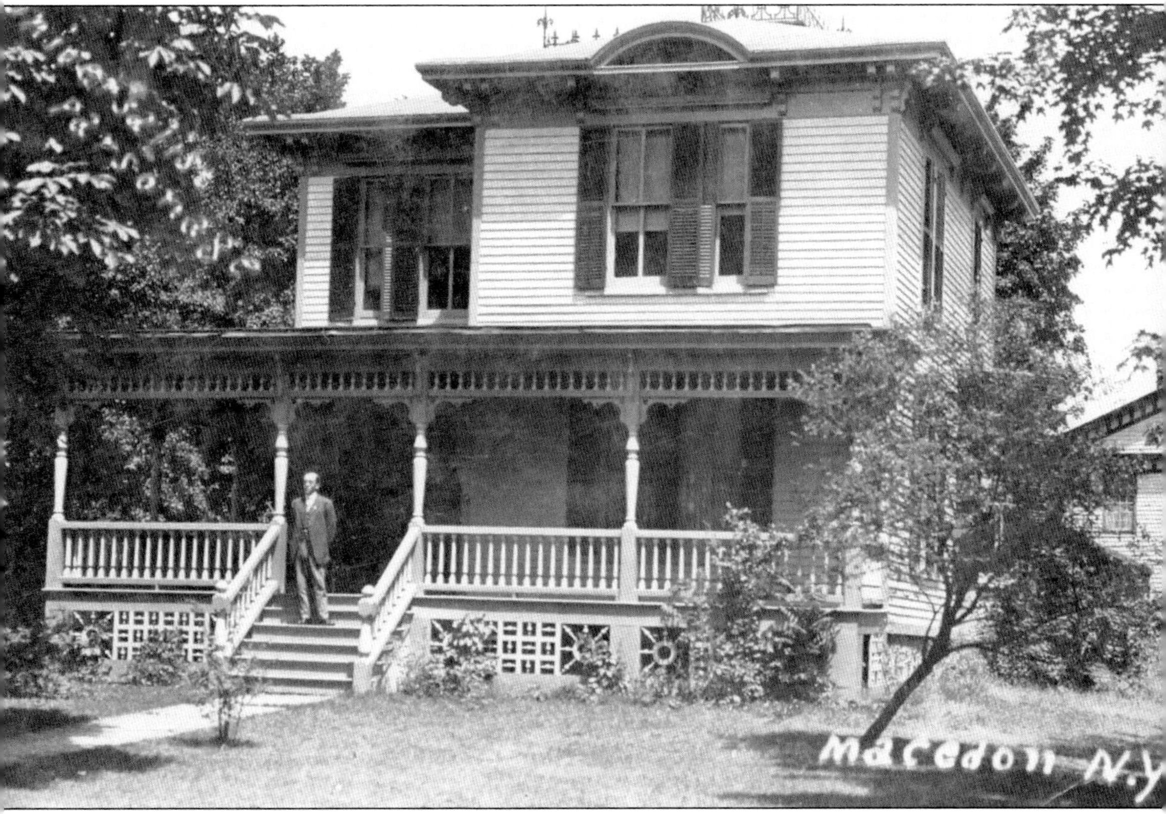

This house at 5 Center Street is pictured when it was the parsonage for the Universalist church next door. The ornamental iron widow's walk on the roof has since been removed, but this is still a single-family residence today. (Courtesy of Hod Conant.)

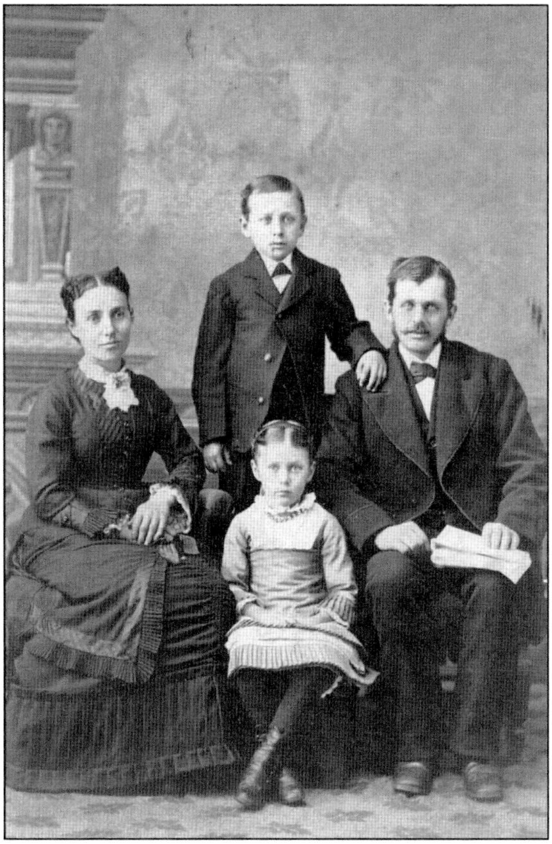

The Wiedrick family sits for this studio portrait about 1880. Martin Wiedrick (right) and Ella Galloway (left) were married in 1876. Posing with them here are their daughter, Eva, and son, Duane. Family records note that Ella died in 1883, just three years after this photograph was taken. (Courtesy of Macedon Historical Society.)

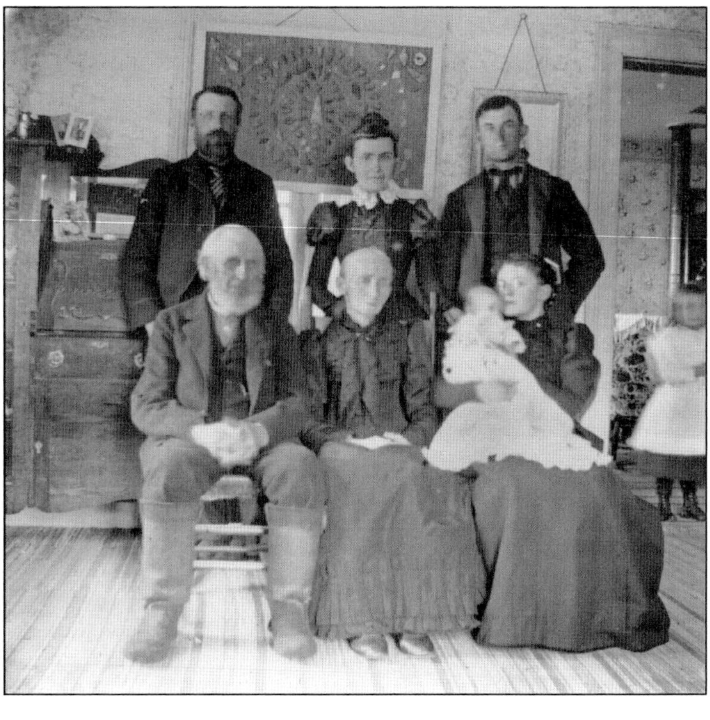

This family photograph was taken about 1887. Shown here are, from left to right, (first row) William Eldredge, Julia Eldredge, and an unidentified woman, probably Bert Brownell's sister, Lena, and her unidentified child; (second row) James Harbou, Helen Harbou, and Bert Brownell. The identity of the little girl in the doorway is not known. On the wall hangs a display case full of arrowheads. (Courtesy of Macedon Historical Society.)

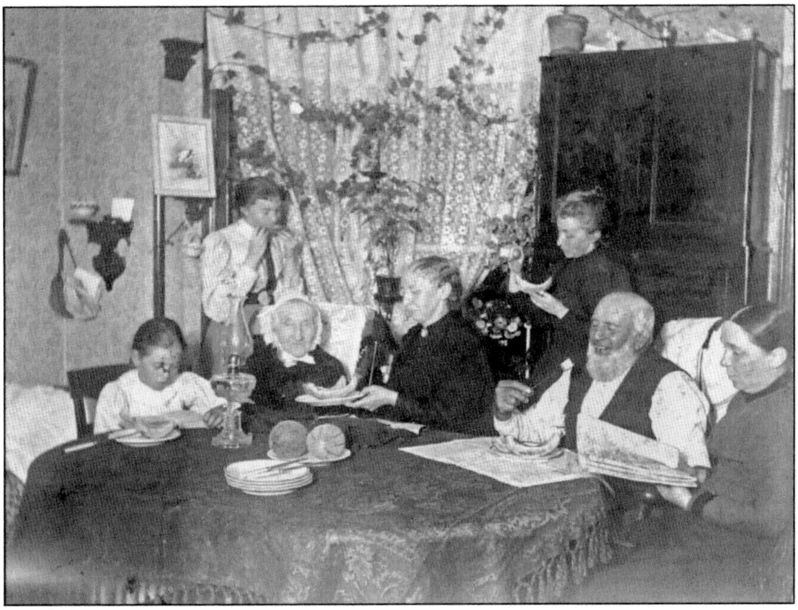

The inscription on the back of this photograph reads, "The Herendeen Family wish you a Merry Christmas." The family appears to be enjoying some melon. (Courtesy of Macedon Town Historian.)

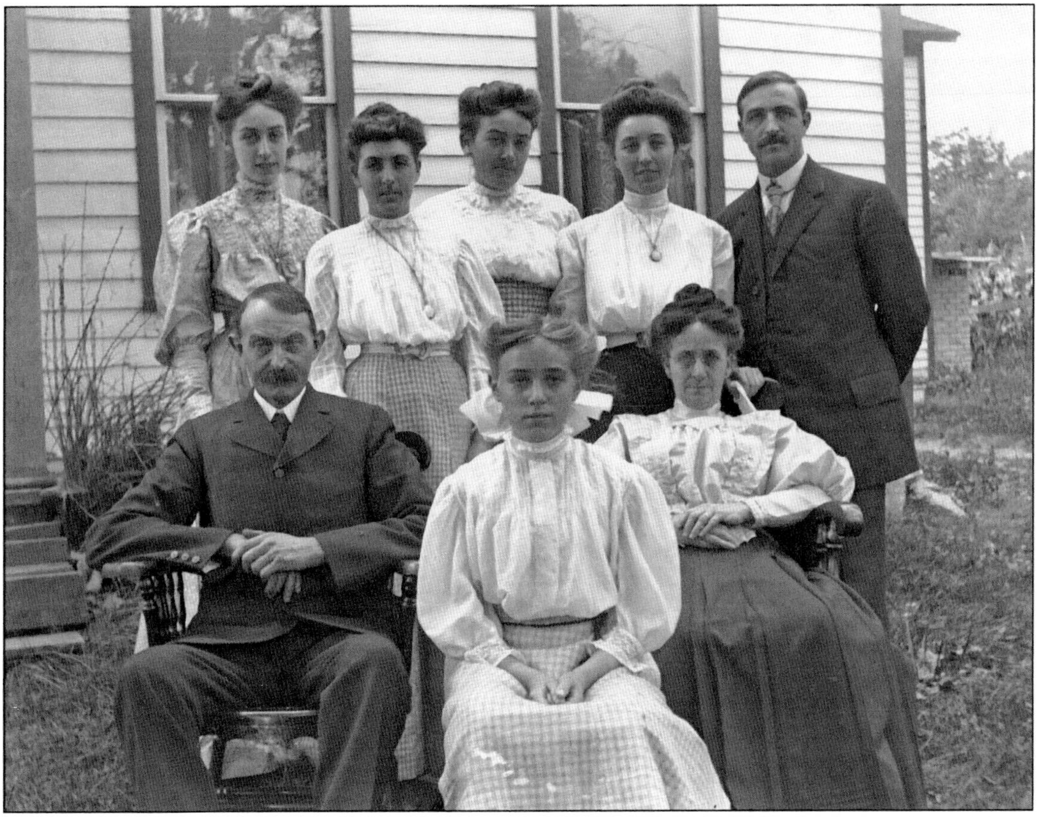

Members of the Beal family pose for a photograph about 1906. Shown here are, from left to right, (first row) Bernard Beal, Blanche Beal Richards, and Julia Servoss Beal; (second row) Bess Beal Sawyer, Hat Beal, Lois Beal Gridley, Mayme Lapham Jaffrey, and Aner Beal. (Courtesy of Marlene Zimmer LeMoyne.)

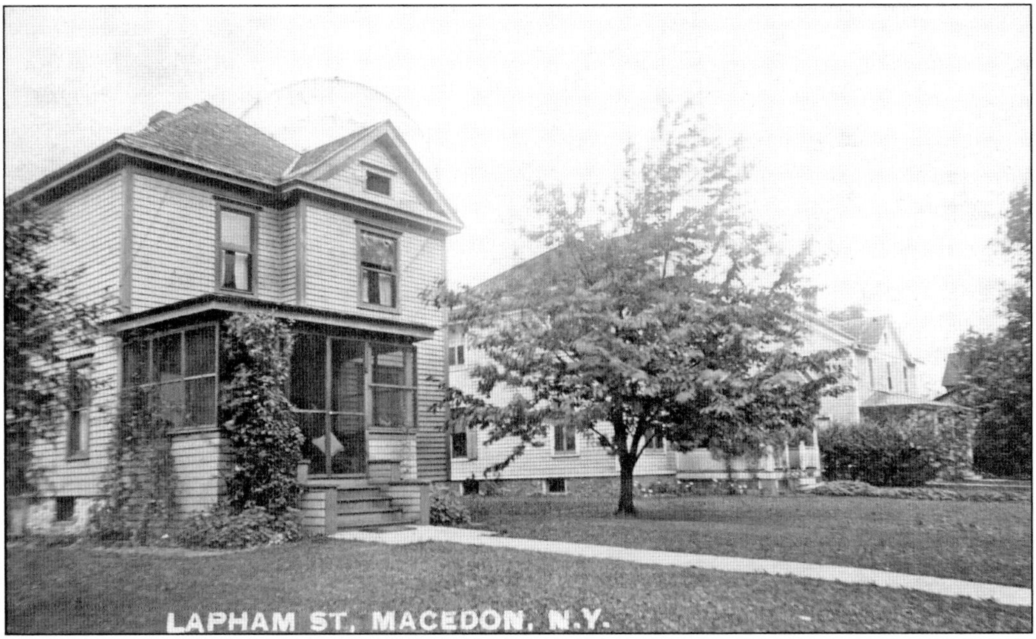

This house at 16 Lapham Street is pictured in the early 1900s. Lapham Street was previously known as School Street, because the Macedon Union Free School, popularly known as Macedon High School, was located there. The school was on the west side of the street, near what is today 12 Lapham Street. The school was constructed in 1887 to replace a school building that had been destroyed by fire the previous year. (Courtesy of Hod Conant.)

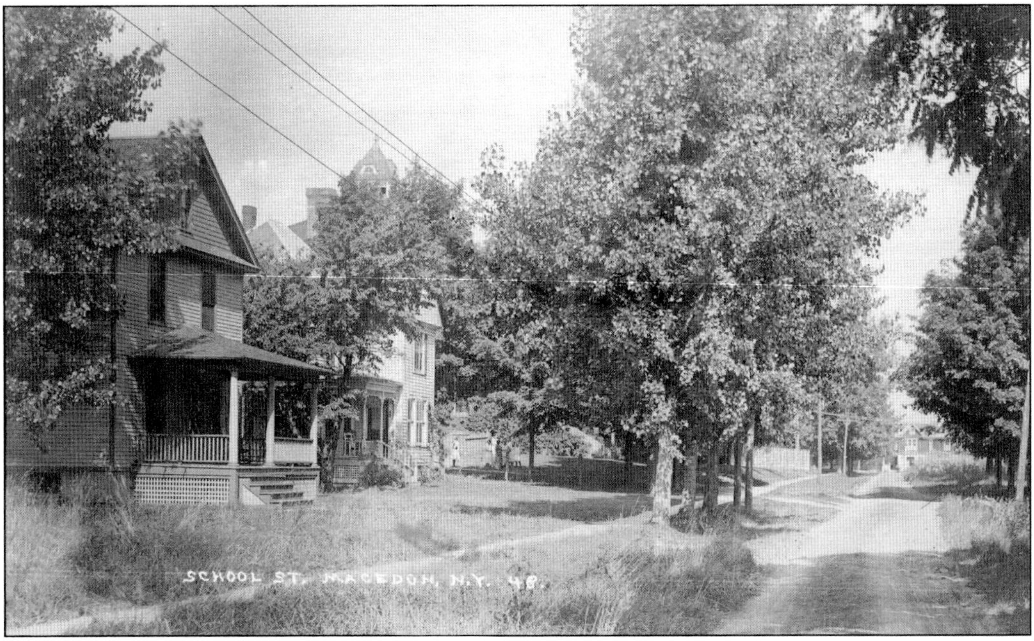

The house on the left is at 6 Lapham Street. The cupola of the old Macedon High School is just visible over the tops of the trees. The school building continued to be used for some functions even after the new high school was built on West Street in 1928. The school building was finally demolished in 1947. (Courtesy of Hod Conant.)

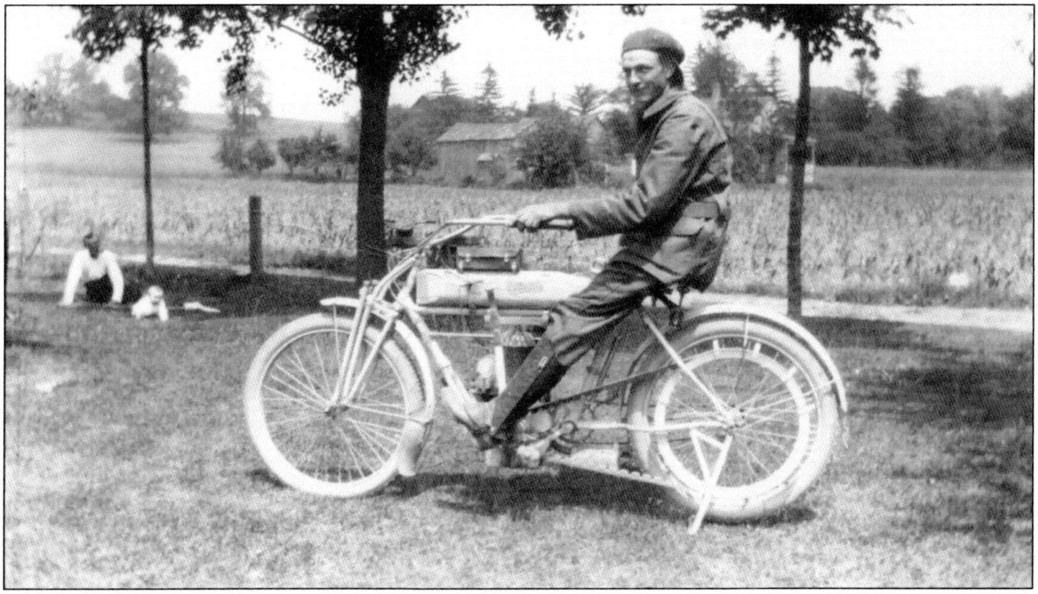

Henry Kemp poses on an early motorcycle around 1914. Motorcyclists in New York State were not required to wear helmets in those days. The man in the background is Henry's older brother Fred Kemp, who ran the Macedon Hardware store for many years. The child is Fred's oldest son, Milton. (Courtesy of Hod Conant.)

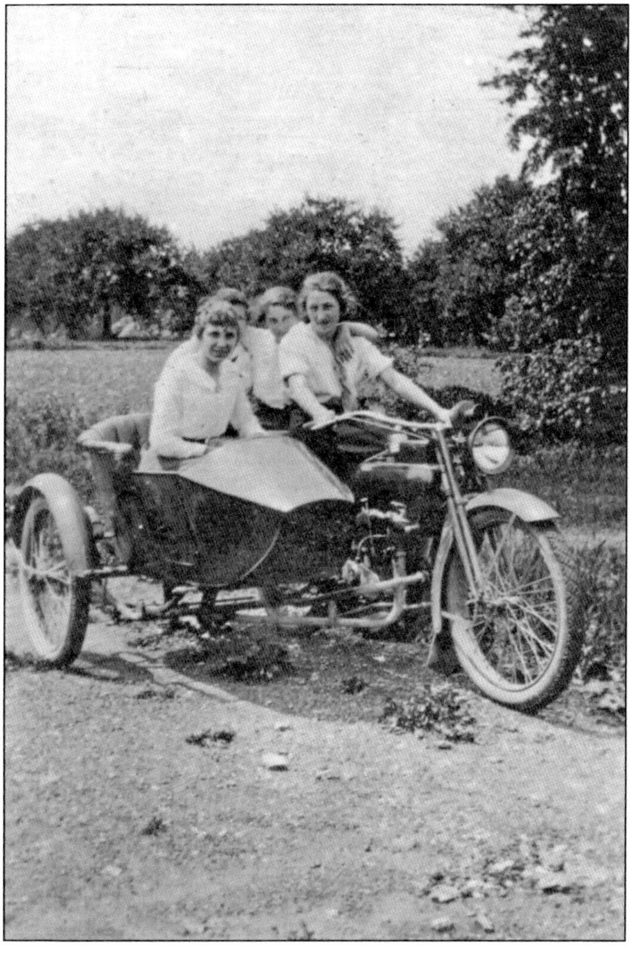

Emma Kemp Conant is at the driver's seat of this motorcycle. Hazel Crocker Henning sits directly behind her. The photograph does not identify the other two women. When motorcycles became popular, sidecars for passengers soon followed. This photograph was taken in the 1920s. (Courtesy of Hod Conant.)

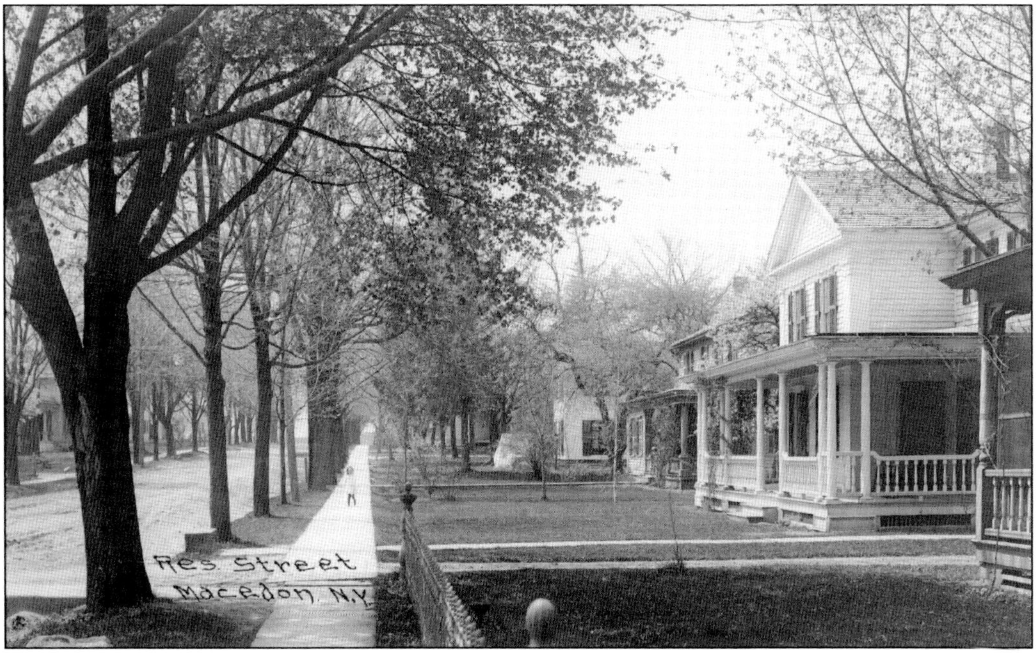

This photo postcard is labeled "Res [Residential] Street." In fact, it is the north side of Bickford Street. The ornamental cast-iron fence in the foreground used to stand in front of 20 Bickford Street. This view is looking west along Bickford Street, which at one time was known as North Main Street. (Courtesy of Hod Conant.)

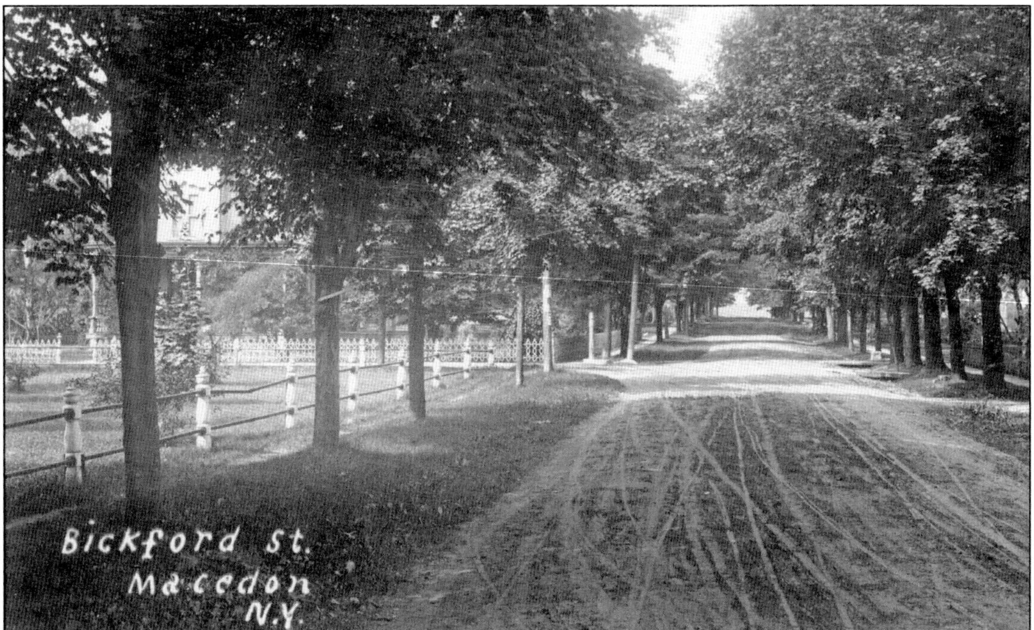

The fence on the left once marked the northern edge of Bickford Park. The park is on the east corner of the intersection of Center and Bickford Streets. Lyman Bickford donated the land for the park, which is across the street from his former home. (Courtesy of Hod Conant.)

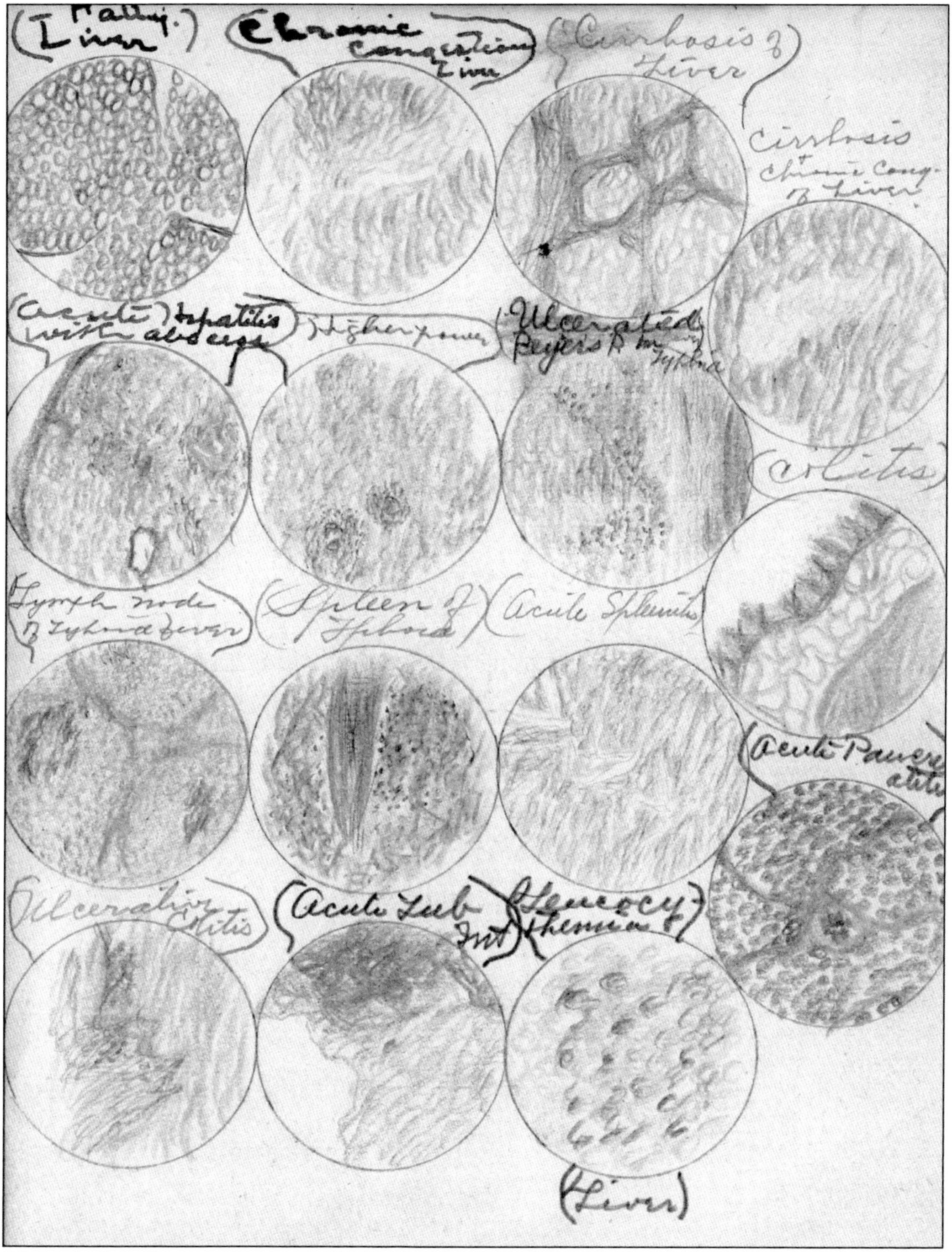

This is a page from a laboratory notebook kept by Dr. Cyrus Packard Jennings when he was a medical student in 1892. He viewed various kinds of pathological tissues through a microscope and made drawings of them. The original sketches are in color. This notebook, and a similar notebook of microscopic views from a course in histology, contain Dr. Jennings's notes from his courses at medical school. Dr. Jennings practiced medicine in Macedon for several decades. (Courtesy of Macedon Historical Society.)

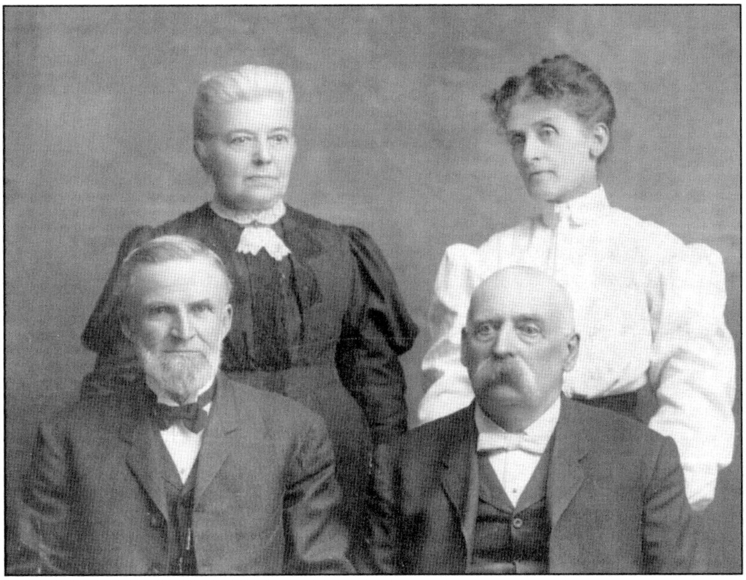

The husband and wife on the left in this c. 1899 photograph are Myron Hoag and Alice Smith Hoag. On the right are Alice's brother Lucius Smith and his wife, Ida. (Courtesy of Margaret Hartsough.)

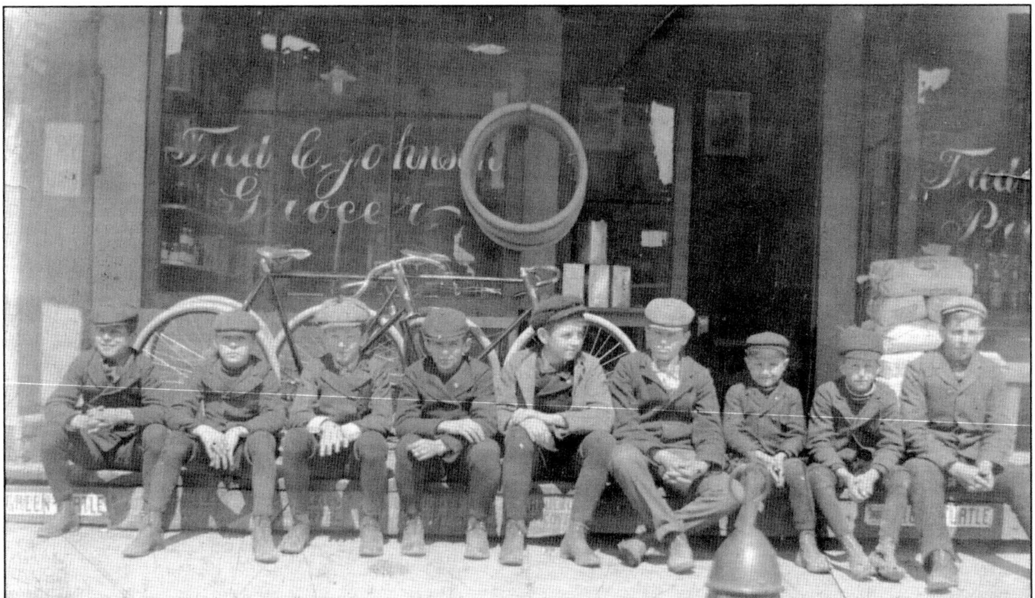

Among the boys lounging with their bicycles in front of the Fred C. Johnson Grocery Store on Main Street around 1895 are Isaac Dean, Eddie Fitzgibbons, Ralph Breese, Hiram Newton, Leo Fuller, Leon Hare, Willard Baseman, Elmer Phelps, and Ralph Hawes. (Courtesy of Macedon Town Historian.)

Three

Macedon Children and Schools

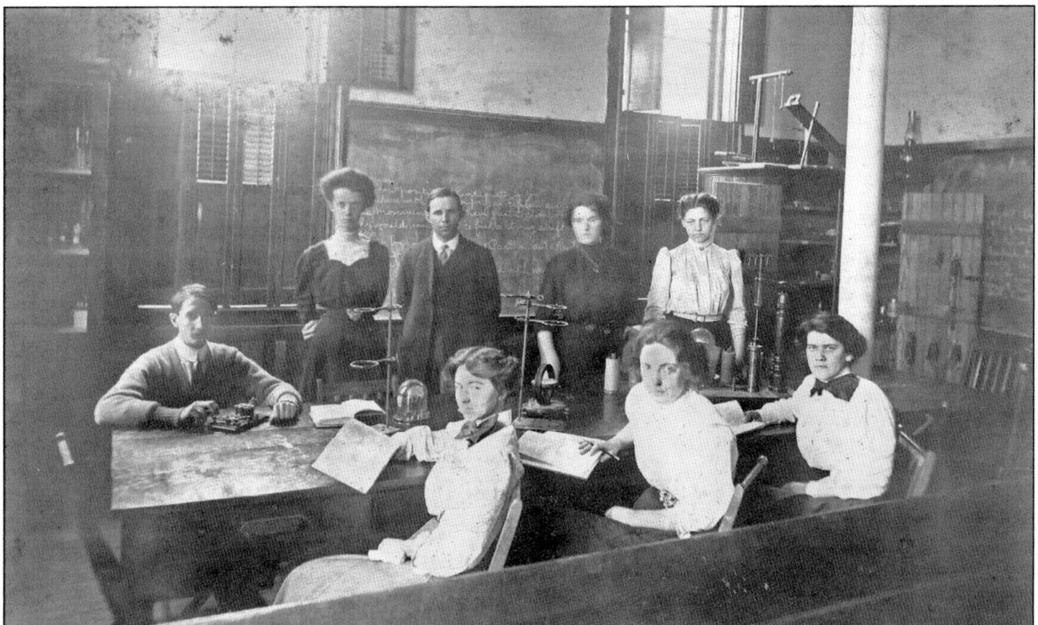

This is the science laboratory at Macedon High School in 1910. Pictured are, from left to right, (seated in front) Edna Wilcoxen, Bernadine McGarry, and Annie Neary; (on the other side of the table) Joseph Farrell, Phoebe Cahill, Freeman Crane (principal), Mary O'Neil, and Nettie Bullis. Farrell is working with a telegraph apparatus. On the lab bench are devices for magnetic, electrical, and vacuum experiments. Stored on a shelf at top right are physics experiments for demonstrating a pendulum and an inclined plane. The kerosene lamp next to the shelf suggests that this laboratory had not yet been wired for electrical lighting. (Courtesy of Hod Conant.)

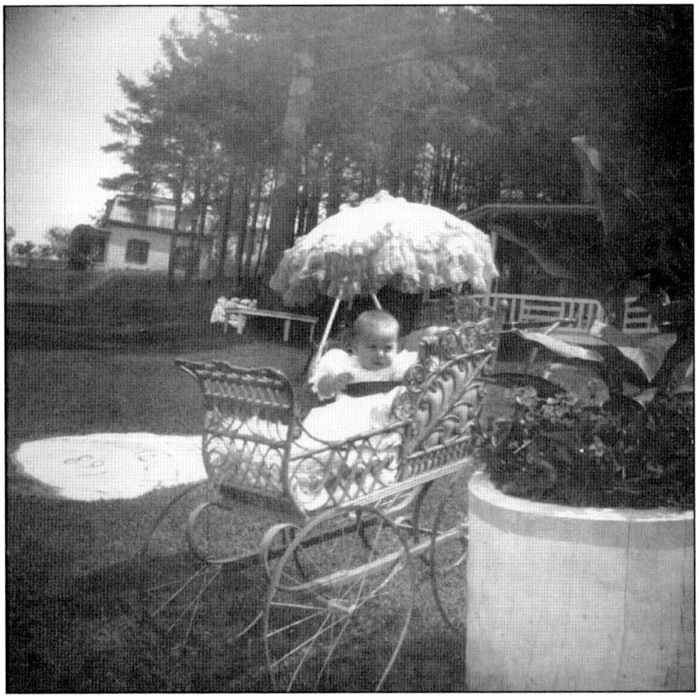

Baby Viola Brundage rides in a fancy carriage in 1891, protected from the sun by a little parasol. Because there were few paved surfaces, carriages needed large-diameter wheels than today's strollers. There were no seat belts or safety features, and, unlike modern baby carriages, those from a century ago did not fold up. Carriages like this were expensive and were passed down through the family. (Courtesy of Macedon Town Historian.)

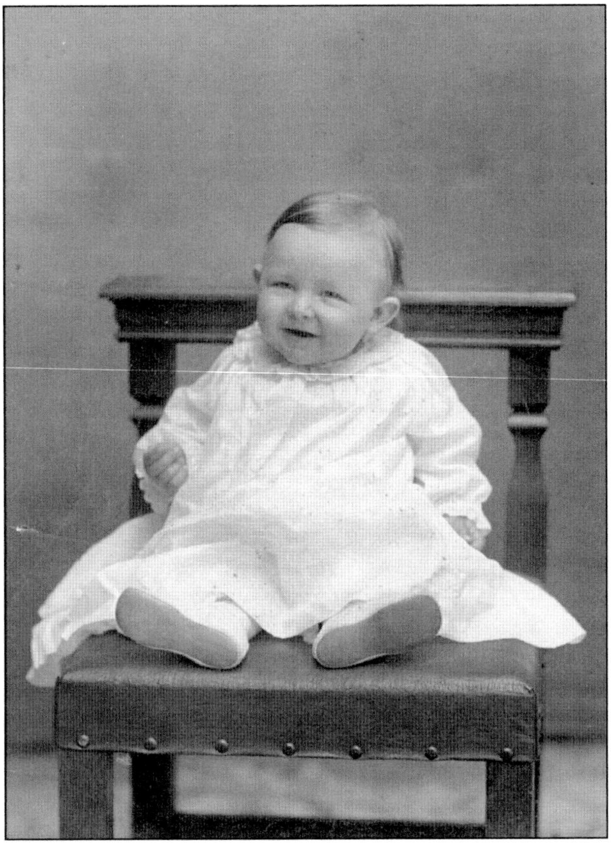

This happy baby is Marvin Eggert, son of Macedon residents Fred and Gertrude Eggert. The photograph was taken about 1910, probably in the Eggert home, since a studio portrait would typically have featured a more elaborate chair and background scenery. The Eggert family later moved from Macedon to Palmyra, where grown-up Marvin became a truck driver for a coal company. (Courtesy of Macedon Town Historian.)

Marion Hoag poses with her doll for a studio portrait around 1884. She later graduated from Macedon Academy and married Lewis F. Allen of Farmington. (Courtesy of Margaret Hartsough.)

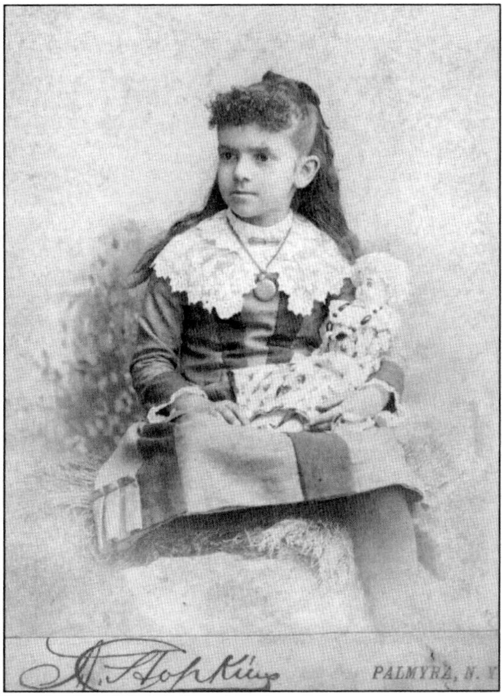

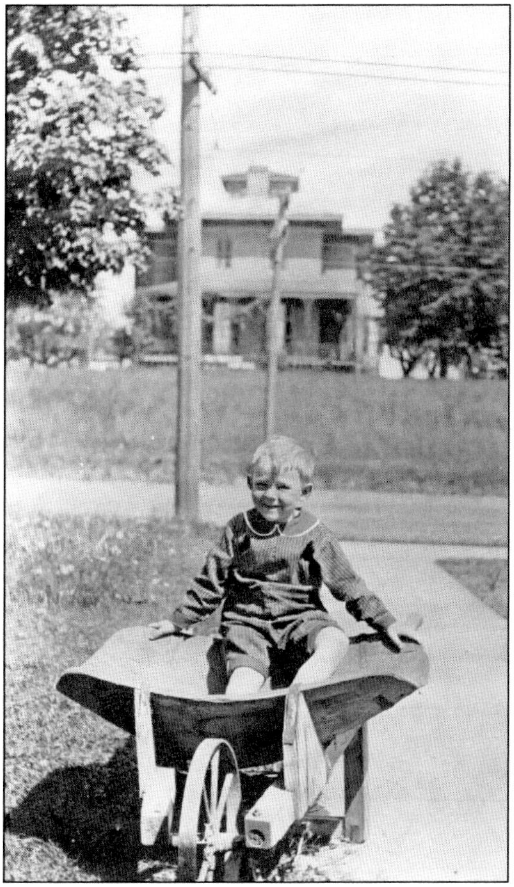

Why is this little boy sitting in a wheelbarrow? Perhaps he is waiting for someone to give him a ride. The inscription on this c. 1915 photograph identifies the boy as Roger Hawes. He is on the sidewalk across Main Street from the Lapham house. (Courtesy of Hod Conant.)

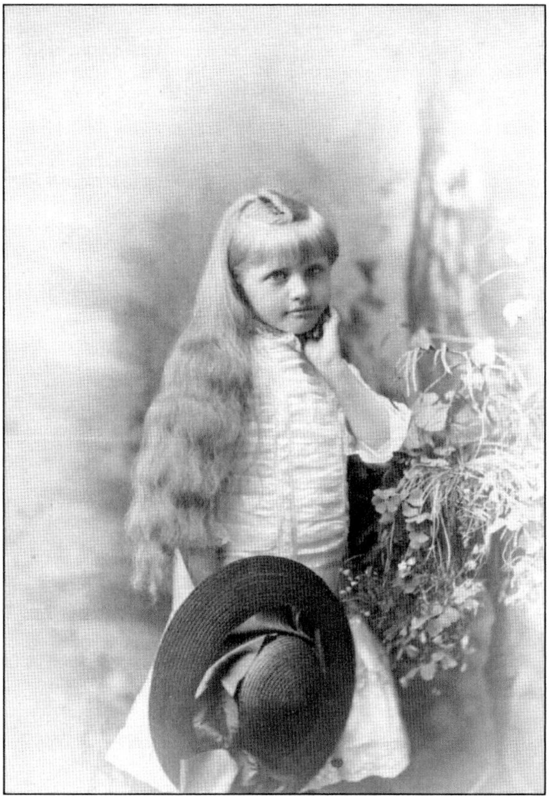

Little Maude Lapham poses for this photograph about 1882. The photographer chose to have her hold the hat to reveal her long golden hair. Maude became a teacher at Macedon High School in the 1900s. Although it was called a high school, lower grades were also taught. Maude taught first and second grades. (Courtesy of the Macedon Public Library, Bullis Collection.)

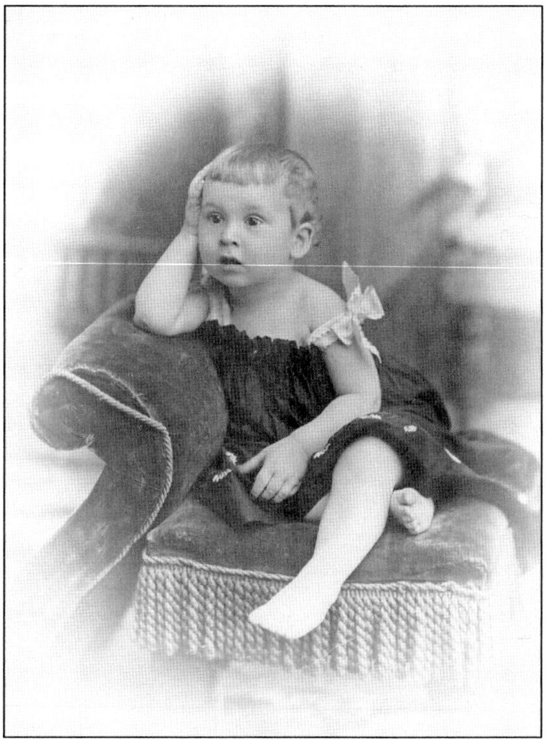

This studio portrait of Floyd Brundage, grandson of DeWitt Clinton Brundage, was taken in August 1893, when Floyd was one year, nine months old. In this era, it was customary for boys to wear dresses until they were several years old. (Courtesy of Macedon Town Historian.)

Floyd Brundage (left) and his brother Frank Brundage Jr. pose for a photograph around 1903. Their father, Frank Sr., died in 1883, and their widowed mother, Phebe, later married Richard Edsall. The boys' baggy, knee-length trousers were called knickers. That style enjoyed a brief revival in the 1930s, but is seldom seen today. (Courtesy of Macedon Town Historian.)

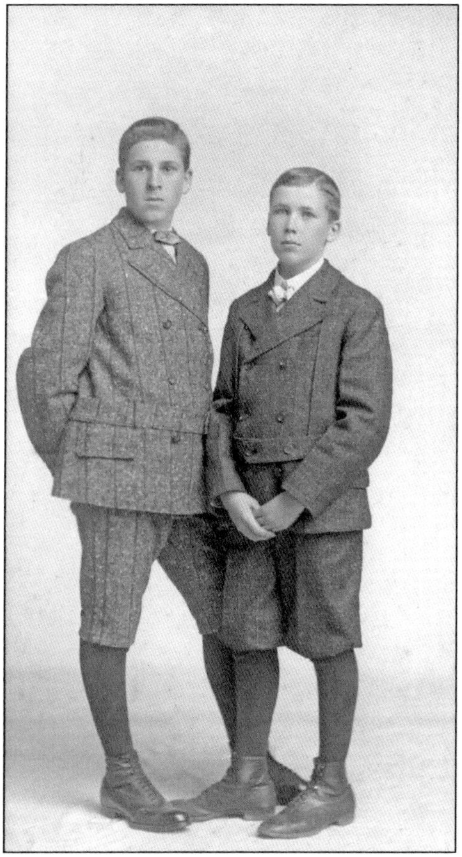

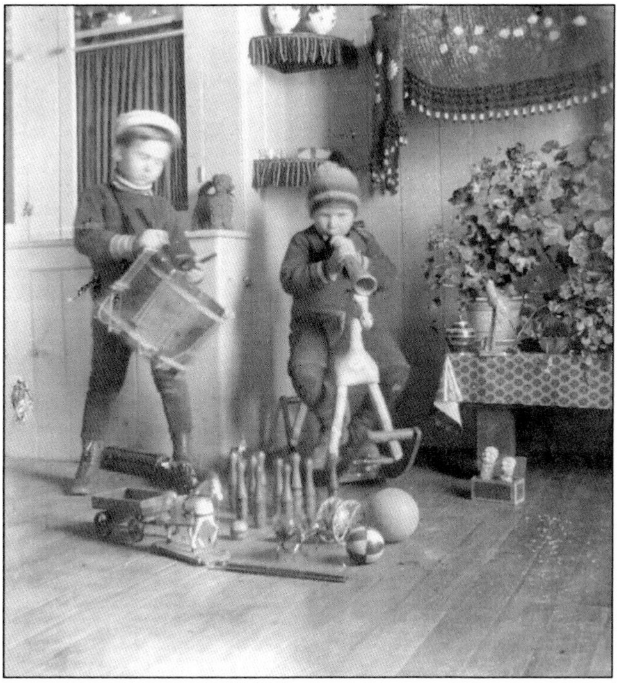

Floyd (left) and Frank Brundage are shown with their Christmas presents about 1897. Among the gifts are a drum, a bowling set, a jack-in-the-box, a hobbyhorse, and a toy wagon. (Courtesy of Macedon Town Historian.)

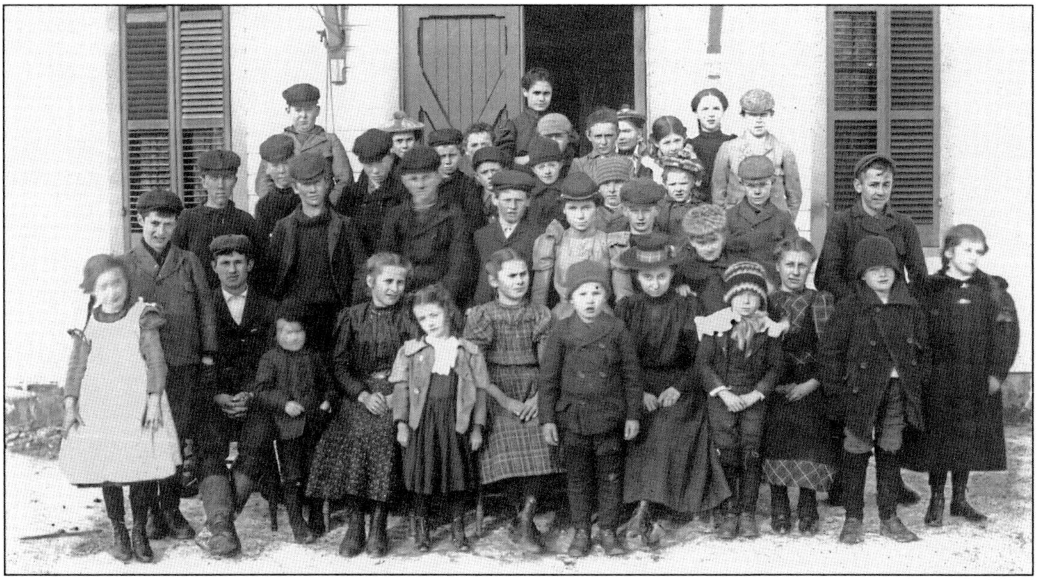

The inscription for this photograph reads "The Stone School, Macedon, New York. Teacher Alberta Arnold Smith." The children vary in age, because district schools like this one typically taught grades one through eight. All of the grades were taught by a single teacher, who rotated instruction through each grade during the school day. Older students were expected to assist the teacher. (Courtesy of Macedon Town Historian.)

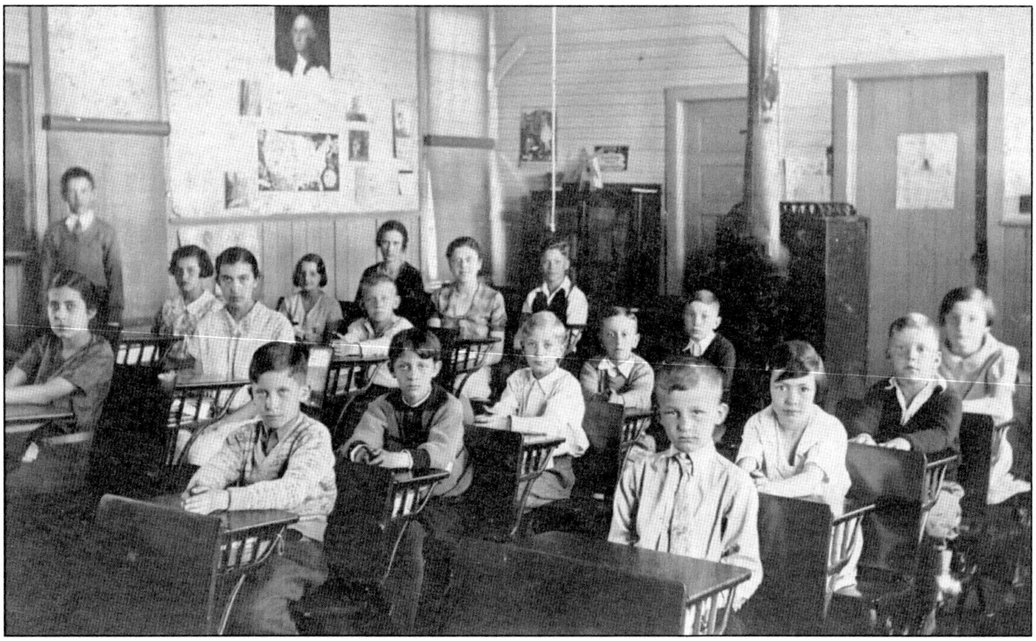

This photograph was taken in District 5 school about 1931. Among the children pictured here are Ruth Getzman, Betty Cummings, Erwin Martz, Joe Pulvino, Everett Schrader, Robert Vane, Emma Weigert, Dorothy Weigert, Dick Erdle, Marge Reeves, Robert Reeves, Bob Schrader, Esther Vane, Pearl Schrader, and Edmund and Hod Conant. The rope in the rear of the photograph probably rang the school bell. The teacher is the Conants' cousin Edna Kemp. Hod is the second person from the right. Other persons positions are not known. (Courtesy of Hod Conant.)

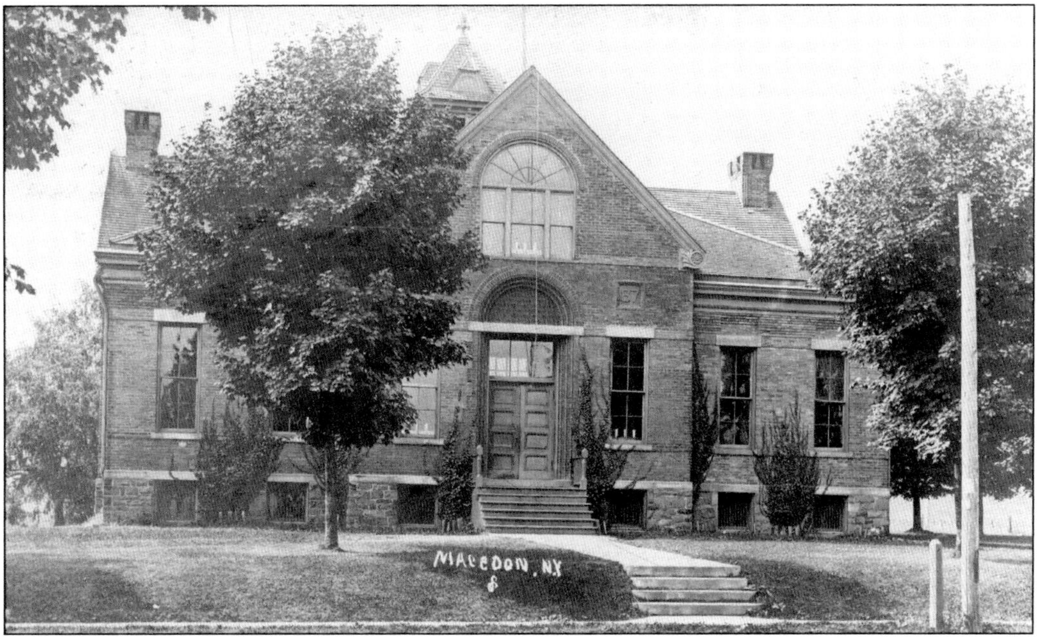

The former Macedon High School was on Lapham Street, which was then called School Street. This is a rare photograph of the building as originally constructed in 1887, before a second story was added in 1908. A wooden school on this site had been destroyed by fire the previous year. The class of 1905 was the first to graduate from this new incarnation of the school. (Courtesy of Hod Conant.)

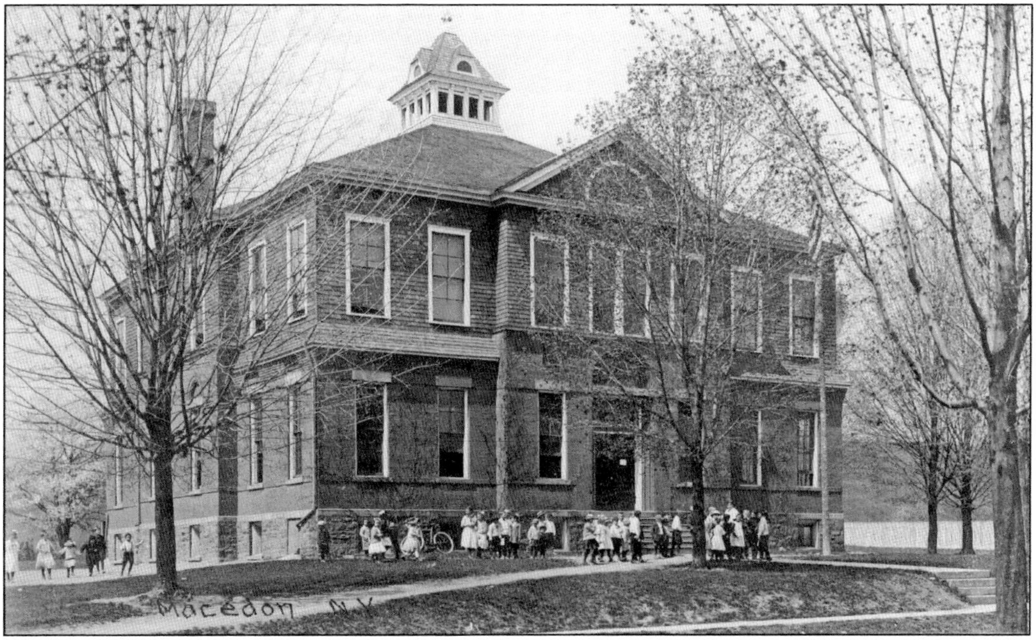

This is the former Macedon High School, after the addition of a second story in 1908. The addition was divided into four large rooms. A bicycle leans against the building, and a group of students has congregated outside. In 1928, a new school was built on West Street. The building shown here was demolished in 1947. (Courtesy of Hod Conant.)

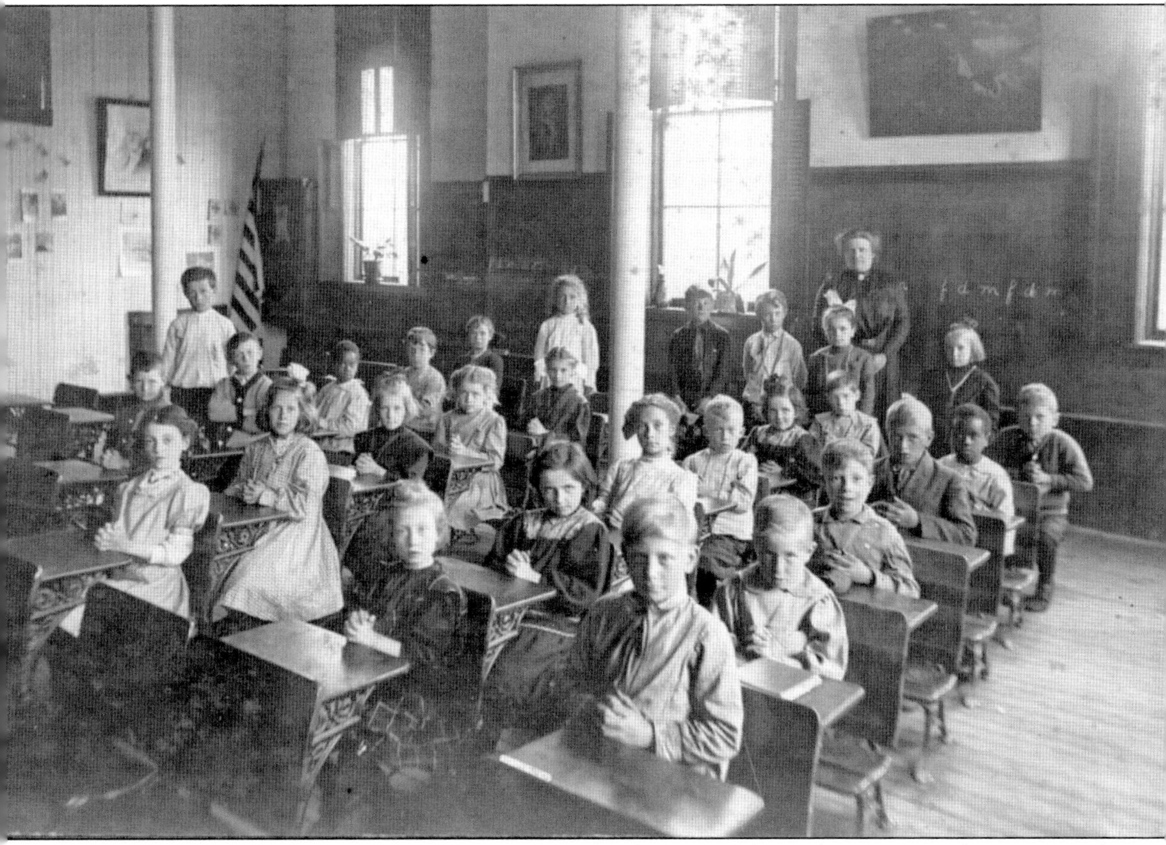

Macedon High School's first- and second-grade classes are shown here on April 21, 1910. The seated children are, from front to back beginning with the near row, as follows: (first row) Howard Cator, Sydney Wesley, Nelson Young, Charles McComb, Babasor Brown, and George Mumby; (second row) Marie Lane, Noreen Daly, Sara Tice, Carl Stevenson, Geraldine Daly, and George Grinnell; (third row) Frances Hilbert, Jennie Worden, Marjorie Easton, Helen Nichols, and Thelma Esley; (fourth row) Earl Knox, Francis O'Brien, Orville Brown, Keith Briggs, and Mary Belle Carter. The students standing in back are, from left to right, Asher Lawrence, Emma Pompa, Bruce Smith, Robert Burhaus, Elizabeth Turner, and Arloa Kennedy. The teacher is Maude Lapham. The children had probably been instructed to fold their hands on their desks. That the school was racially integrated is demonstrated by the presence of two African American students. (Courtesy of Hod Conant.)

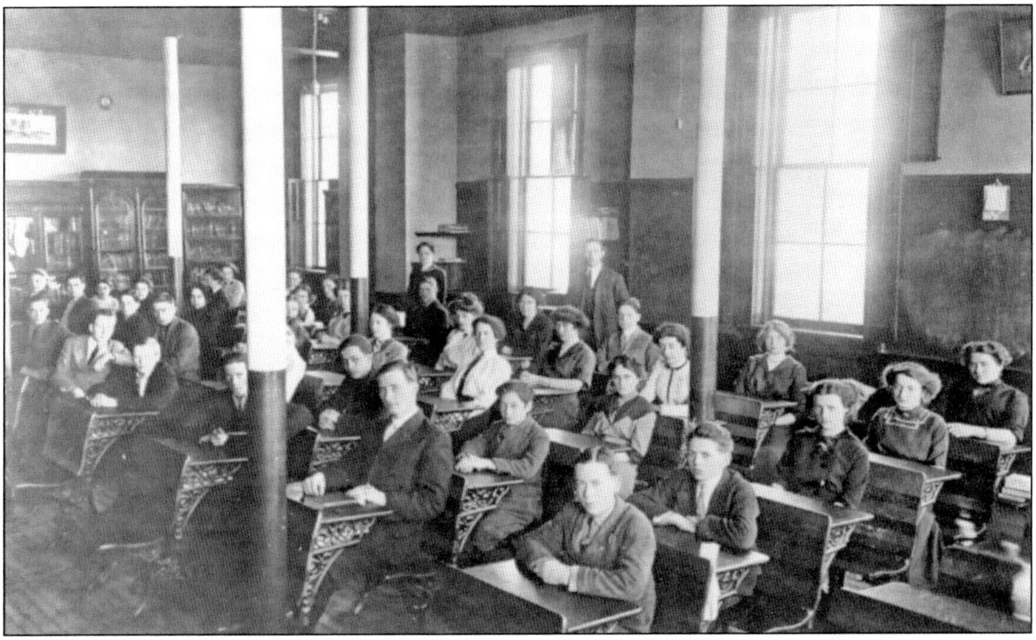

This 1920s photograph shows the interior of the old Macedon High School. Both students and teachers appear to be included here. The tall, thin windows and structural support columns are characteristic of this school's classrooms. The ornamental iron scrollwork at the sides of the desks is typical for this period. (Courtesy of Macedon Town Historian.)

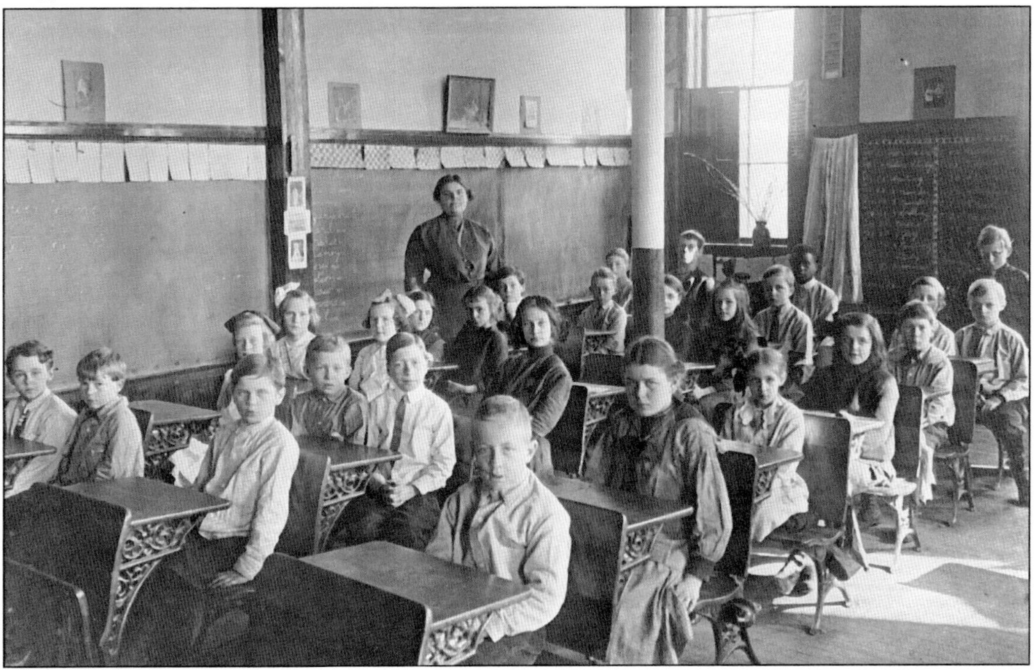

This is the third- or fourth-grade class at Macedon High School. Carrie Turner is the teacher. Despite its being labeled a high school, this institution included instruction of lower grades. Some lessons are visible, written on the blackboard. The students' facial expressions cover the spectrum, from detachment to mild interest to apparent hostility. (Courtesy of Marlene Zimmer LeMoyne.)

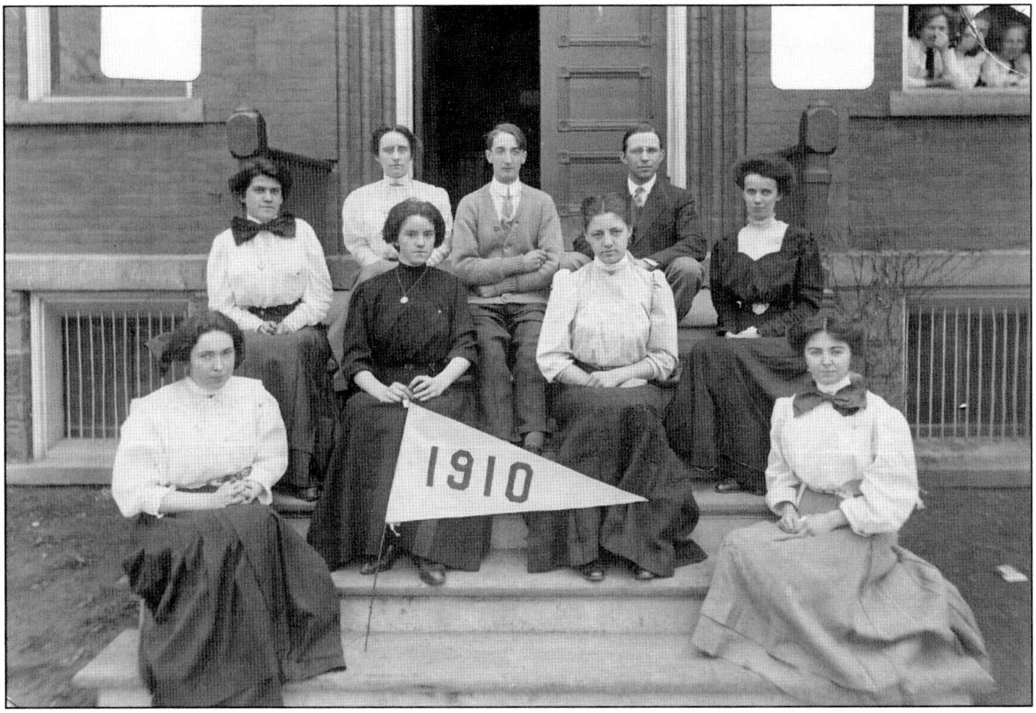

Students and faculty of Macedon High School pose in 1910. Shown here are, from left to right, (first row) Bernadine McGarry and Edna Wilcoxen; (second row) Annie Neary, Mary O'Neil, Nettie Bullis, and Phoebe Cahill; (third row) Mrs. Freeman Crane (teacher), Joseph Farrell, and Freeman Crane (principal). Bullis did not graduate with this class, due to illness. Adelaide Ransom was a member of the class but is not in this photograph. Note the onlookers in the window at top right. (Courtesy of Macedon Town Historian.)

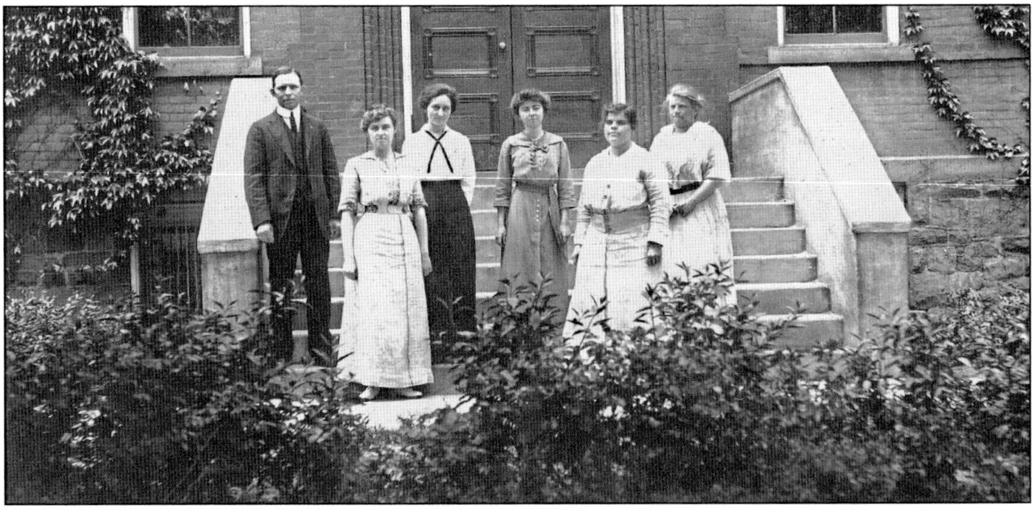

The faculty of Macedon High School poses in 1914–1915. Shown here are, from left to right, principal Freeman Crane, high school teacher Zoe Morrison, seventh- and eighth-grade teacher Lena Jeffery, fifth- and sixth-grade teacher Edna Wilcoxen, third- and fourth-grade teacher Carrie Turner, and first- and second-grade teacher Maude Lapham. (Courtesy of Macedon Town Historian.)

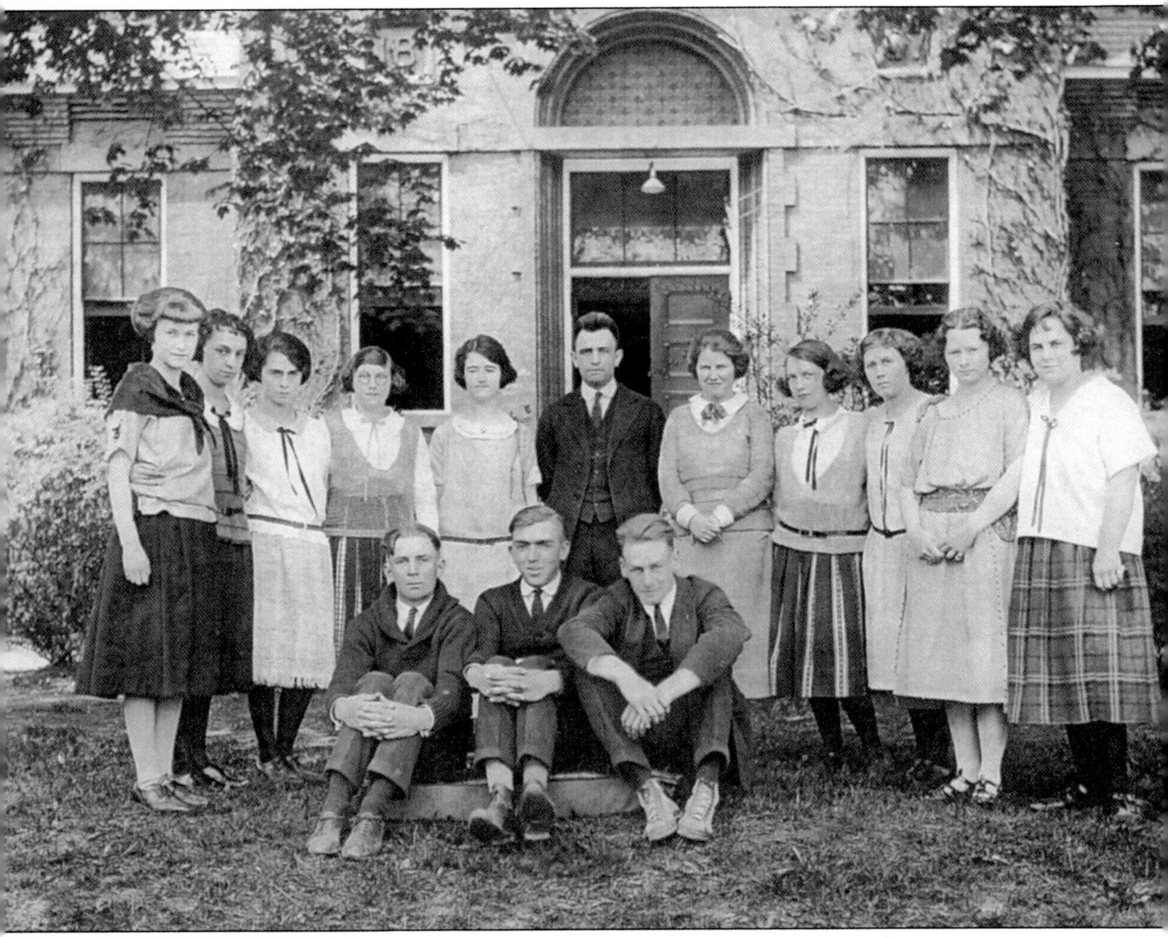

The girls outnumber the boys in the 1923 senior class at Macedon High School. Posing here are, from left to right, (first row) Francis Herendeen, George Allen, and Ernest Diebold; (second row) Minnie Jennings, Mildred Clark, Leona Fuller, Charlotte Exton, teacher ? Scanlon, principal Wesley Francis Williams, teacher ? Egan, Carol Lent, Margaret Herendeen, Emma Reynolds, and Harriet Crane. (Courtesy of Macedon Town Historian.)

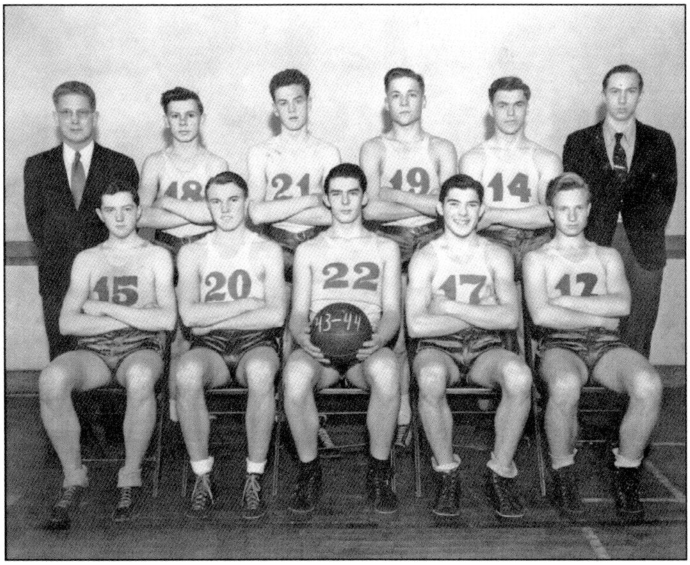

The 1943–1944 Macedon High School basketball team poses for a photograph. Shown here are, from left to right, (first row) Glen Doyle (captain), John Donk, Skip Marsh, Ed Bradley, and Buddy Frank; (second row) Walter McKean (coach), Don Kemp, Jack Dillon, Roger Blazey, Jack Eggleton, and an unidentified coach. The inscription notes that the cheerleaders for that year were Dorothy Donk, Elizabeth Packard, Janice Baker, and Arline Williamson. (Courtesy of Macedon Historical Society.)

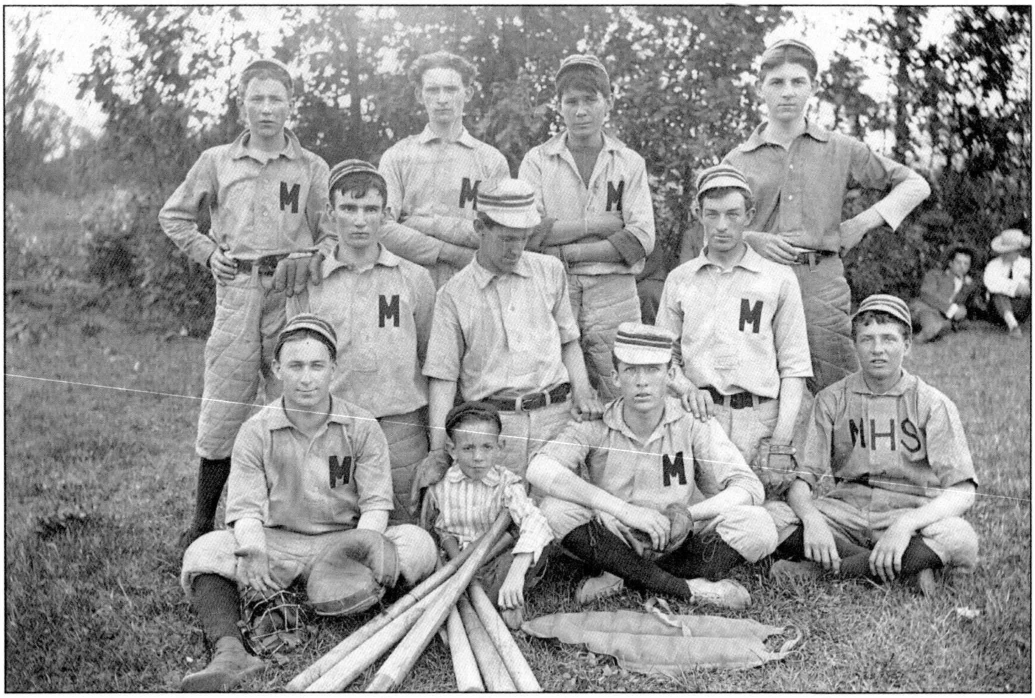

The members of the Macedon High School baseball team pose with their bats and protective gear. The photograph does not identify any of the individuals. The year is not known, but the clothing style suggests that this photograph was taken in the early 1900s. Nine players and a batboy were the standard team size. The man in the first row at far left is evidently the catcher. In the right background, a couple of loungers watch the photography session. (Courtesy of Macedon Town Historian.)

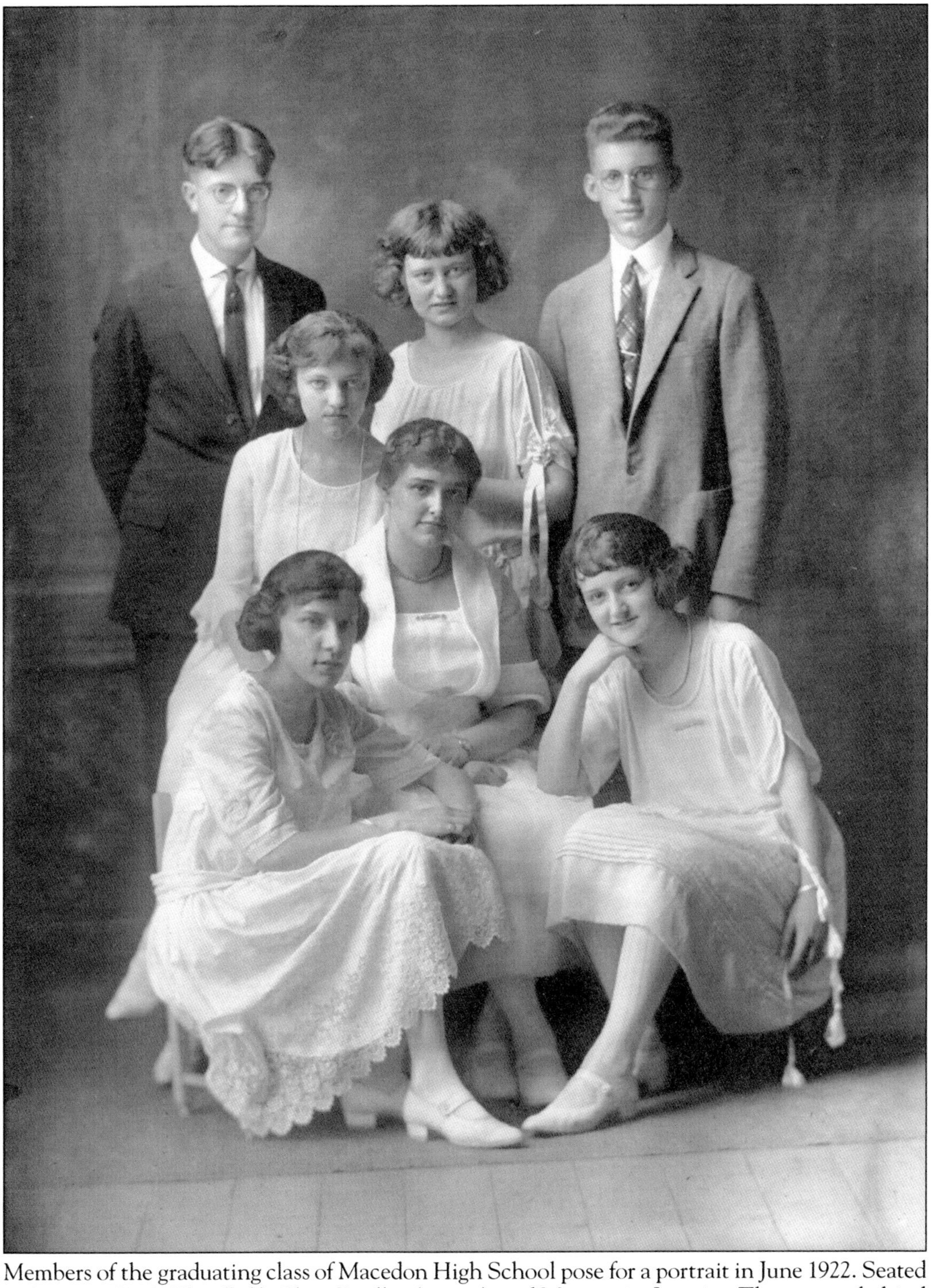

Members of the graduating class of Macedon High School pose for a portrait in June 1922. Seated in front are Ruth Klee (left), Clara Bradley (center), and Marguerite Lovejoy. The woman behind Bradley is Doris Mann. The students standing in back are Nelson Young (left), Marie Lane (center), and Howard Bradley. This was one of the last classes to graduate from the old Macedon High School on School Street. (Courtesy of Macedon Historical Society.)

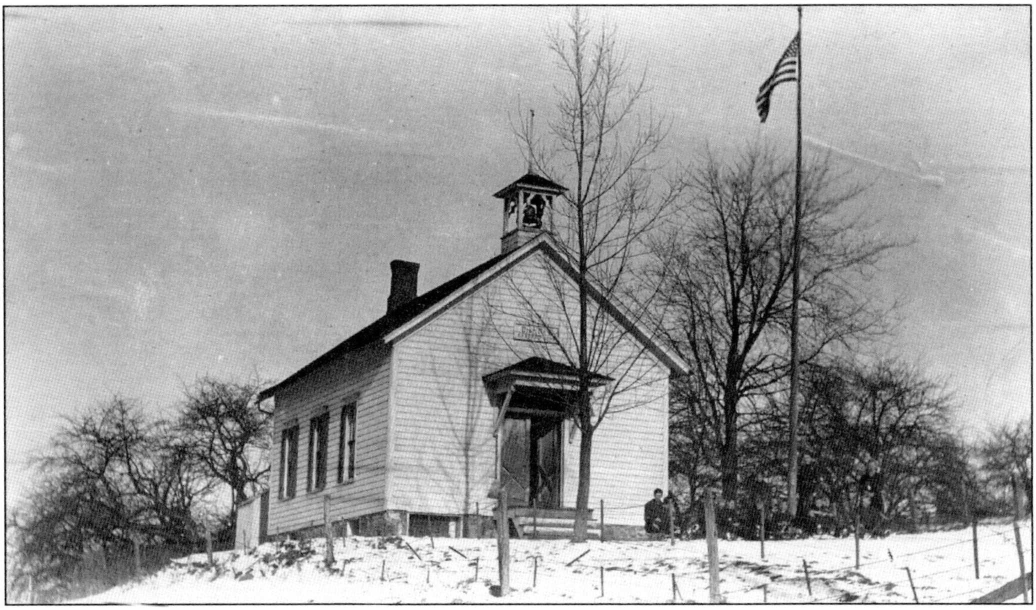

A few students are standing out in the snow at the old Science Hill School, District No. 8. The building, erected in 1873, was located just east of the intersection of State Routes 350 and 31F, in the triangle of land bordered by Macedon Center Road, Route 350, and Scott Road. The building still exists, but it has been converted to a private residence. (Courtesy of Hod Conant.)

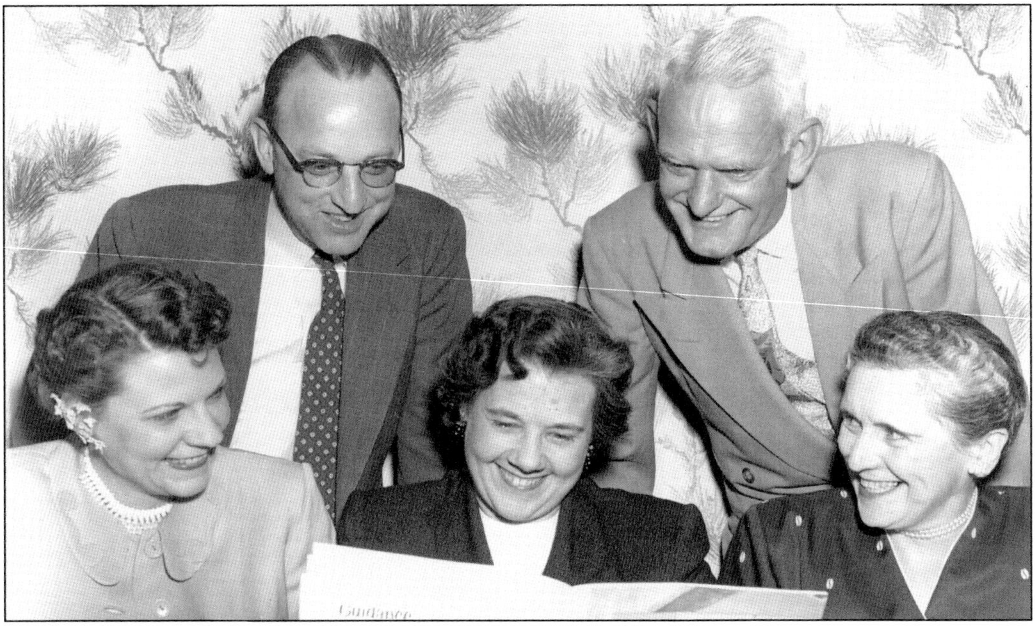

These are the members of the Palmyra-Macedon Central School Board of Education in 1954. The ladies are Mrs. Robert Hornsby (left), Mrs. R.C. Brigham (center), and Mrs. Lynn Schultz. Standing behind them are Eugene C. McGuire (left) and Dennis Church. (Courtesy Macedon Town Historian.)

Four

Macedon Center and Macedon Academy

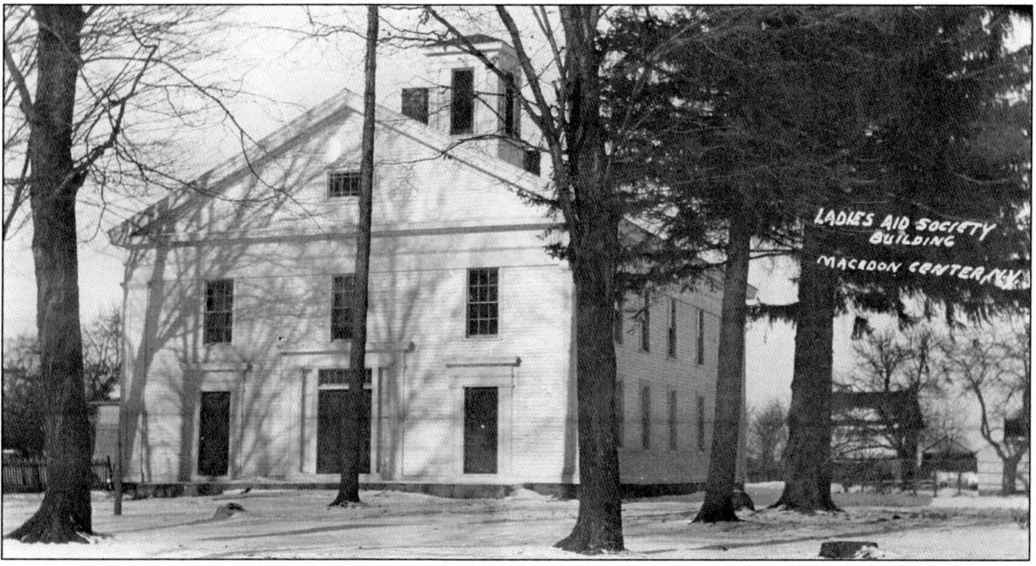

Macedon Academy, founded in 1841, was incorporated by the New York State Legislature on April 11, 1842. The building pictured here was constructed in 1853, and it still looks like this today. This image, from a photo postcard, shows the building shortly after the academy had ceased operation as a school in 1904. It then became the home of the Ladies Aid Society for a few years. Today, the building houses the Macedon Historical Society, a repository for an impressive collection of documents, photographs, and artifacts of early Macedon history. The building, currently undergoing substantial improvements, is one of the few surviving examples of a late-19th-century center for instruction beyond grade school. Subjects included Latin, astronomy, algebra, and history, and some college preparatory courses were also taught. Macedon Academy graduates met for their last reunion in 1947. (Courtesy of Hod Conant.)

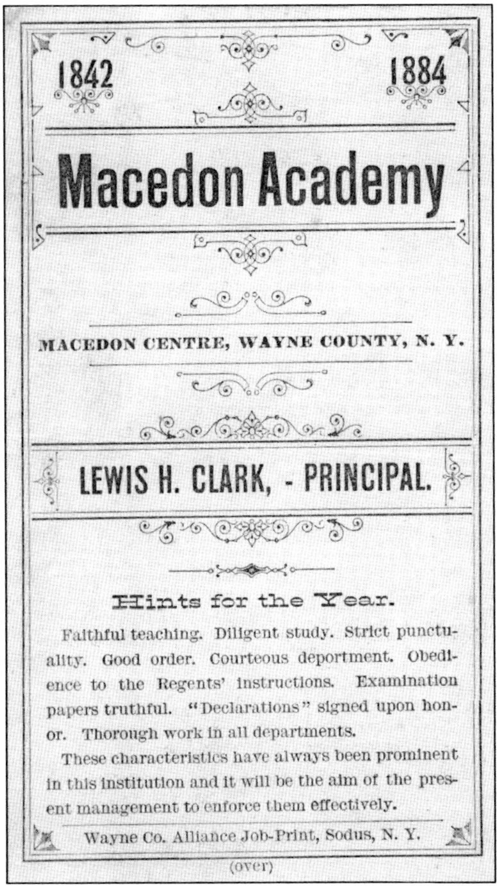

1842 1884

Macedon Academy

MACEDON CENTRE, WAYNE COUNTY, N. Y.

LEWIS H. CLARK, - PRINCIPAL.

Hints for the Year.

Faithful teaching. Diligent study. Strict punctuality. Good order. Courteous deportment. Obedience to the Regents' instructions. Examination papers truthful. "Declarations" signed upon honor. Thorough work in all departments.

These characteristics have always been prominent in this institution and it will be the aim of the present management to enforce them effectively.

Wayne Co. Alliance Job-Print, Sodus, N. Y.

(over)

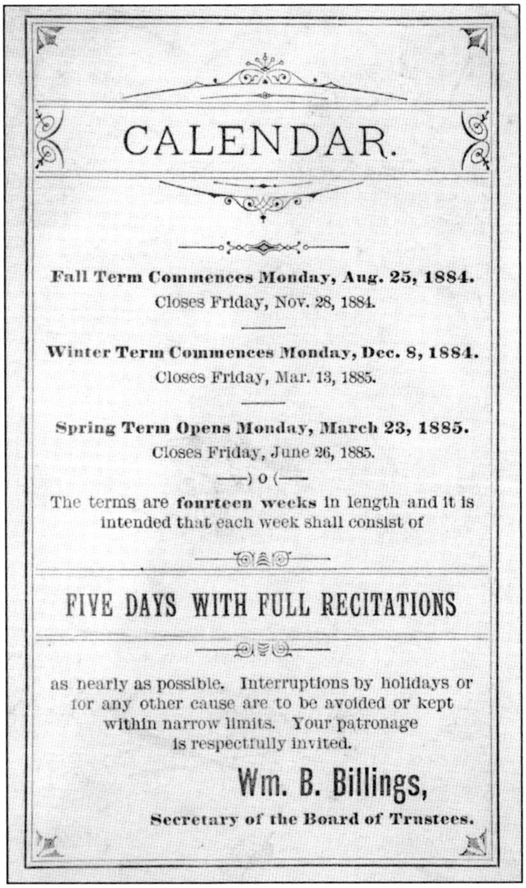

CALENDAR.

Fall Term Commences Monday, Aug. 25, 1884.
Closes Friday, Nov. 28, 1884.

Winter Term Commences Monday, Dec. 8, 1884.
Closes Friday, Mar. 13, 1885.

Spring Term Opens Monday, March 23, 1885.
Closes Friday, June 26, 1885.

—) o (—

The terms are **fourteen weeks** in length and it is intended that each week shall consist of

FIVE DAYS WITH FULL RECITATIONS

as nearly as possible. Interruptions by holidays or for any other cause are to be avoided or kept within narrow limits. Your patronage is respectfully invited.

Wm. B. Billings,
Secretary of the Board of Trustees.

Here are two pages from the 1884–1885 Macedon Academy catalog. When the academy was established in 1842 as an institution of higher learning, most children attended a local district school, which was often a one-room schoolhouse, with one teacher for grades one through eight. The few who could afford it went on to "high" school, grades nine through twelve. Macedon Academy in Macedon Center was such an institution. Classes were held in the academy building, which is currently the home of the Macedon Historical Society. Some of the subjects taught were English composition, algebra, physical geography, vocal music, and instrumental music. Both Regents and non-Regents courses were available. Tuition and board were $3.75 per quarter, with additional charges for each course varying between $4.50 and $5.25. The catalog notes that "the whole expense need not exceed forty-seven dollars per term for students from abroad, and is much less for those near the institution." (Both, courtesy of Hod Conant.)

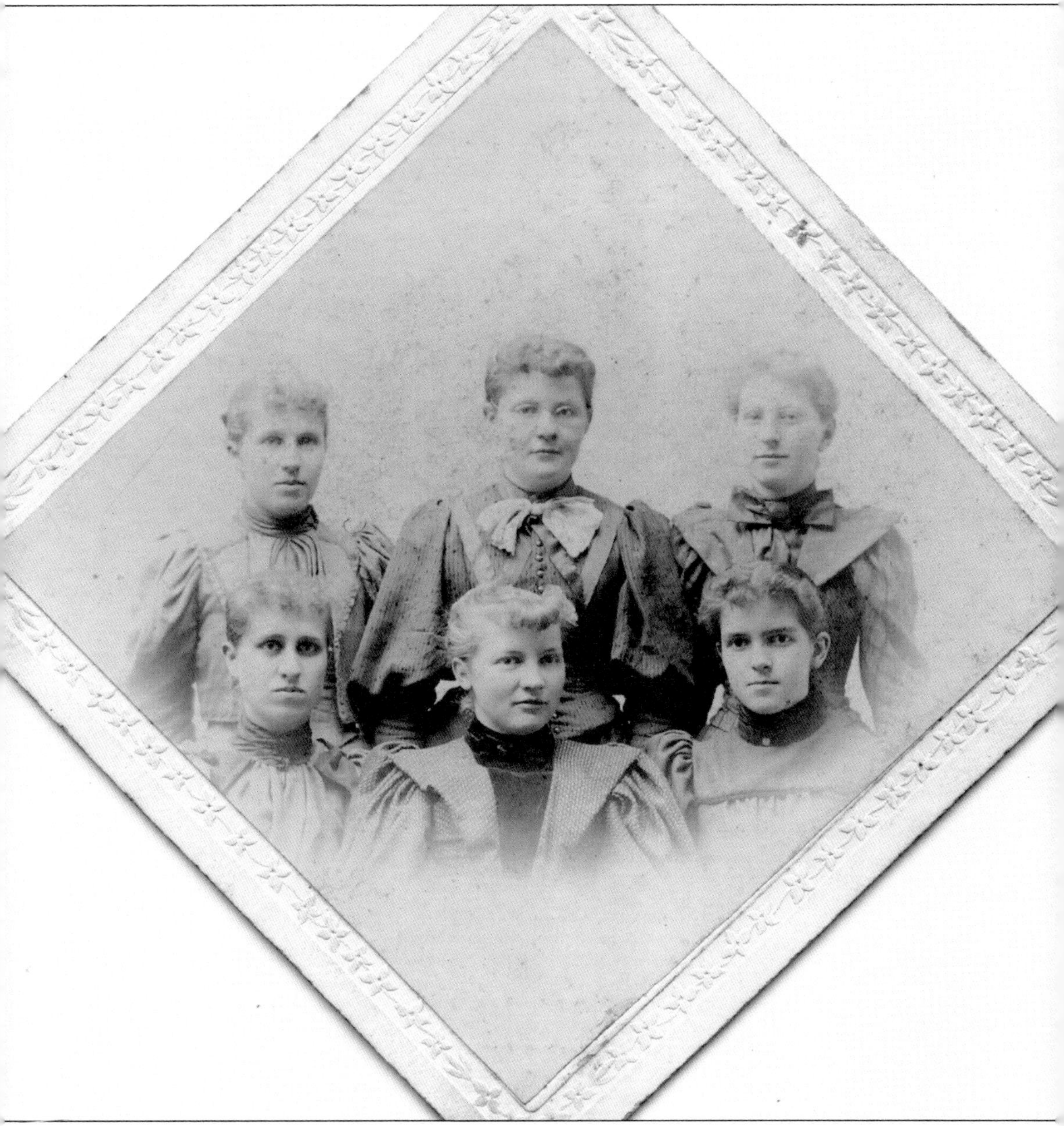

These six serious young ladies were gathered for an important occasion: they were taking the required examinations for aspiring teachers. Shown here are, from left to right, (first row) Lillian Pilcher, Della Chase, and Marion Hoag; (second row) Grace Gage, Flora Gage, and Lena Harbou. The photograph was taken on January 10, 1895, in Marion, New York. (Courtesy of Margaret Hartsough.)

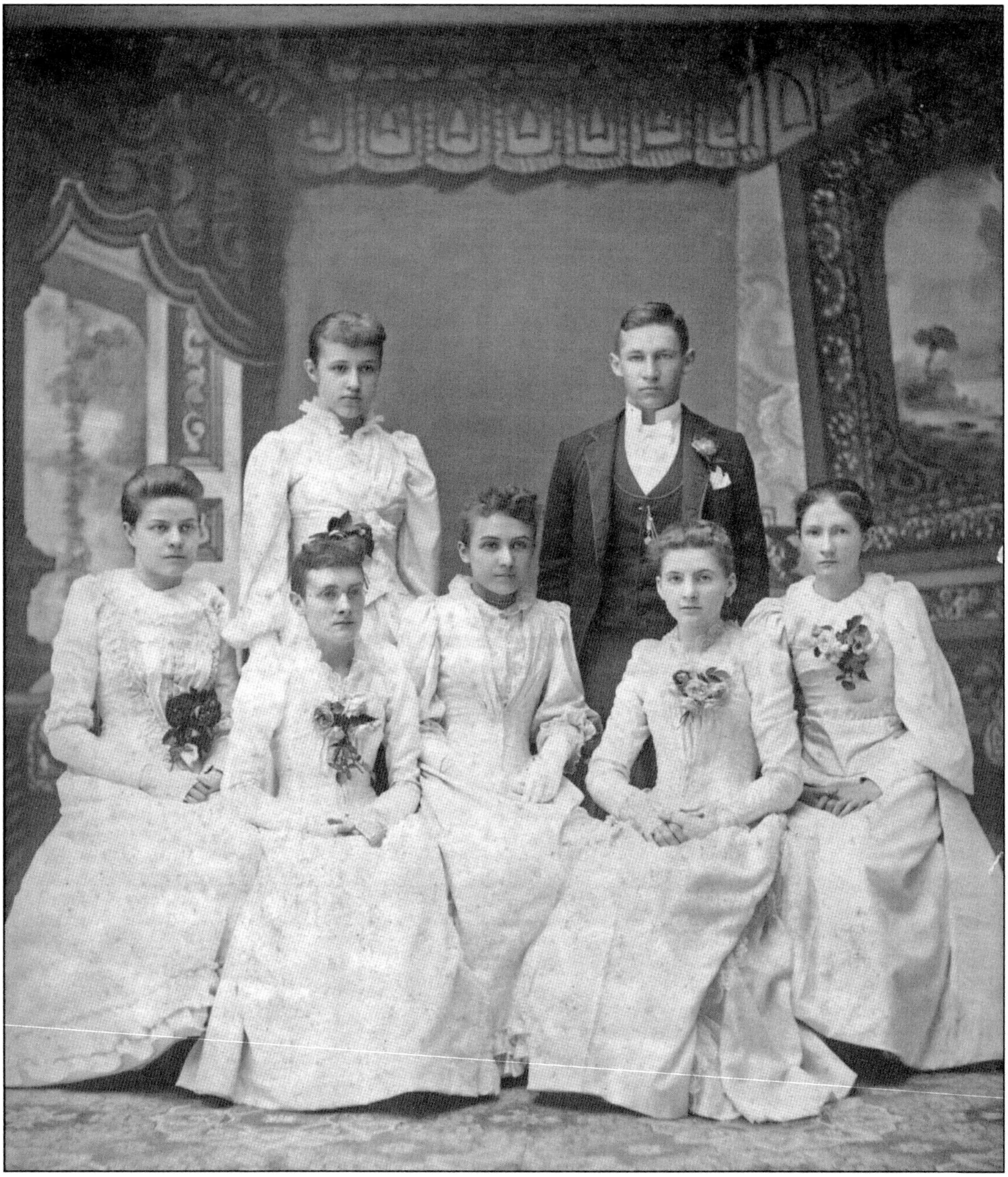

This is a Macedon Academy graduating class, but the year and the names of the individuals are not known. Based on the clothing styles and the fact that the academy's last graduating class was in 1902, this photograph was probably taken in the late 1880s or early 1890s. (Courtesy of Macedon Historical Society.)

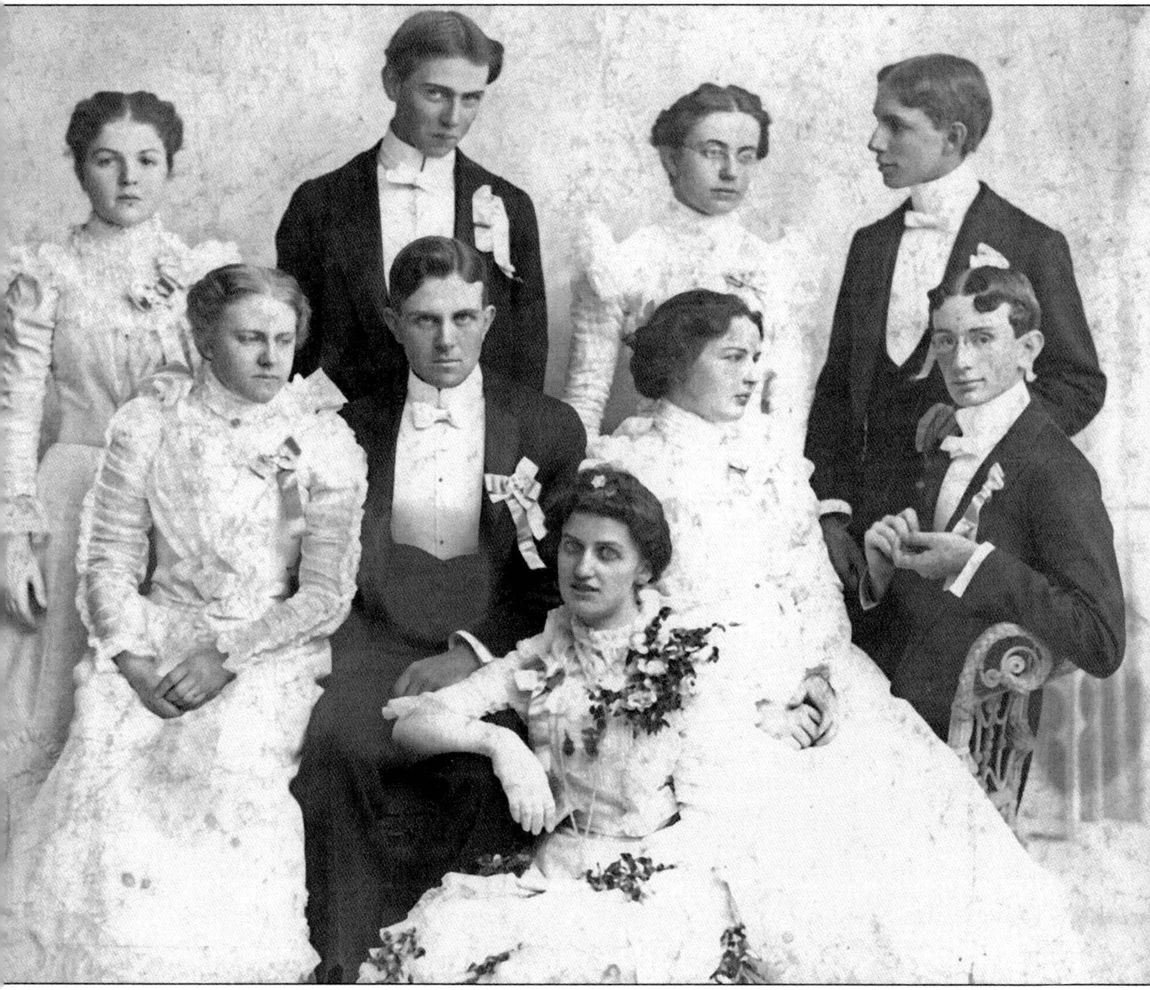

The members of the Macedon Academy graduating class of 1899 pose for a photograph. The young men and women have a wide variety of facial expressions, and several are not even looking at the camera. One suspects that the photographer liked this charming candid shot more than the usual formal one. Shown here are (seated in front) Edna Geraldine Brennan; and, from left to right, (first row) Carrie Allen, Isaac Jay Furman, Helen Thayer, and Stewart Hoxie Breese; (second row) May Gardner, Charles Thomas Fuller, Clementine Hoag, and George Gallup. The class officers were Breese (president), Allen (vice president), Hoag (secretary), and Thayer (treasurer). (Courtesy of Macedon Town Historian.)

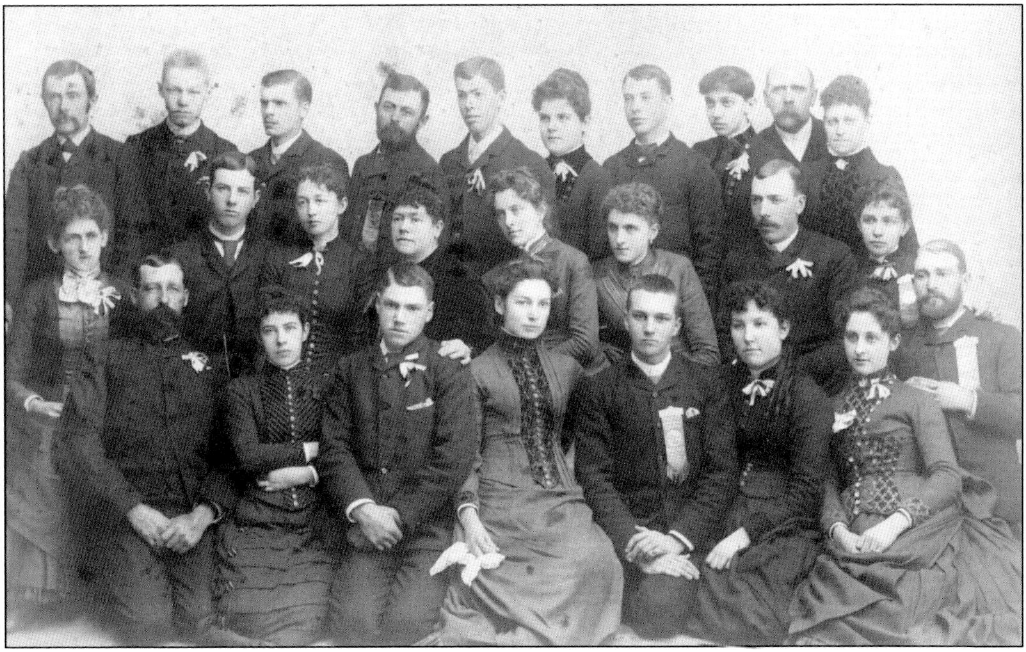

These undated photographs show members of the Macedon Center Lodge 371 of the Independent Order of Good Templars (IOGT). Many are wearing their member badges and insignia. The IOGT was a 19th-century organization dedicated to promoting abstinence from alcohol. The organization enjoyed popular support for its cause. In 1907, the IOGT had 350,000 members in the United States, and it had branches in Europe, Asia, Africa, and Australia. In an age when most lodges were fraternal organizations that excluded women, the IOGT was an exception. Displayed in front of the group in the below photograph is the organization's framed charter, which today hangs on the wall of the Macedon Academy Building. (Above, courtesy of Macedon Historical Society; below, courtesy of Macedon Town Historian.)

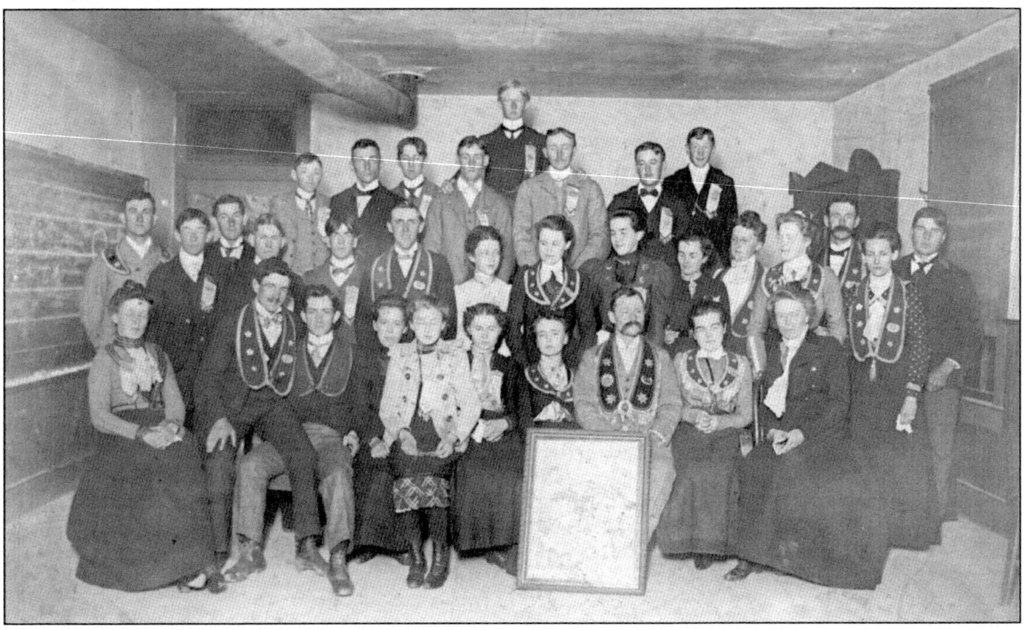

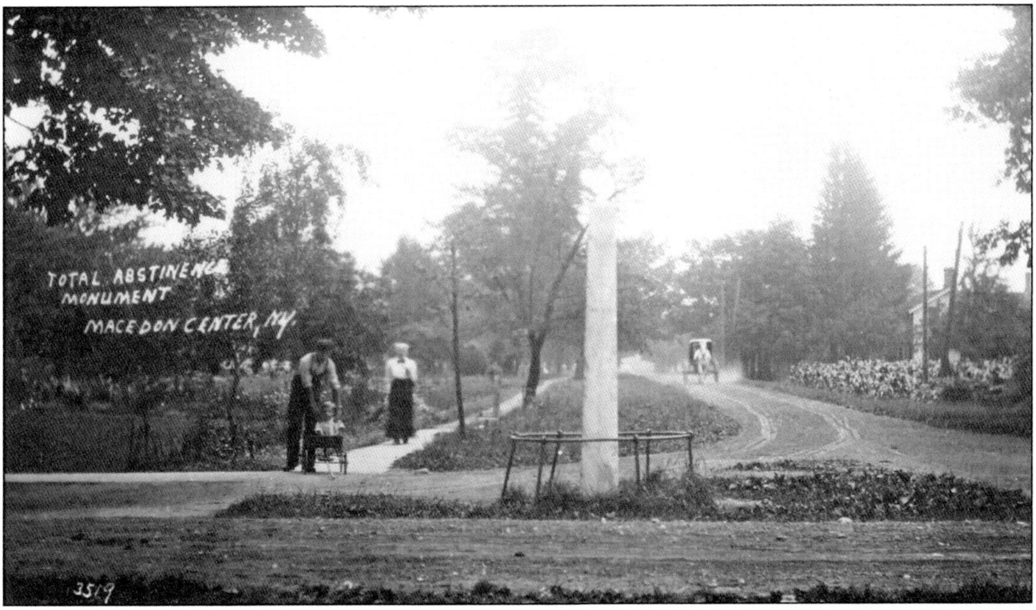

A family walks past Macedon Center's monument supporting temperance, which was a call for abstinence from alcohol. The father is pushing the child in a little cart as the mother follows behind. Down the road at the right, a horse and buggy approaches the intersection. Today, a replica of this monument stands near the southeast corner of the intersection. (Courtesy of Hod Conant.)

The Abstinence Monument is shown in its original location in the center of the intersection of State Route 31F and Canandaigua Road. In the background is the Hicksite meetinghouse. The monument was erected by Ira Lapham in 1845 as a symbol of community support for the temperance movement. Lapham purchased the stone from a quarry in Vermont and had it shipped to Macedon on the Erie Canal. (Courtesy of Hod Conant.)

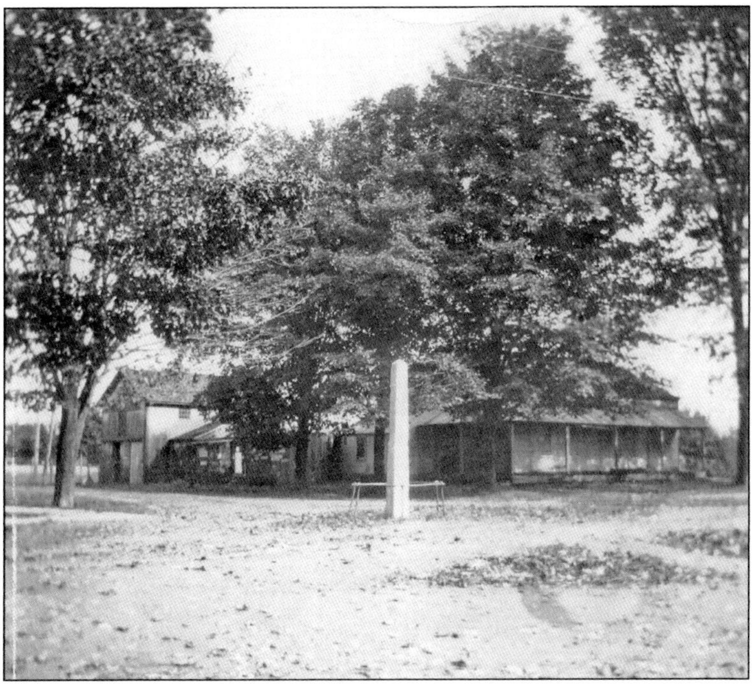

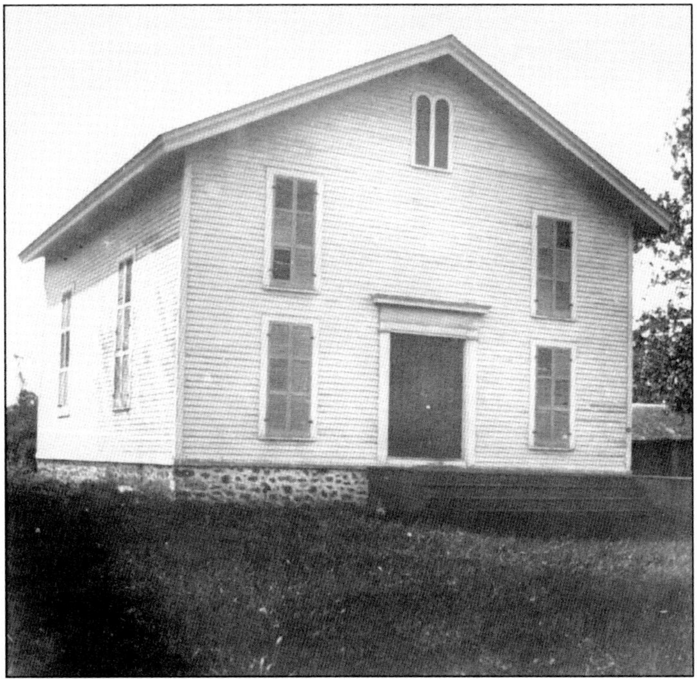

This building on the southeast corner of Canandaigua Road and Route 31F has assumed many identities over the years. It was originally the Macedon Center Orthodox Quaker Meetinghouse. The building is currently occupied by Sew What Sewing Service and Contractors. Directly across Route 31F was the Hicksite Quaker meetinghouse, which no longer exists. (Courtesy of Macedon Town Historian.)

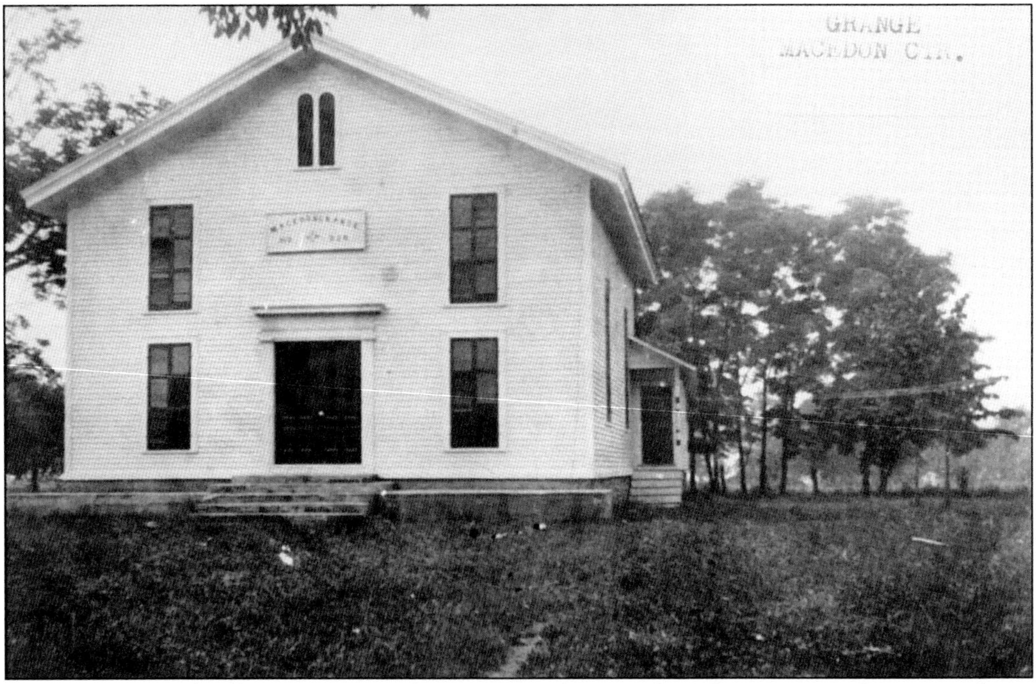

This is the same building as seen in the previous photograph. After it was no longer used as a Quaker meetinghouse, it became the home of the Patrons of Husbandry 326, also known as the Macedon Center Grange. The Grange, a nationwide organization representing farmers, was an enormously popular organization in the late 19th century. The Grange successfully lobbied for new governmental programs that benefited farmers, such as Rural Free Delivery. (Courtesy of Macedon Town Historian.)

This is a reunion of Macedon Academy graduates and faculty. Prof. Wesley Williams is at the center in the back row. Some of the other individuals are, in no particular order, Minnie Jennings Kinsman, Mildred Clark Content, Leona Fuller Wiedrick, Charlotte Easton Bradley, Madeline Scanlan, Alice Eagan Benjamin, Emma Reynolds, Harriet Crane Fluker, Francis Herendeen, George Allen, and Ernest Diebold. (Courtesy of Macedon Town Historian.)

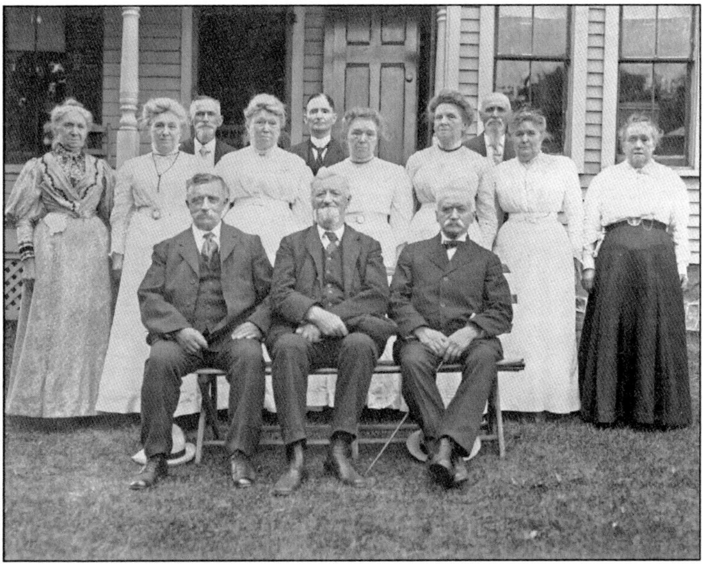

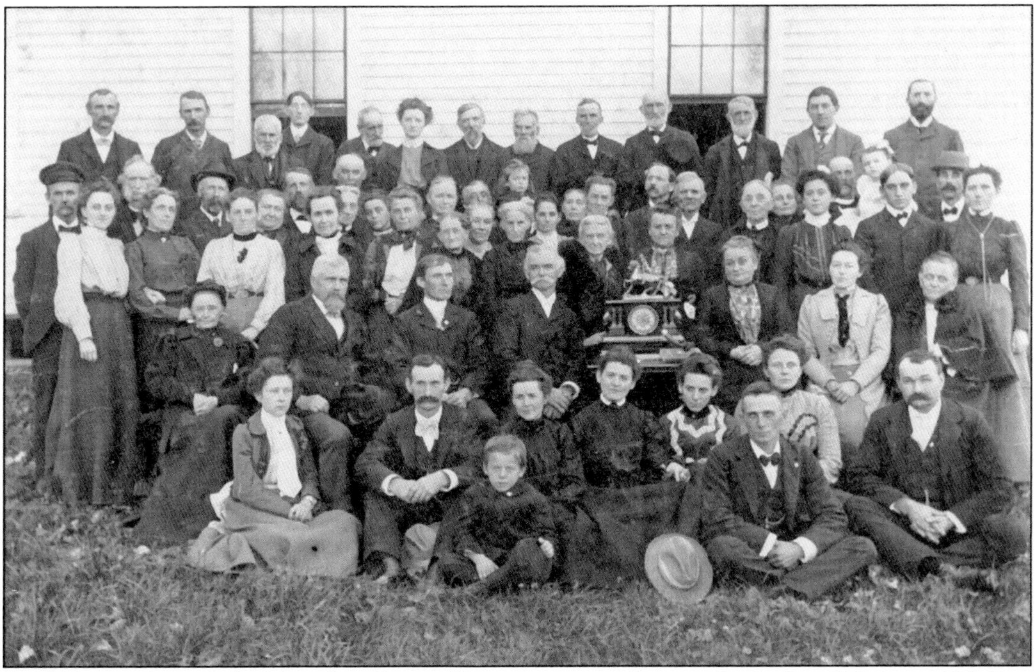

In 1902, members of the Macedon Center Grange presented a mantle clock to Edwin and Melissa Mead as a going-away present. The Meads were Grange leaders who were leaving for Cornwall. They are in the center, on either side of the clock. Some of the other individuals in this photograph include Charles Diebold, Cyrus Packard, Arthur Carman, Stella Herendeen, and Burton Durfee. (Courtesy of Macedon Historical Society.)

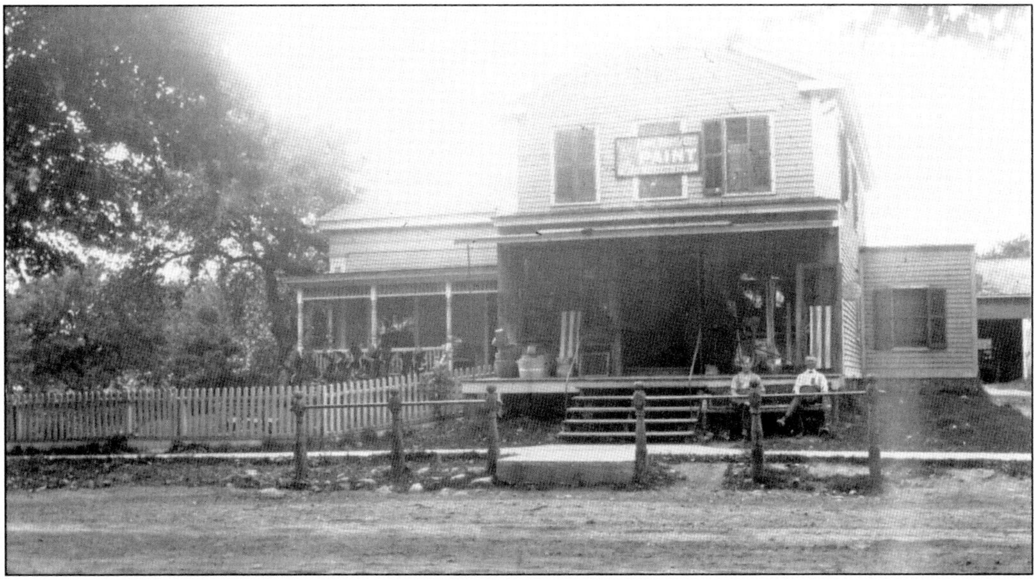

For decades, the Hicks Country Store and Post Office was a fixture in Macedon Center. In this view from the early 1900s, a paint advertisement sign appears over the open porch. Two men sit on a bench in front of the store, where several hitching posts are available for shoppers' horses. Although the road is unpaved, there appears to be a sidewalk in front of the store. (Courtesy of Macedon Town Historian.)

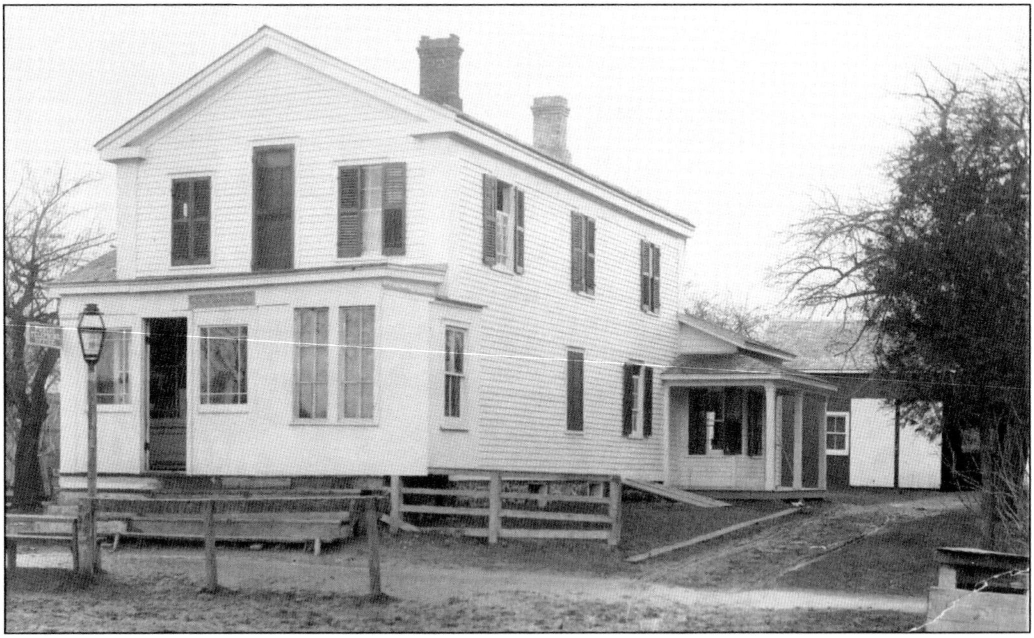

In this later view of the Hicks Country Store, there is no sidewalk, the hitching posts have been replaced by a fence, and the porch has been enclosed. A small sign sticking out from the building on the left side of the photograph reads "Public Telephone Office," and a larger sign over the door reads "Boots & Shoes, Groceries, Dry Goods, Hardware &c. F.H. Hicks, Macedon Centre." This latter sign is one of the historical artifacts preserved at the Macedon Historical Society. (Courtesy of Macedon Town Historian.)

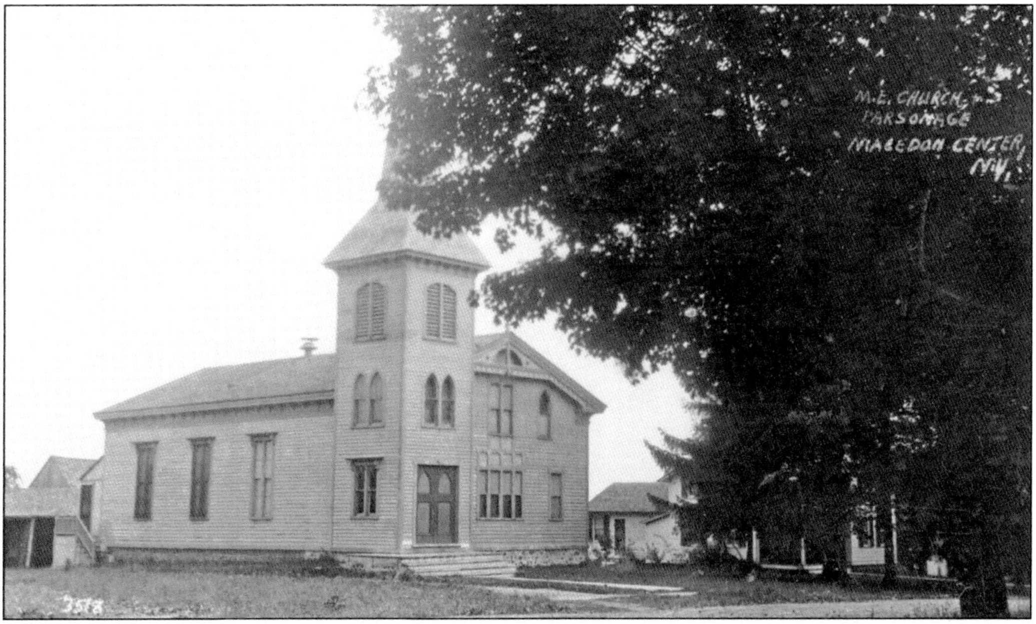

The Macedon Center Methodist Episcopal Church is seen here about 1900. Although the front view looks much the same today, there have been several additions to the structure. The steeple is currently painted a very distinctive yellow. (Courtesy of Macedon Town Historian.)

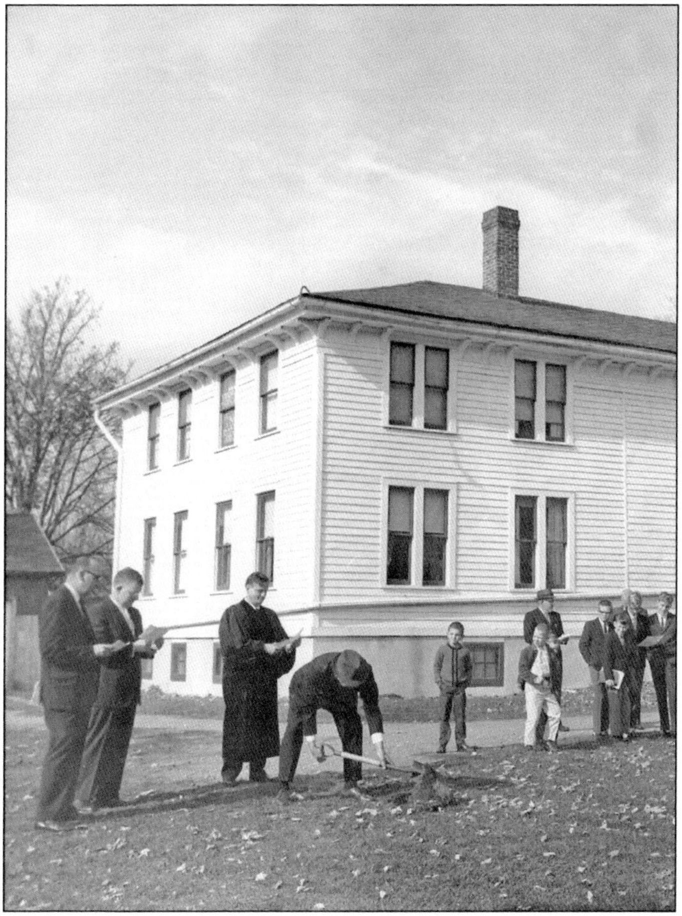

This photograph was taken at the ground-breaking ceremony for an addition to the Macedon Center Methodist Church, on November 11, 1965. The officials shown here are, from left to right, Leonard Bennett, Mike Burrows, Rev. Victor Smith, and Walt Wiedrick. (Courtesy of Macedon Town Historian.)

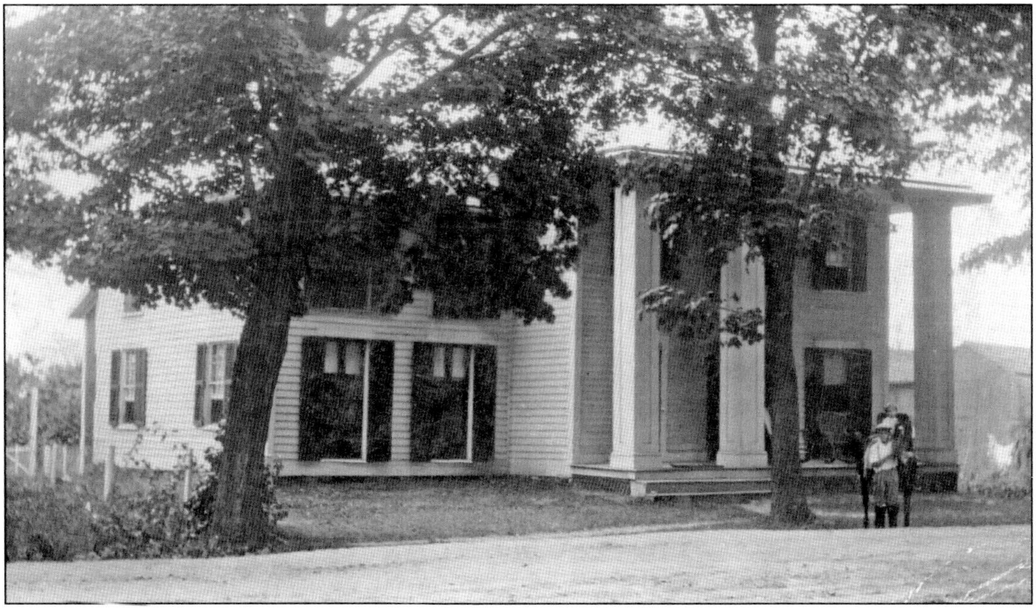

This photo postcard is postmarked "Macedon Center, March 21, 1912." This home is still at 1188 Macedon Center Road (State Route 31F). The columns and windows look a little different today than they did 100 years ago. The individuals standing in front are not identified. (Courtesy of Hod Conant.)

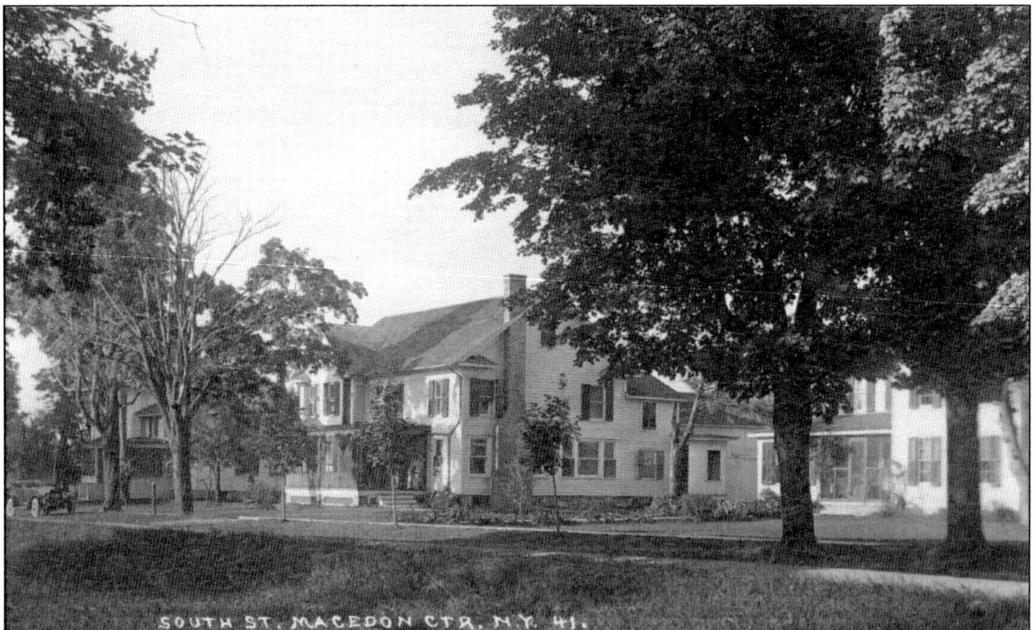

The inscription on this photograph reads: "From all writers this house come good wishes for the best Christmas and Happiest New Year Possible. The Eldredges, Dec. 1919." This house is in Macedon Center at 2393 Canandaigua Road. (Courtesy of Hod Conant.)

Five

TRAINS, TROLLEYS, AND THE CANAL

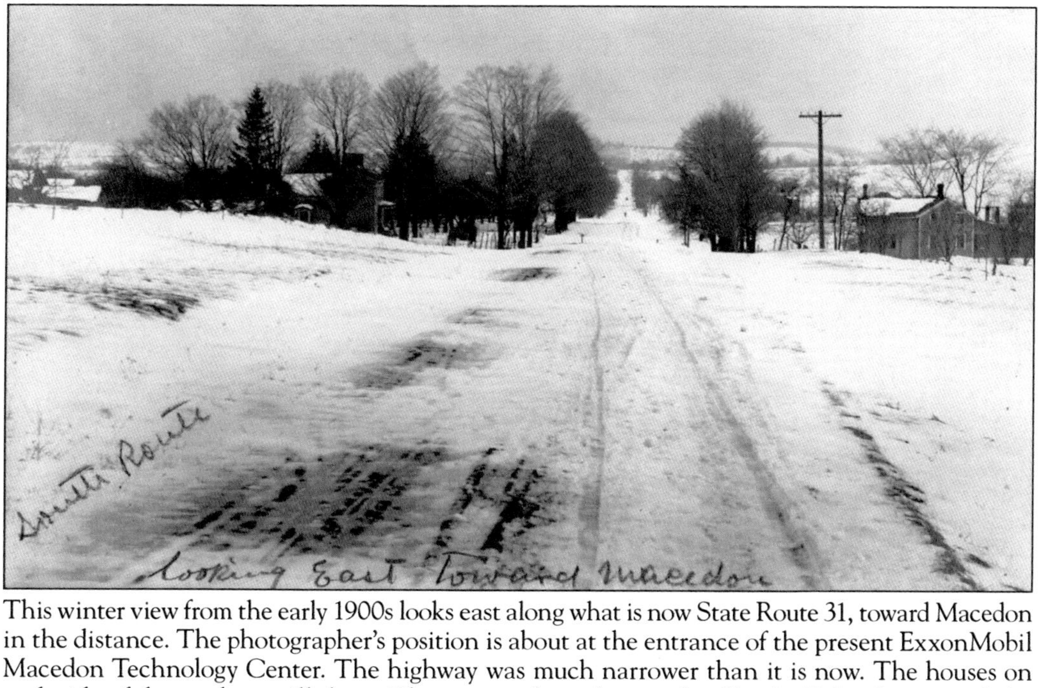

This winter view from the early 1900s looks east along what is now State Route 31, toward Macedon in the distance. The photographer's position is about at the entrance of the present ExxonMobil Macedon Technology Center. The highway was much narrower than it is now. The houses on each side of the road are still there. The one on the right was the Charles Baker home, and the one on the left was the Byron Allen home. The line of sight to the Beebe Road substation for the Rochester, Syracuse & Eastern Electric Railway (RS&E) trolley line is obscured by the trees on the right side of the road. A few hundred yards down the road, the trolley line swings in from the right, crossing the highway on its way to Main Street in downtown Macedon. (Courtesy of Macedon Town Historian.)

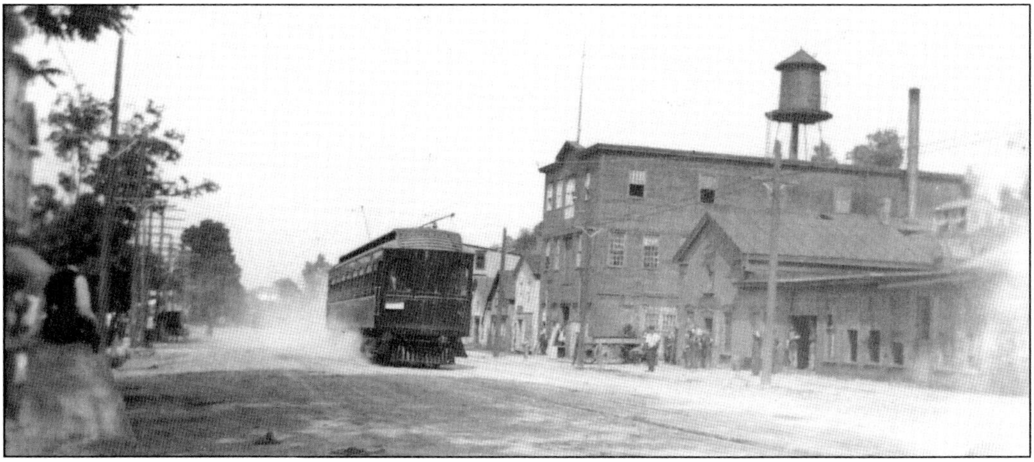

According to this photograph's inscription, this is the first trolley to travel through Macedon, heading west. It is raising a cloud of dust on June 21, 1906. This must have been a trial run, as the records show that the official first day of operation to Macedon was July 2 of that year. By that time, the RS&E railway had extended the trolley line east from Rochester as far as Lyons. By 1909, the line from Rochester to Syracuse was complete. At the left, a blurry pedestrian scurries to get out of the way. (Courtesy of Macedon Town Historian.)

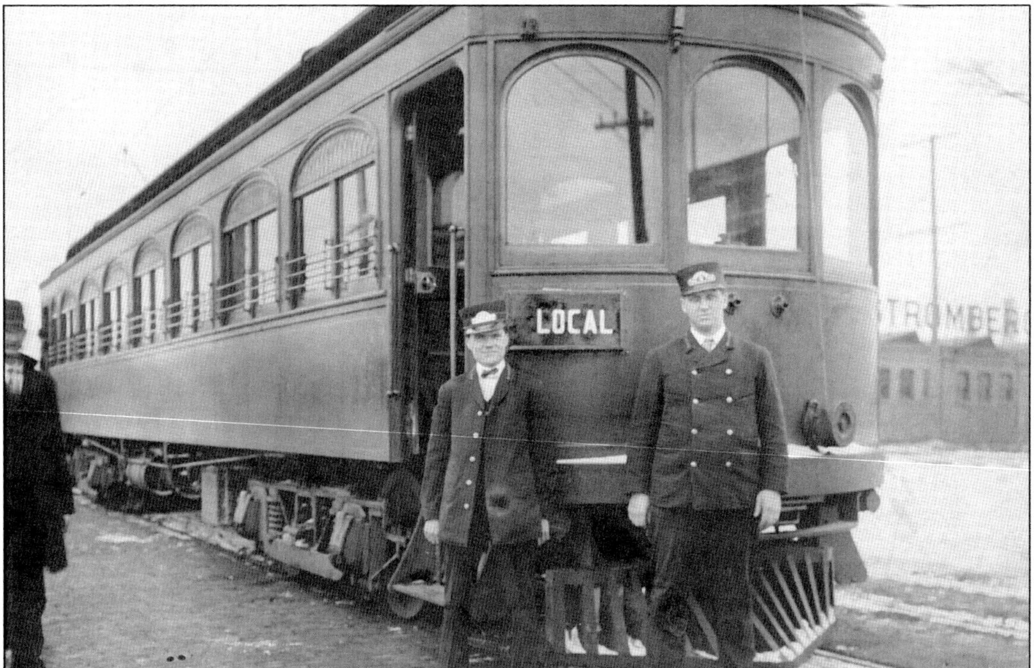

This Easter 1907 photograph from the collection of Macedon resident and trolley rider Gail Thistlethwaite Youngman was personally inscribed to her by motorman Morris Clark (right) and conductor Charles Soper (center). The photograph was taken at the Culver Road and University Avenue trolley station in Rochester. At the right edge of the photograph is part of the Stromberg-Carlson Company's sign. Gail was a steady customer during the time she was a student in Rochester. This car, staffed by these two men, carried passengers from Macedon to Rochester and back. (Courtesy of Macedon Historical Society.)

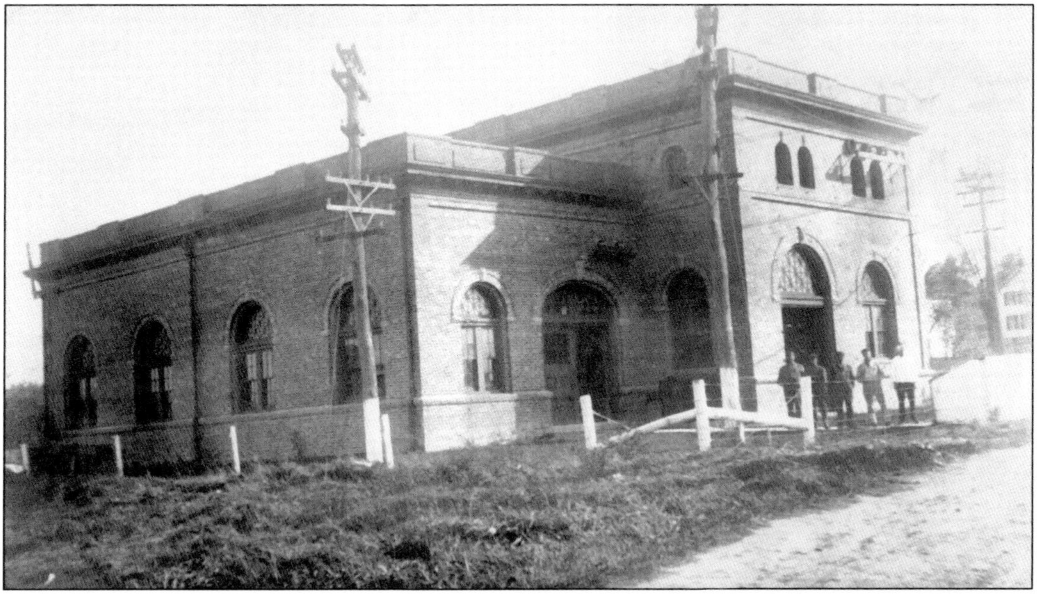

Trolley workers pose outside the RS&E power substation on Beebe Road. This power plant was one of several substations along the trolley's route that transformed high-voltage transmission-line power to the lower voltages used by local trolley motors. This building, which still stands, has been converted to other uses. (Courtesy of Hod Conant.)

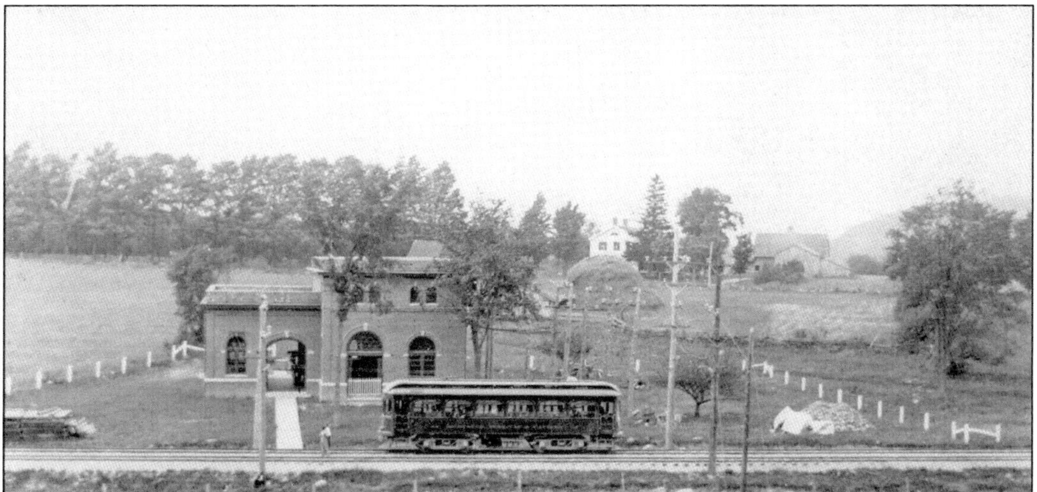

This is another view of the substation building, with a trolley passing in front of it. This was known as the Beebe Station. The station and Beebe Road were named for C.T. Beebe, general manager of the RS&E company. The trolley line passed south of the building. This view looks north toward State Route 31. (Courtesy of Hod Conant.)

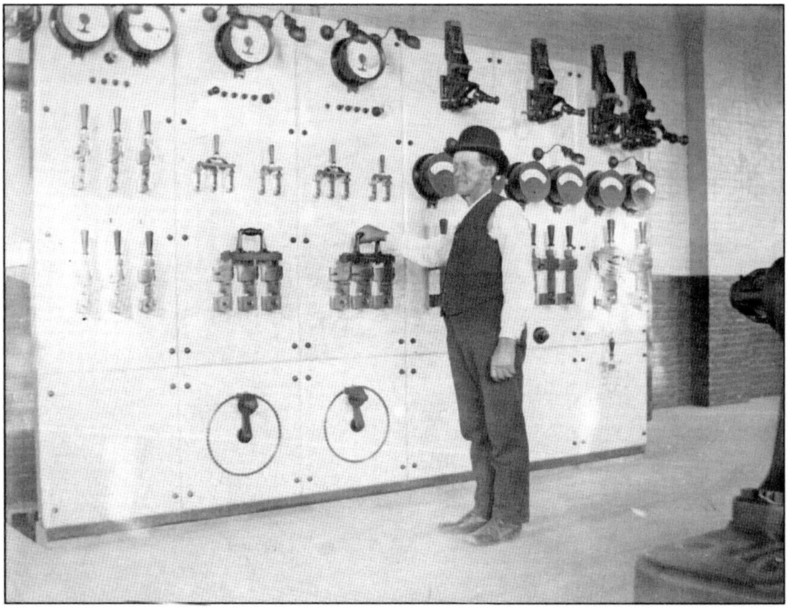

Inside the RS&E substation, an operator stands ready to adjust the controls that keep electricity steadily powering the trolley line. Today, this array of meters, switches, and manual controls would probably be replaced by a more complex, smaller, but more reliable automated system. (Courtesy of Macedon Town Historian.)

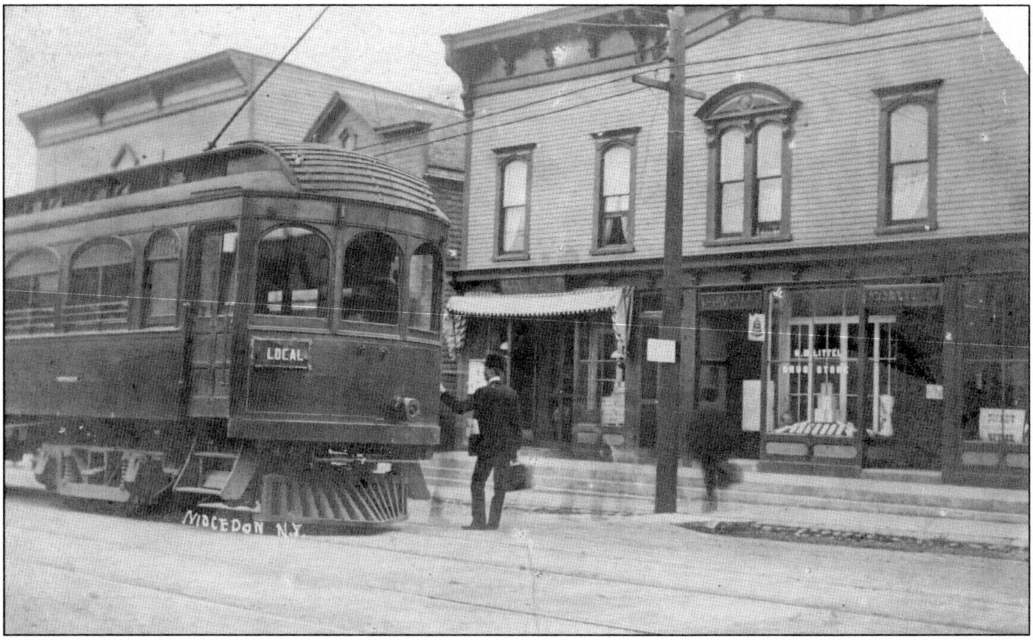

A passenger with a briefcase waits to board the trolley on Macedon's Main Street, in front of the H.M. Littel Drug Store. Another passenger near the utility pole moved during the photograph and is just a blur. The trolley was immensely popular with passengers, but its business plan depended on freight traffic that never materialized. As automobiles proliferated, the trolley lost ridership, and it went out of business in 1930. (Courtesy of Macedon Historical Society.)

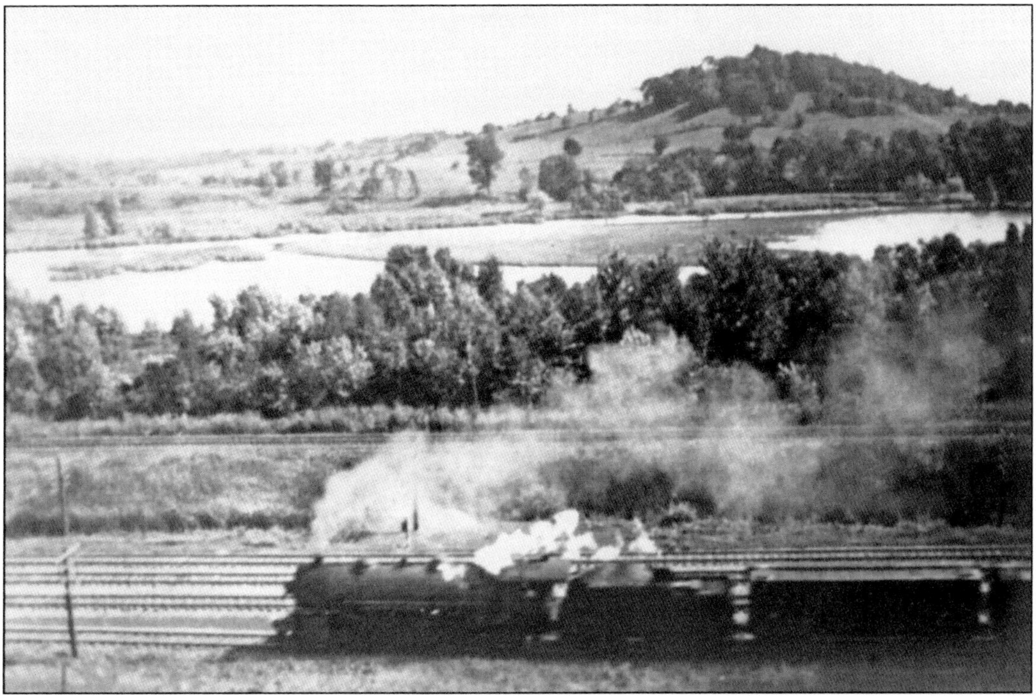

This photograph's inscription says that this train was one of the last locomotives powered by steam to pass through Macedon on the New York Central Railroad. The c. 1930 photograph was taken from a hill on the Eldredge farm on Quaker Road, a little east of Wayneport Road. The view is to the south, with the New York Central tracks in the foreground, the single-track West Shore line just beyond, and the Barge Canal in the background. (Courtesy of Macedon Town Historian.)

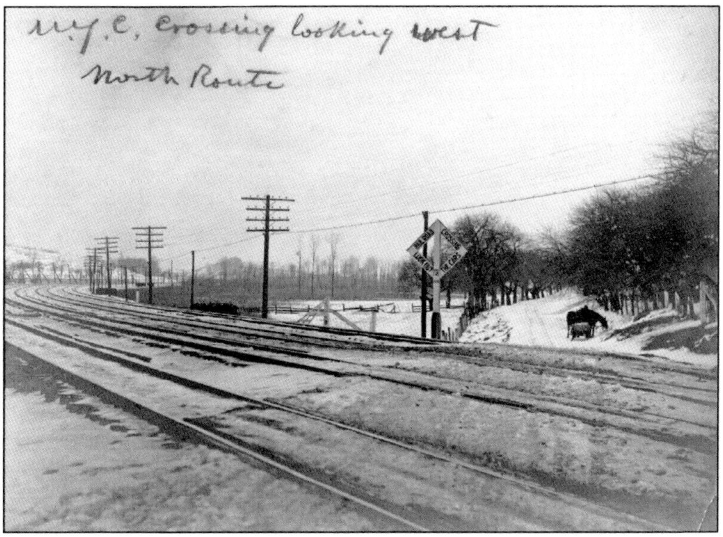

This winter scene from the late 1800s or early 1900s looks west along Quaker Road at the New York Central tracks. A horse-drawn sleigh pauses at the side of the road. Today's view is very similar, although the line has been reduced to two tracks, automatic crossing gates have replaced the simple warning sign, and the rail bed has been raised several feet. (Courtesy of Macedon Town Historian.)

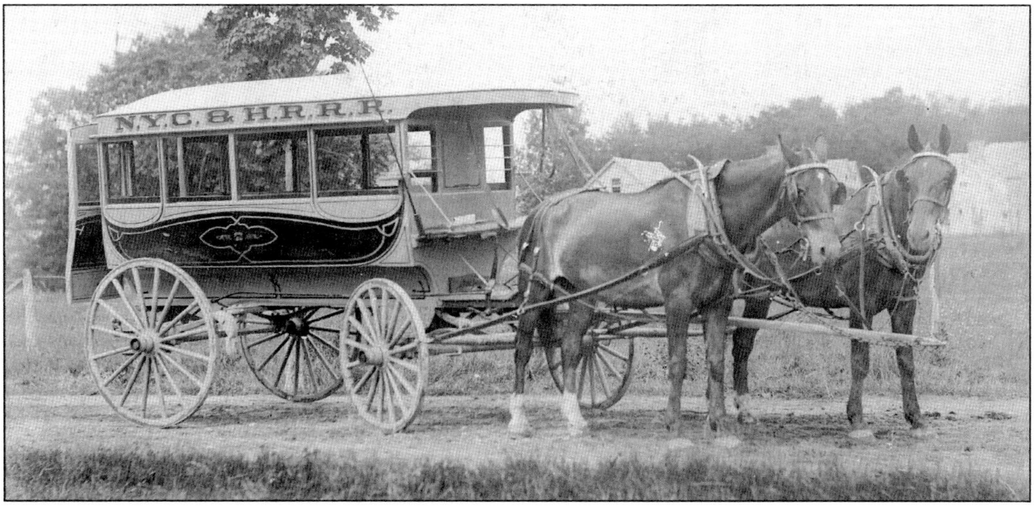

This stagecoach transported travelers between the railroad stations and hotels or other local destinations. It also picked up mail and delivered it to the Macedon Post Office, next to the Purdy store. The New York Central & Hudson Railroad terminal was next to the tracks, by the underpass for State Route 350/31F. Today, some of the abandoned terminal buildings are visible just west of the underpass. (Courtesy of Macedon Town Historian.)

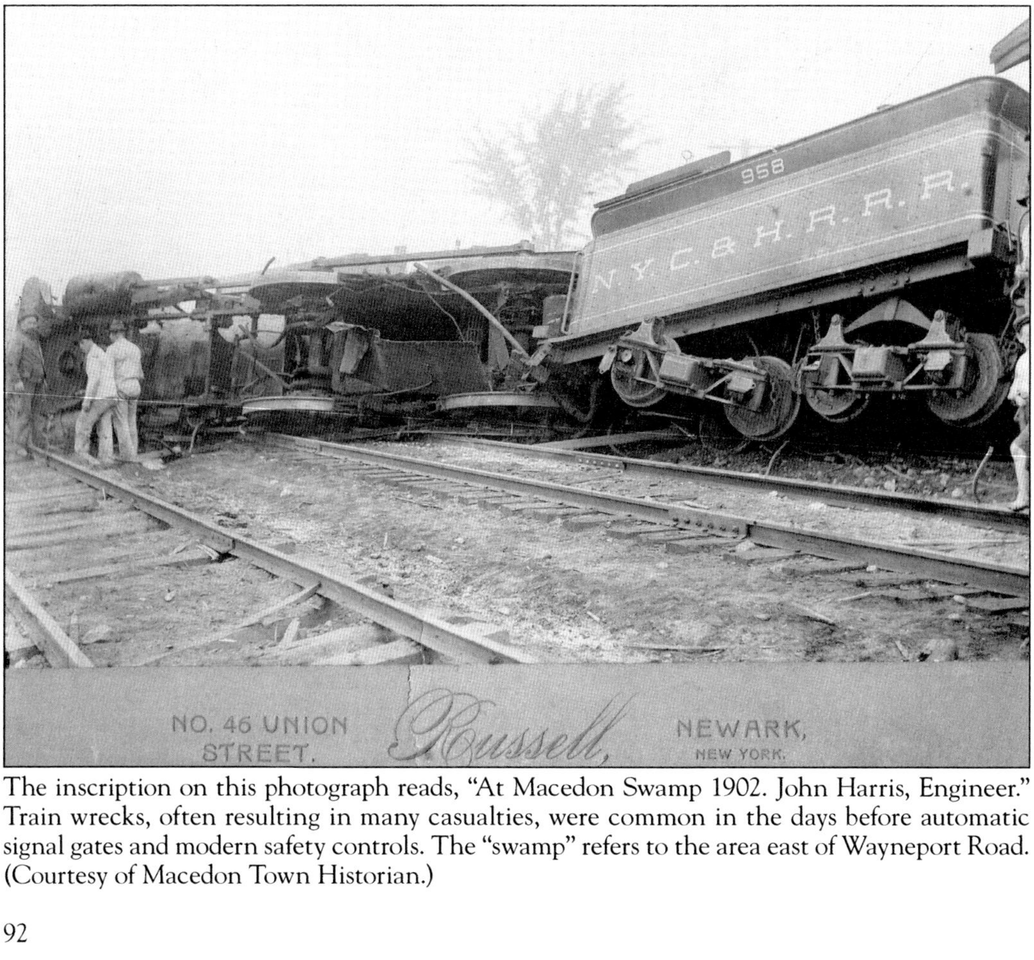

The inscription on this photograph reads, "At Macedon Swamp 1902. John Harris, Engineer." Train wrecks, often resulting in many casualties, were common in the days before automatic signal gates and modern safety controls. The "swamp" refers to the area east of Wayneport Road. (Courtesy of Macedon Town Historian.)

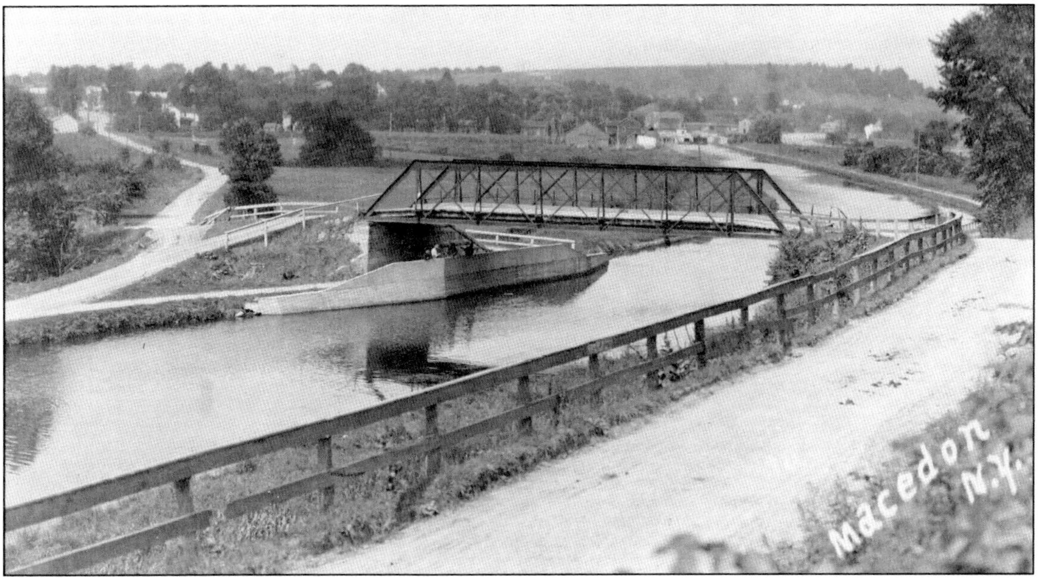

This view looks west along Quaker Road where it intersects with O'Neil Road. This bridge was one of the few double bridges on the old Erie Canal. Road traffic between Macedon and Palmyra went across the bridge in the foreground. The road at the left turned into Main Street in Macedon. It is almost impossible to see in the photograph, but directly behind the foreground bridge is a separate bridge for canal traffic, where the towpath changed from the north side to the south side. Today's O'Neil Road Bridge and Erie Canal are about 150 feet south of this location. The remains of the bridge abutment and canal bed can be seen today, west of the intersection of O'Neil and Quaker Roads. (Courtesy of Hod Conant.)

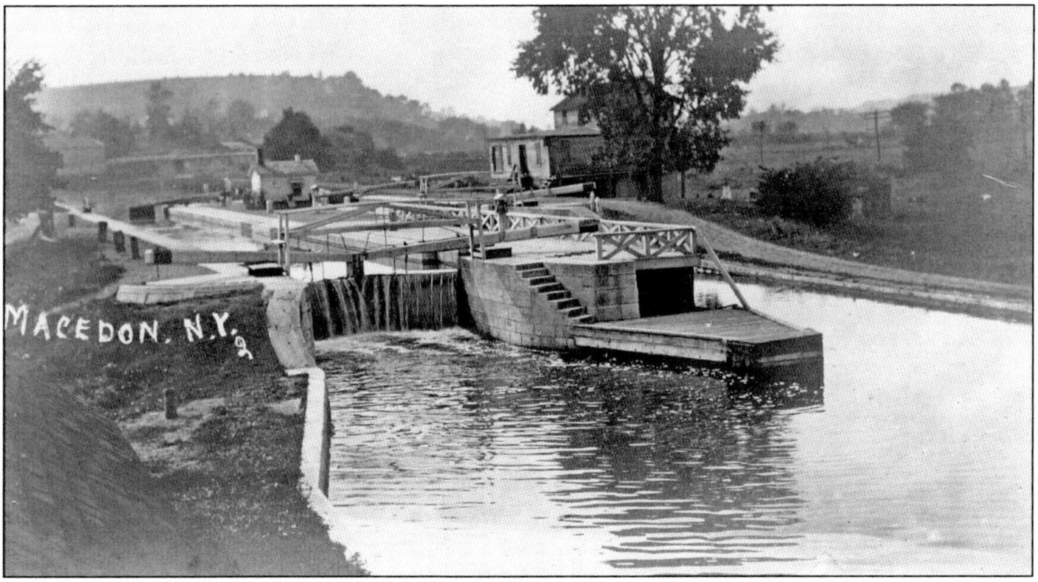

This view of this photo postcard looks west from the lower level of Erie Canal Lock 61. The inscription notes that the buildings on the spillway at right are the McCann house and store. The cupola of the old Macedon High School is barely visible in the distance, just over the tops of the trees on the left. Much of the stonework from this old lock is still visible near the south edge of today's Lock 30 Park on the east side of the village. (Courtesy of Hod Conant.)

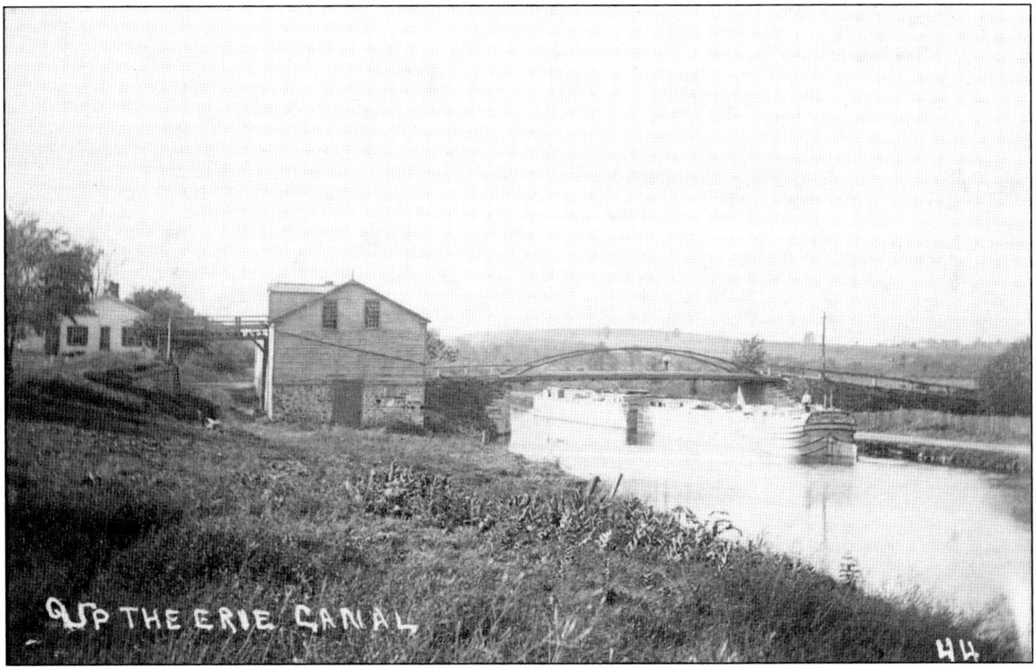

Two barges pass under the Erie Canal's Railroad Avenue Bridge in Macedon. This is a so-called bowstring bridge, also called a Whipple bridge, after its designer, Squire Whipple. The view is toward the west. On the left is the C.J. Servoss warehouse. Later, the new Barge Canal will be excavated in an area just to the right of this scene. (Courtesy of Macedon Historical Society.)

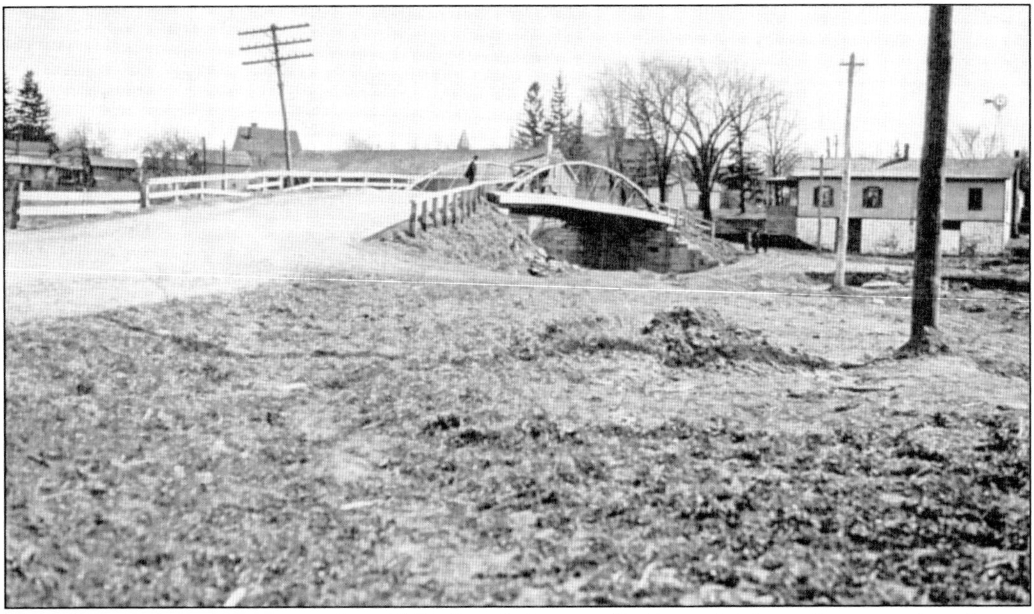

This view looks south across the old Railroad Avenue Bridge, which no longer exists. It was replaced by a new bridge, just east of today's Macedon Canal Park. The park is actually an island that occupies most of the area between the old Erie Canal and the new Barge Canal. That future Barge Canal will be constructed directly behind the position of this image's photographer. (Courtesy of Macedon Town Historian.)

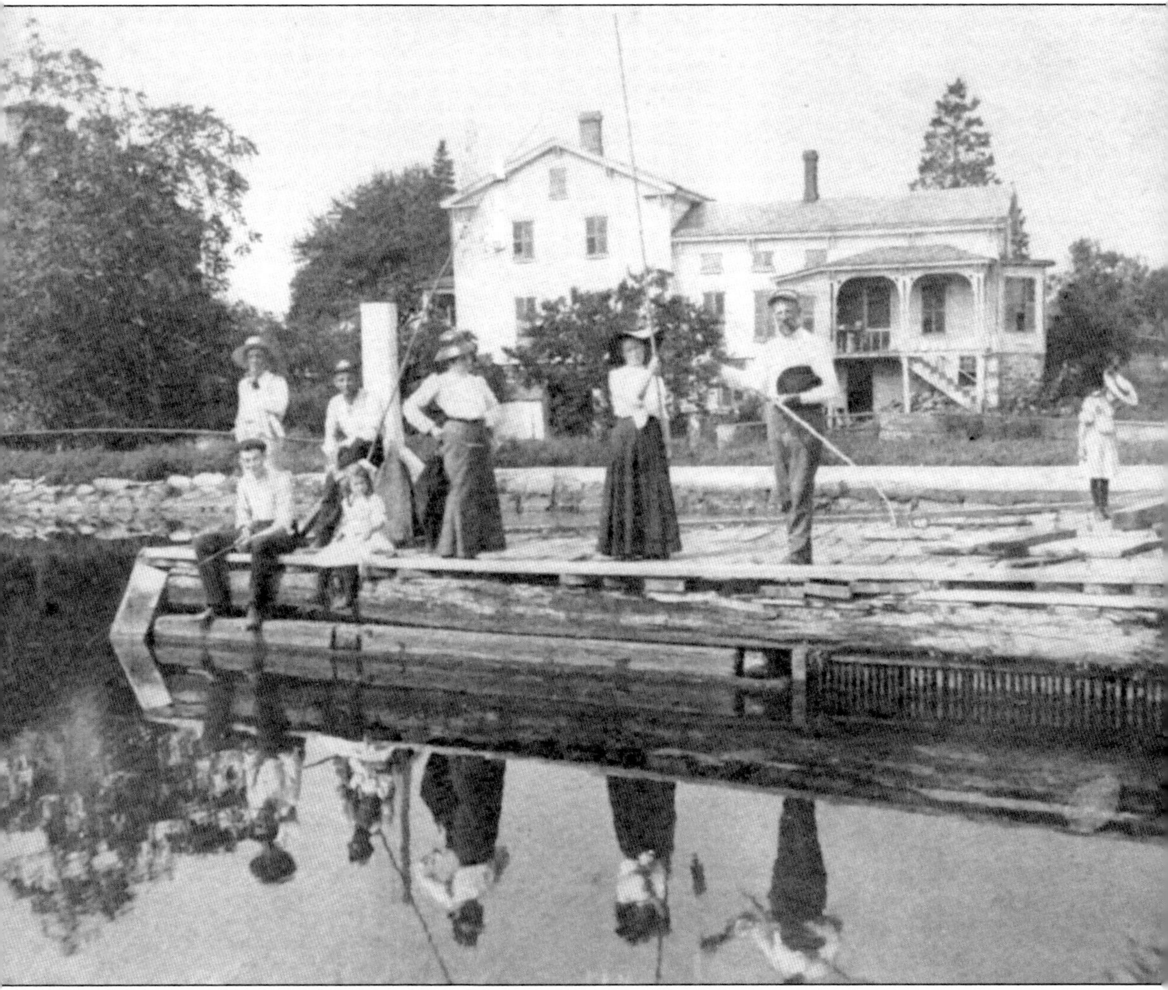

The Aldrich family takes advantage of a quiet day on the canal to enjoy some fishing at Erie Canal's Lock 60. The long fishing rods of the time did not have reels. It must have required some fancy footwork to land a fish once one had a bite. This house and the remains of Lock 60 are on Quaker Road, a few hundred yards east of the intersection with O'Neil Road. (Courtesy of Macedon Town Historian.)

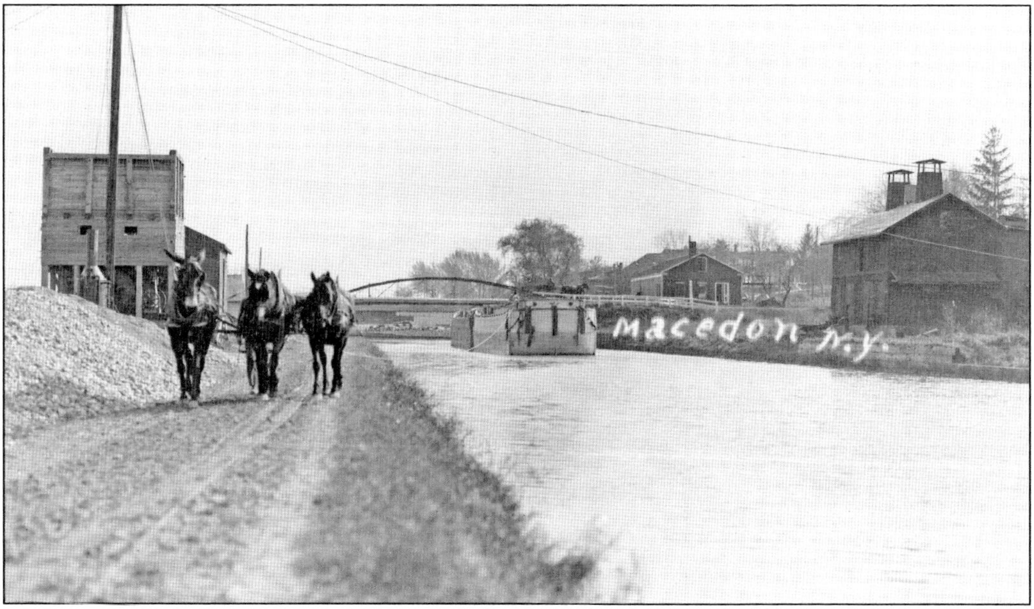

This is a barge under tow on the old Erie Canal, just west of the Railroad Avenue Bridge, which is visible in the background. Three mules strain against the towline. The canal speed limit was four miles per hour. Westbound canal traffic typically carried manufactured goods and immigrants headed for the frontier. Eastbound traffic carried flour, wheat, fruit, whiskey, and lumber. (Courtesy of Hod Conant.)

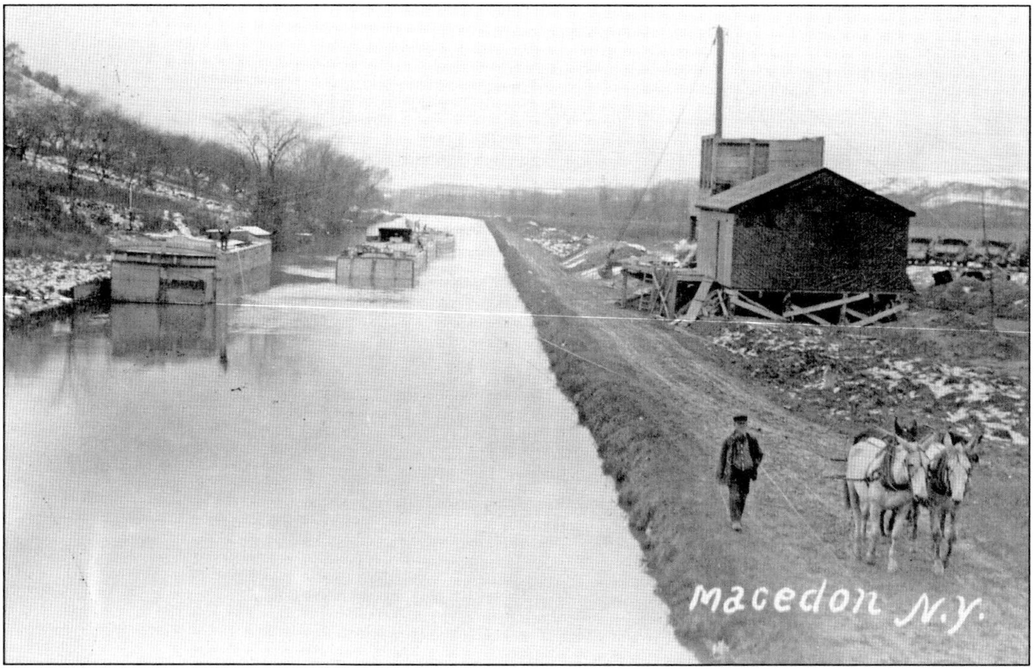

This photograph appears to have been taken looking west from the Railroad Avenue Bridge. One barge is docked at the side of the Erie Canal as two other barges are towed past it. In the right foreground are the mules that provide the motive power, along with their handler, known as a hoggee. (Courtesy of Hod Conant.)

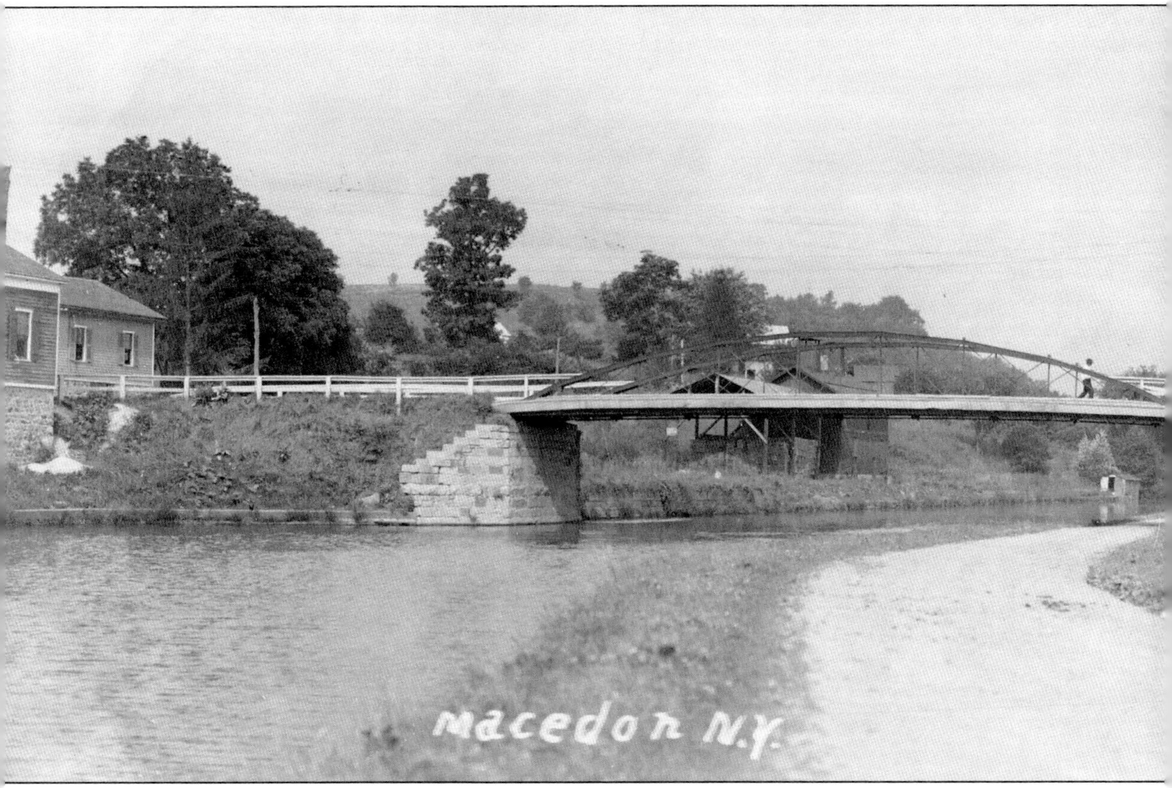

A lone pedestrian crosses the old Railroad Avenue Bridge. This view looks west toward Wayneport. Recently, the Erie Canal name was resurrected to replace the Barge Canal, which was the name given to the canal when a wide range of improvements was made in the 1920s. Just beyond the camera's view on the right is the towpath, now made into a recreational trail. The Canal Trails system is an important recreational resource, not only for Macedon residents, but for trail users across the state. Most trails follow the old Erie towpaths. The Macedon Trails Group helps the State of New York maintain these trails. (Courtesy of Hod Conant.)

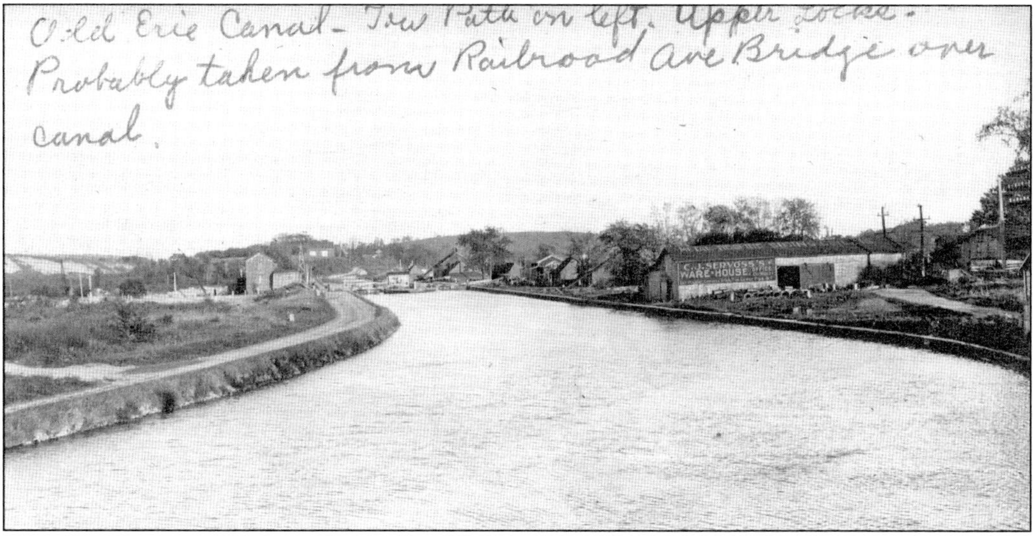

This view of the Erie Canal shows Lock 61 in the distance. As the caption notes, this photograph appears to have been taken looking east from the old Railroad Avenue Bridge. On the right is the C.J. Servoss warehouse. The warehouse's roof advertises "Metal Roofing, Siding and Ceilings." A billboard advertisement on the side offers "Salt, Plaster, Cements, Brick, Tile, Sewer Pipe & C." The Servoss Company had an office on Main Street in Macedon. (Courtesy of Macedon Town Historian.)

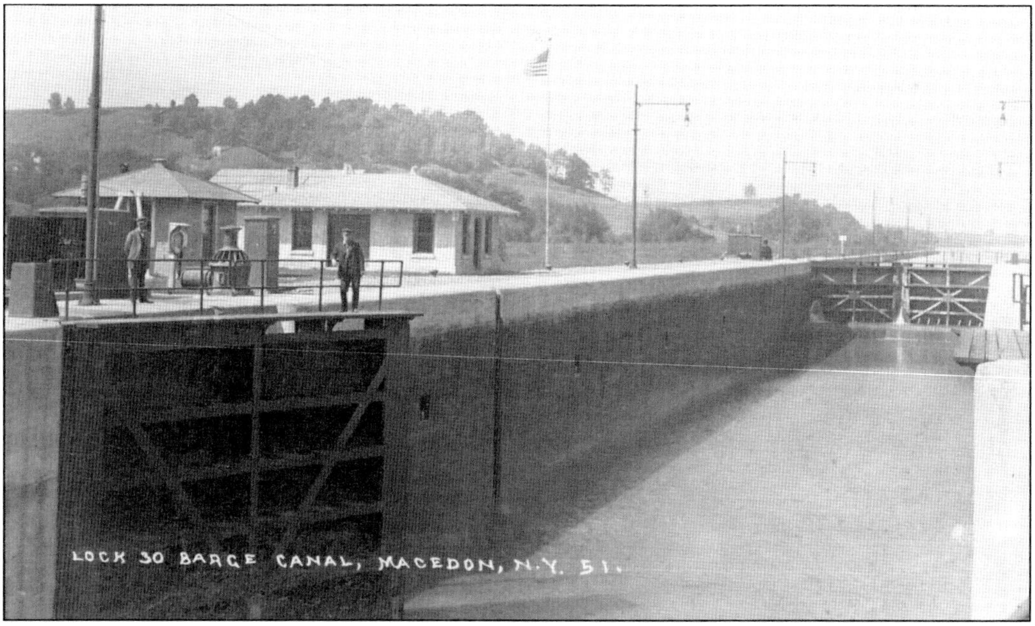

This is Macedon's Lock 30, shortly after its completion in 1918. As the Erie Canal was enlarged and transformed into the Barge Canal, many locks were eliminated or renumbered. The new canal was straighter and deeper. The larger drop at the new Lock 30 eliminated Lock 61 at Macedon and Lock 60 between Macedon and Palmyra. Gates at Locks 29 and 30 were operated by electricity from water turbines at the spillway near Lock 29, just west of Palmyra. When a construction problem sidelined the turbines, electricity from the RS&E trolley line was used for a short time. (Courtesy of Hod Conant.)

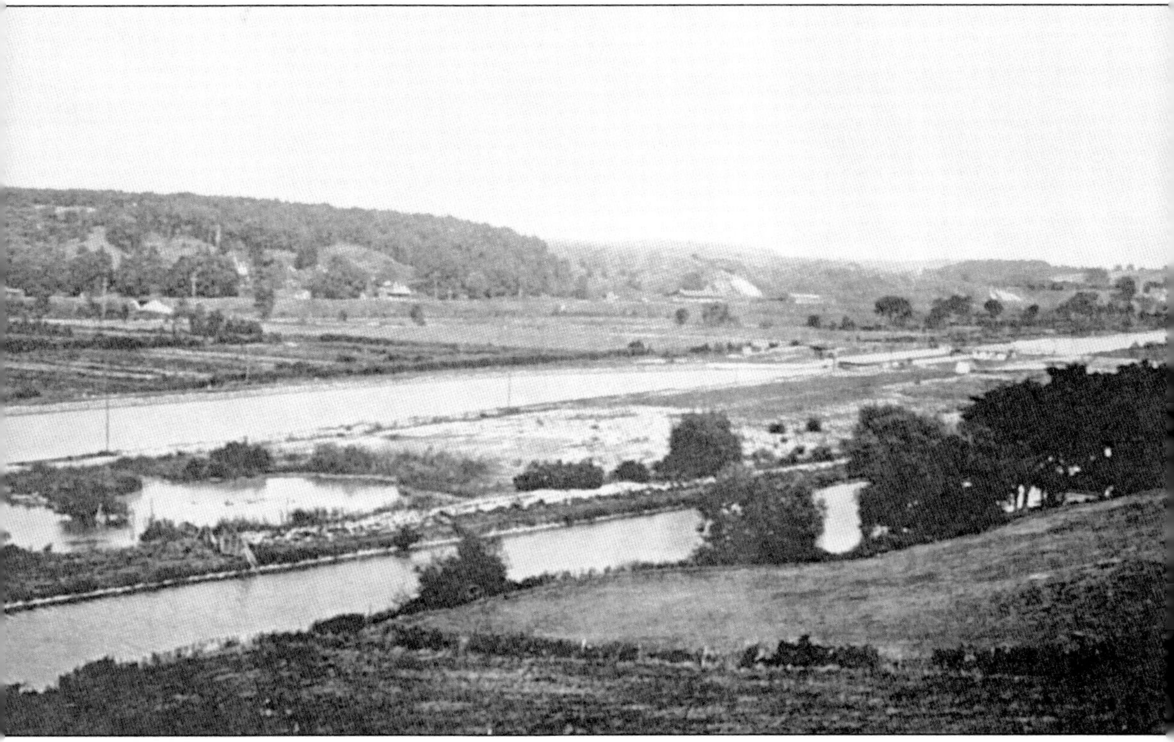

Two canals are visible in this photograph. The Barge Canal runs across the center, and the Erie Canal is below it. This view is to the northeast, toward Lock 30 near the right edge of the photograph. The canal was a main traffic artery for the growing nation in the mid-1800s, and Macedon benefited greatly by being a canal town. The view here suggests that the photographer may have been standing on the north side of Lapham Hill. (Courtesy of Macedon Town Historian.)

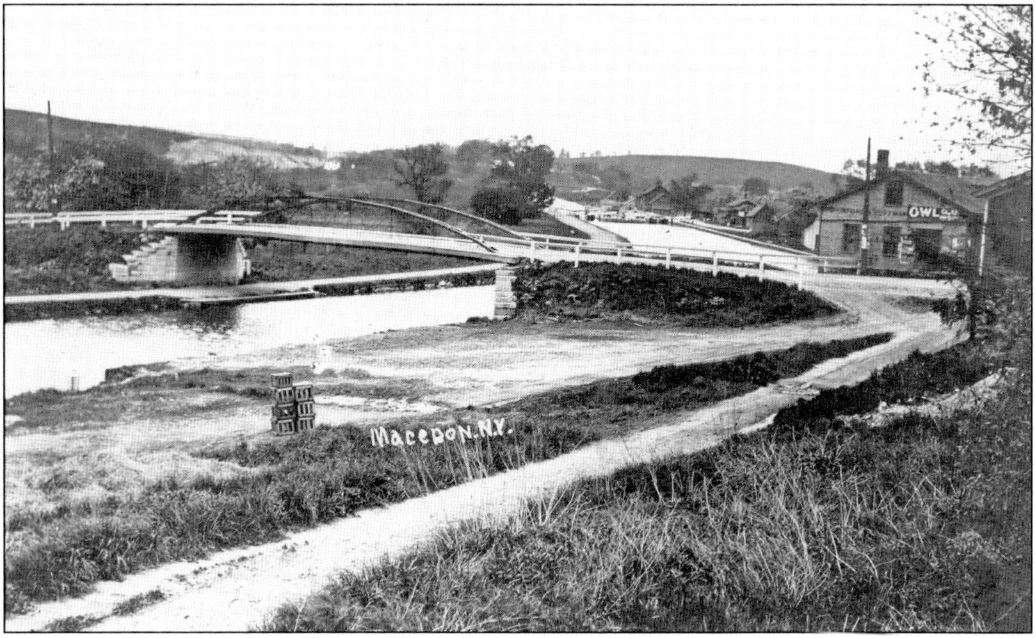

Empty crates sit at the edge of the Erie Canal just west of the Railroad Avenue Bridge. Lock 61 is visible in the distance. The message side of this photo postcard reads, "This is where they load boats with produce for the New York Market. There were thousands of crates of apples and potatoes piled in that space this fall." The warehouse at the right bears an advertisement for Owl cigars and a sign for the Bickford & Huffman Drill Works. (Courtesy of Hod Conant.)

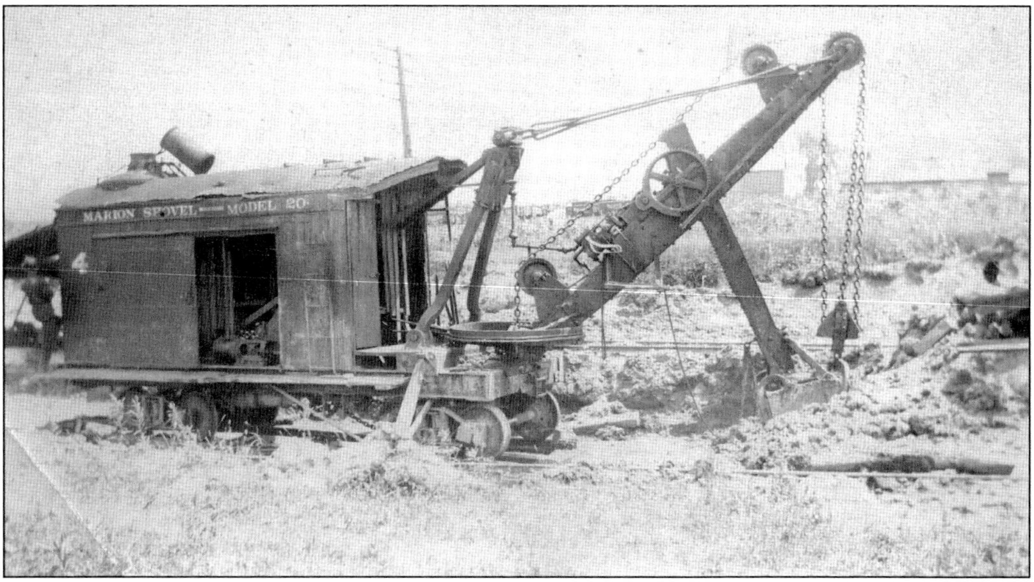

This steam shovel, a Marion Model 20, is working on the Barge Canal at Macedon. Early excavating equipment was powered by steam engines. This machine, typical of the time, was not self-propelled, but had to be moved to the work site on rails. Only the base of the boom rotated, severely restricting the area that could be reached. Today, an entire earthmoving machine can rotate around its vertical axis, and caterpillar tracks allow it to move freely. (Courtesy of Macedon Town Historian.)

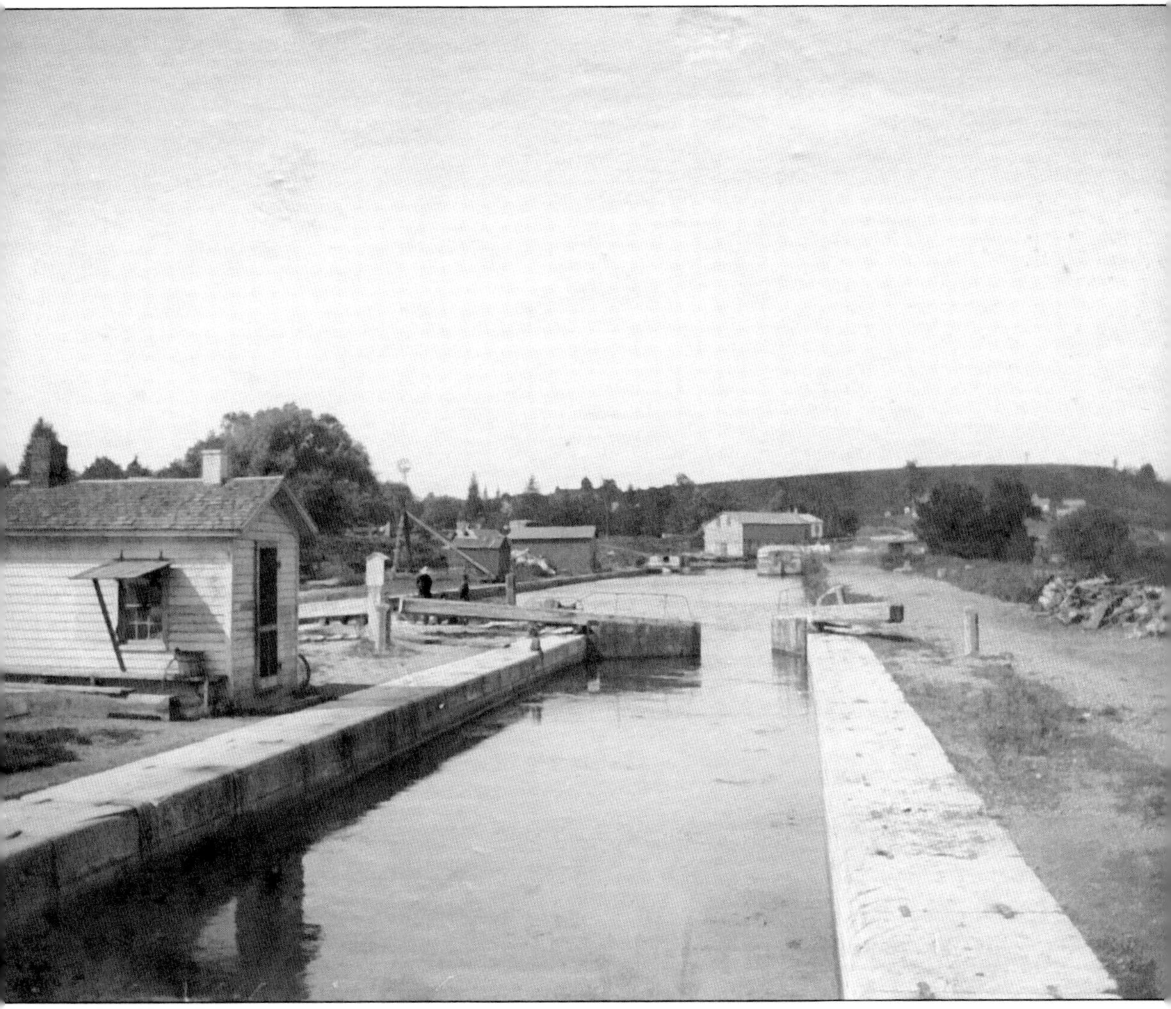

This photograph was taken from inside the south chamber of Lock 61, looking east. On the left is the locktender's house, at the tip of the island dividing the north and south chambers. In the distance are some of the warehouses and commercial enterprises that flourished along the canal. (Courtesy of Macedon Town Historian.)

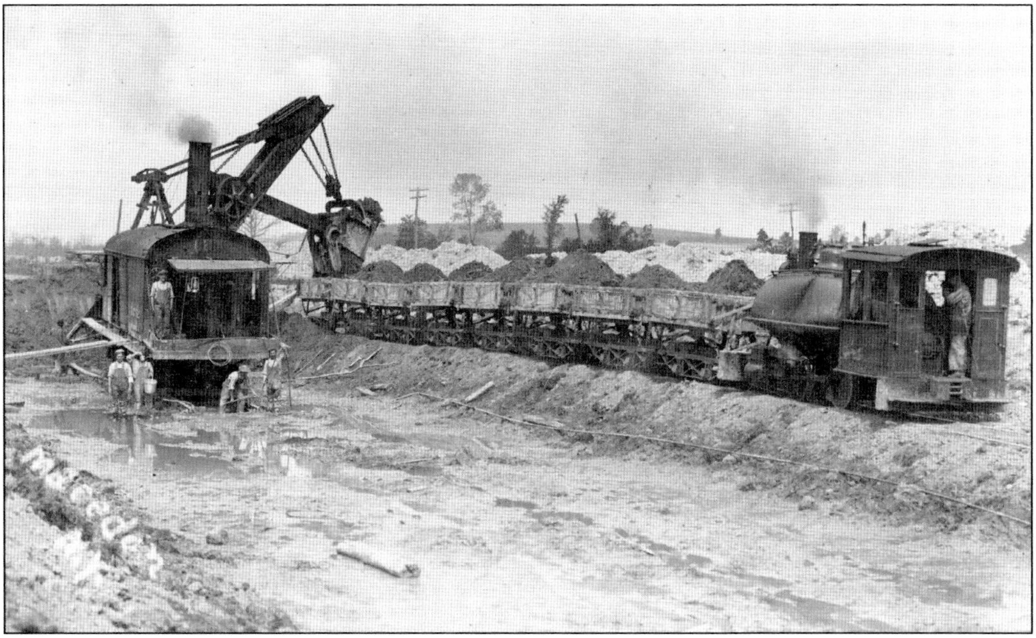

Several workers are standing in the mud near this steam shovel as it loads dirt from the canal excavation into rail-mounted "dump trucks" that will haul the dirt away. This was a difficult, muddy, dirty job. The construction pictured here was part of major improvements that were completed in 1918. At that time, the waterway's name was changed from the Erie Canal to the Barge Canal. In the 1990s, the name change was reversed. (Courtesy of Hod Conant.)

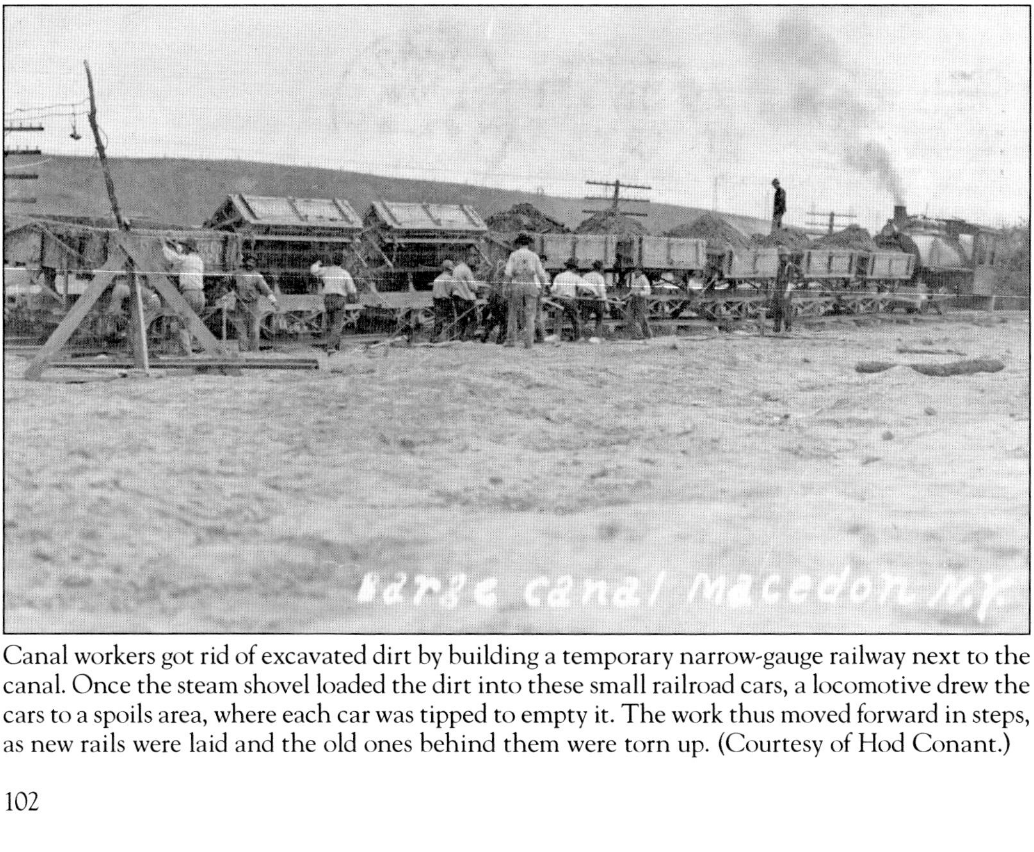

Canal workers got rid of excavated dirt by building a temporary narrow-gauge railway next to the canal. Once the steam shovel loaded the dirt into these small railroad cars, a locomotive drew the cars to a spoils area, where each car was tipped to empty it. The work thus moved forward in steps, as new rails were laid and the old ones behind them were torn up. (Courtesy of Hod Conant.)

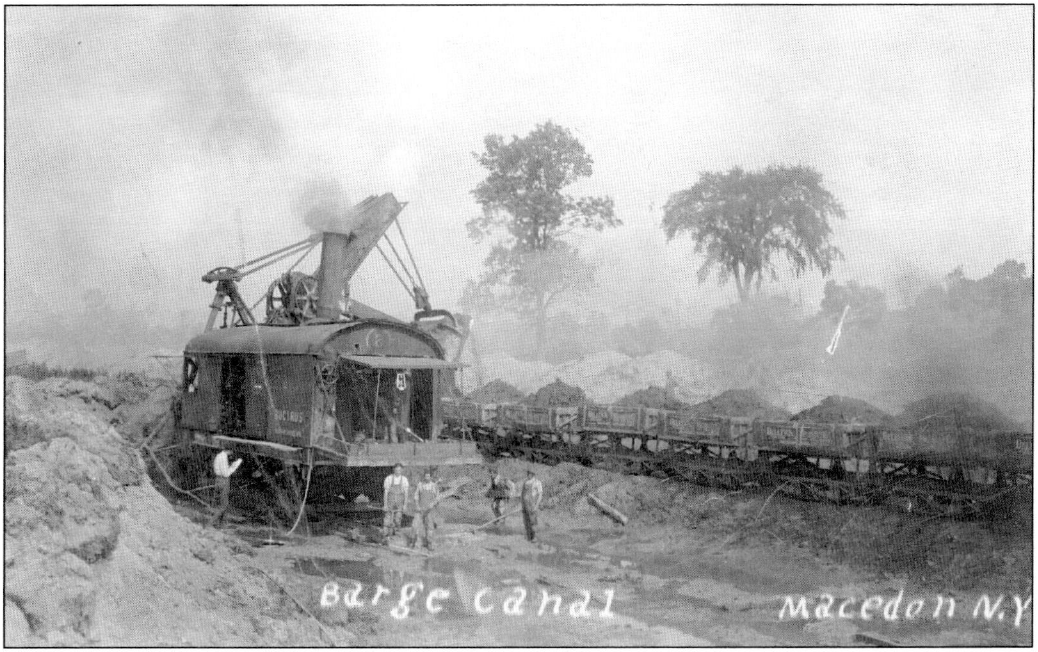

Smoke from the boilers of the steam shovel and from the locomotive hauling the spoils casts a pall over the construction site as excavation for the Macedon section of the Barge Canal proceeds. By 1918, increases to the depth and width of the Erie Canal would make it possible to move more freight through New York State at less cost. (Courtesy of Hod Conant.)

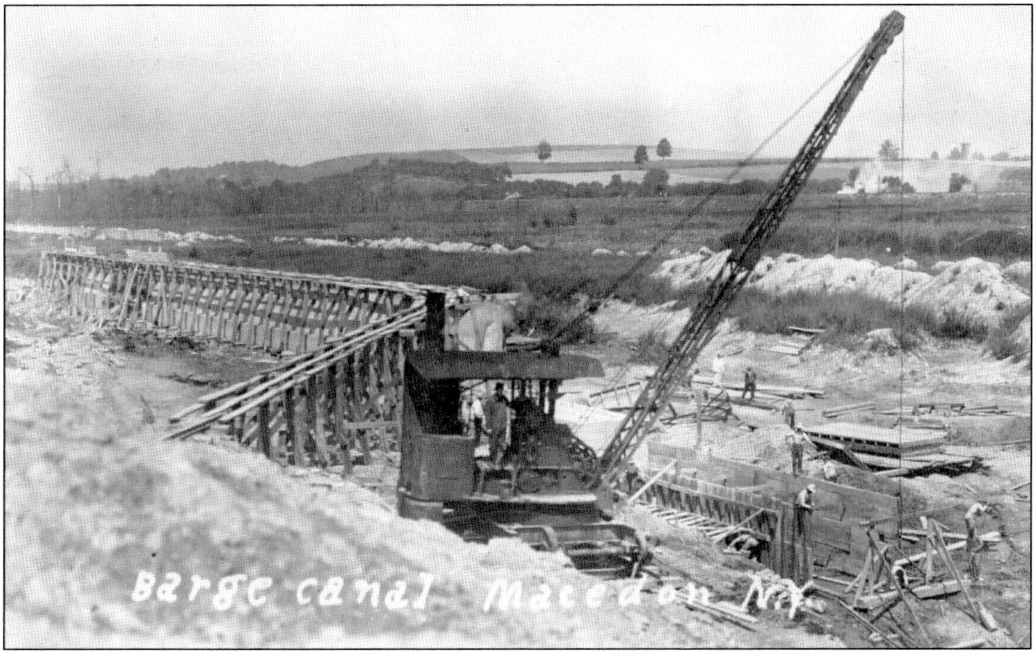

Along with excavation to the proper depth, canal construction requires wooden forms to be built so that the walls of the canal can be reinforced. Concrete foundations will be constructed at locks, where barges are transferred between different water levels. (Courtesy of Hod Conant.)

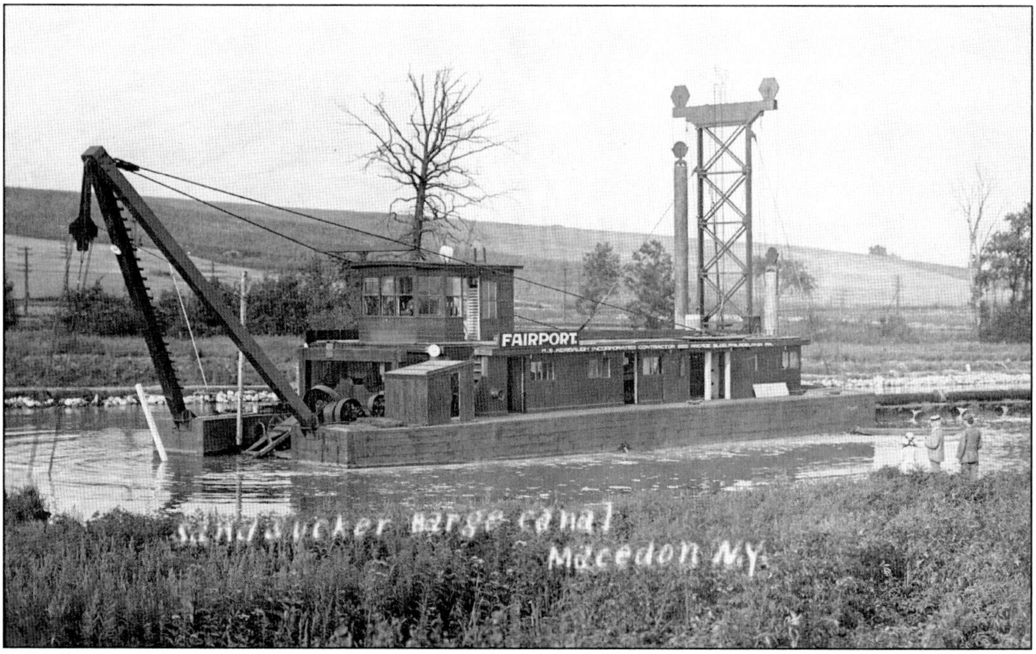

Canals require frequent maintenance. Silt and debris build up at the bottom, reducing the clearance for barge traffic. Dredges like the sand sucker in these photographs restore the original depth. Dredges use buckets or suction pumps to transfer loose material like sand and silt to a nearby empty barge. According to the sign on the side of the dredge, the *Fairport* was operated by H.S. Kerbaugh Inc., a Philadelphia contractor that also built canal bridges. In the above photograph, two men and a woman watch the process from the side of the canal. Below, the dredge operates at one of the wider spots of the canal at Macedon. Both photographs date from the early 20th century. (Both, courtesy of Hod Conant.)

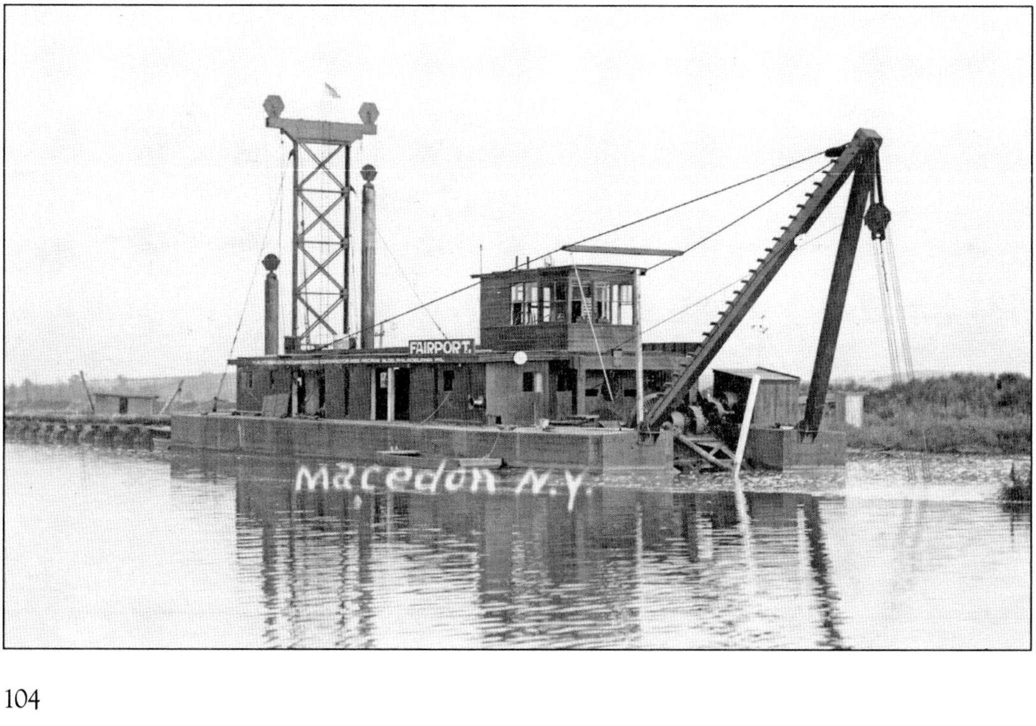

Six

Community Life

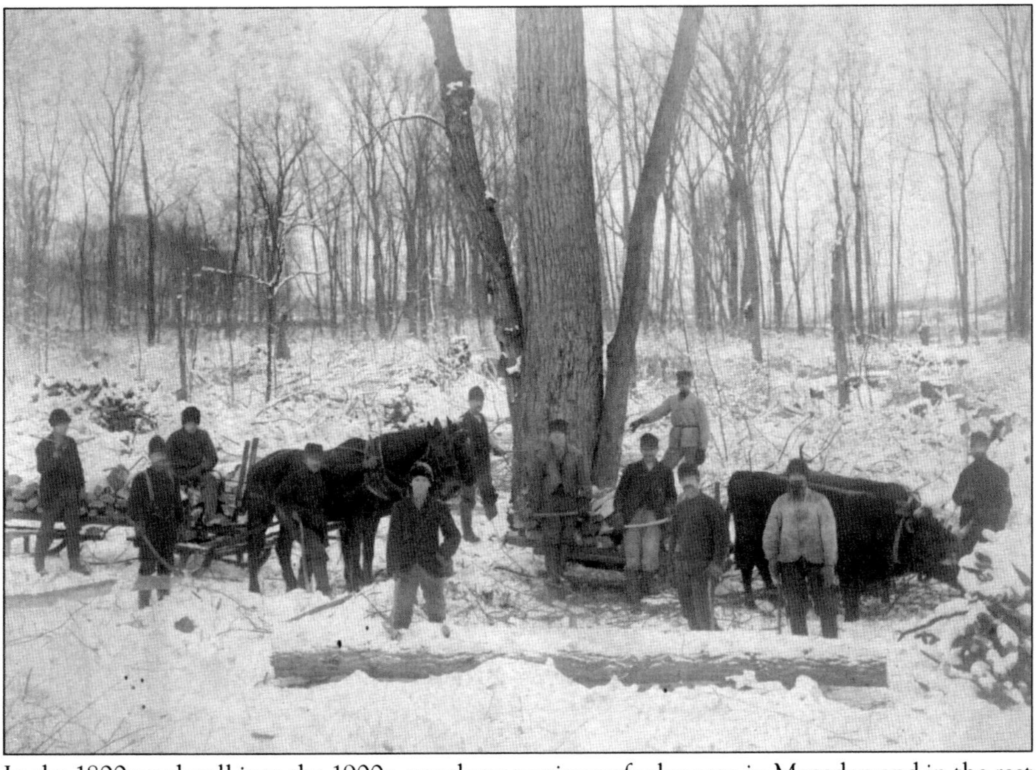

In the 1800s and well into the 1900s, wood was a primary fuel source in Macedon and in the rest of the country. Harvesting wood was a year-round activity. Here, a group of men, heavily dressed against the cold, loads sleighs with wood. The men are using a team of horses for one sleigh and a team of oxen for the other. Most homes had fireplaces and stoves on the ground floor. Often, the only heat available in second-floor rooms was secondhand heat that percolated up through floor grates. Only the well-to-do had central heating in their homes, such as a coal-fired furnace or steam boiler. (Courtesy of Macedon Town Historian.)

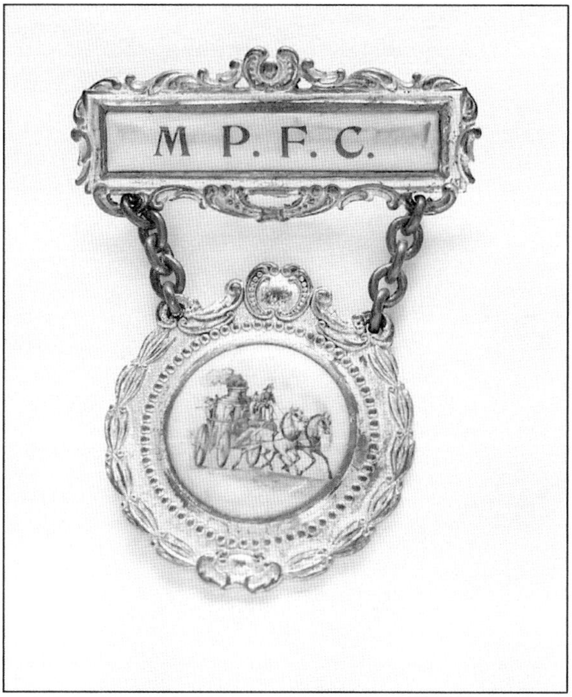

This Macedon Fire Protective Company badge, about three inches high, dates from the early 1900s. The enameled medallion is suspended from the clasp by two chains. It bears a halftone image of horse-drawn fire-fighting apparatus. According to a newspaper item of May 25, 1900, "Consent to the formation of the Macedon Protective Fire Company was filed at the county clerk's office yesterday. It is signed by President Emory Lapham and Trustees J. McNary and David W. Courter. The organizers are Fred C. Johnson, Harry Mitchell, Charles J. Servoss, B.E. Woods, Harry Steiger and John E. Simonds. The membership of the company cannot exceed forty." (Courtesy of Macedon Town Historian.)

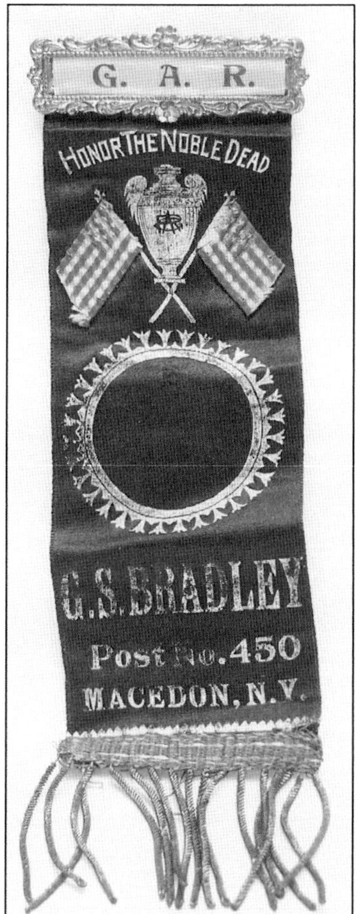

This badge identified the wearer as a member of the Grand Army of the Republic (GAR), Macedon Post 450. The GAR was a nongovernmental organization made up of veterans of the Union army in the Civil War. There were GAR posts in every state of the union and several posts overseas. The enameled clasp has the initials *G.A.R.* in contrasting colors. The gilt fringe at the bottom is typical of decorative fraternal badges of the period. The GAR was dissolved in 1956, when its last surviving member died. (Courtesy of Macedon Town Historian.)

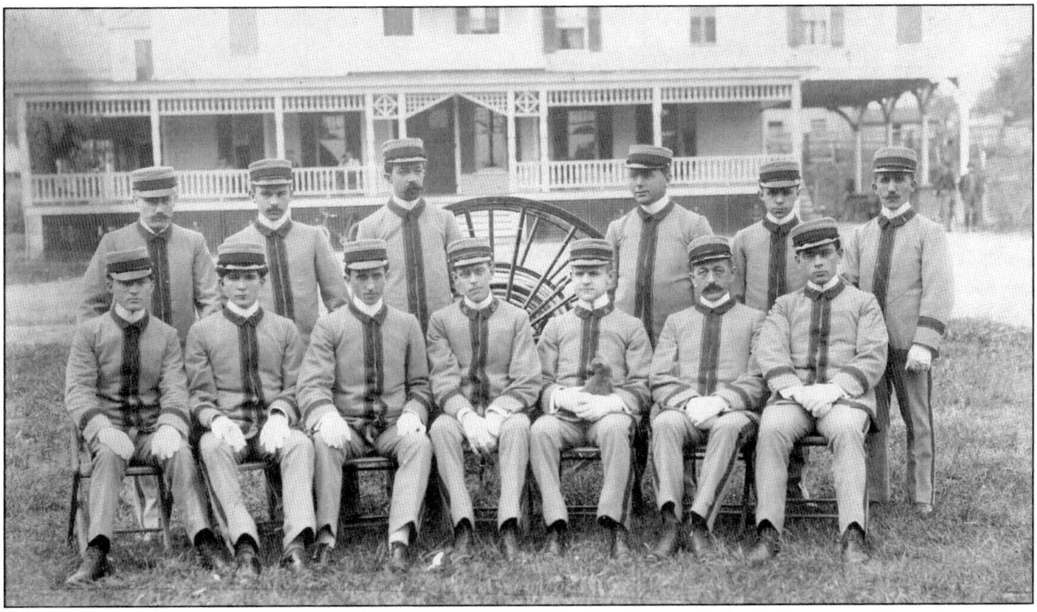

Macedon Protective Hose Company members pose in front of the Macedon Hotel wearing uniforms and gloves. Shown here are, from left to right, (first row) Thomas Quinn, Theron Sutton, Jerome Reed, William Marsh, Thomas Millis, A.B.C. Clark, and Timothy McGary; (second row) George Harp, Ira Hare, Frank Mosher, Charles Shimmia, Edward Hare, and Paul Lutz. Although Dalmatian dogs were the traditional fire company mascot, the animal in Millis's lap appears to be a cat. (Courtesy of Macedon Town Historian.)

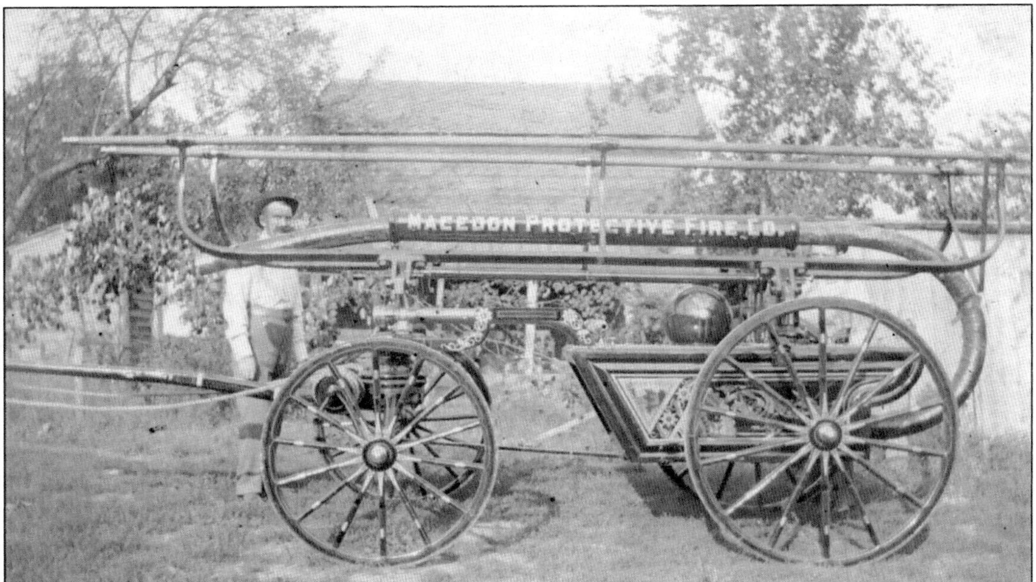

This pumper proudly bears the name of the Macedon Fire Protective Company. It is typical of small-town firefighting equipment in the era before municipal water systems made it possible to locate fire hydrants on many streets. After connecting the pumper's hose to a water source such as a nearby pond, the two long handles at the top were lowered and operated by hand in a see-saw motion to power the pump. (Courtesy of Macedon Town Historian.)

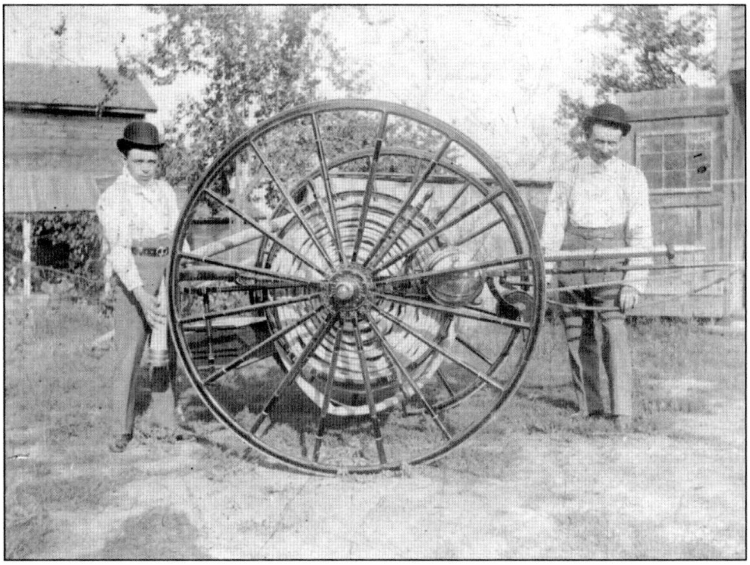

The two men posing with this fire-hose reel are identified only as Sutton and Milton Kemp. Firemen would use the handles at the right to wheel the hose to the location of the fire, then would unreel the hose by hand. In the days before municipal hydrants and engine-powered pumpers, it was much more difficult to save a burning building. (Courtesy of Macedon Town Historian.)

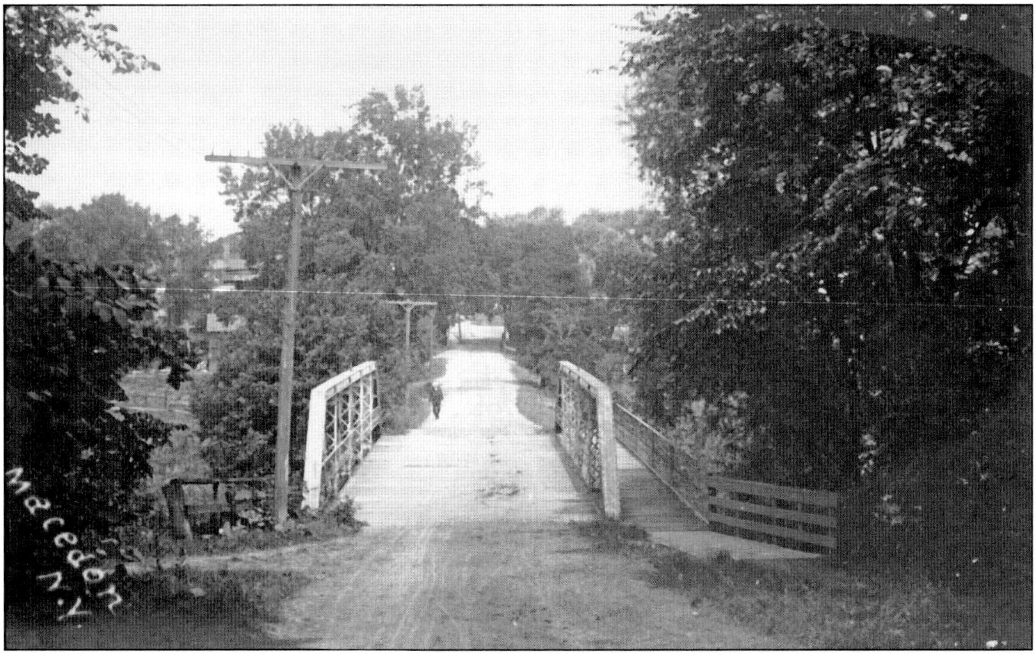

The old Erie Street Bridge spanning Ganargua Creek is seen in this north-facing photograph. The view is toward Main Street. A lone pedestrian heads toward the bridge. Today, this is old Erie Street. There is a new Erie Street extension, which begins at the Route 31/350 stoplight and joins the old road on the other side of Ganargua Creek. (Courtesy of Hod Conant.)

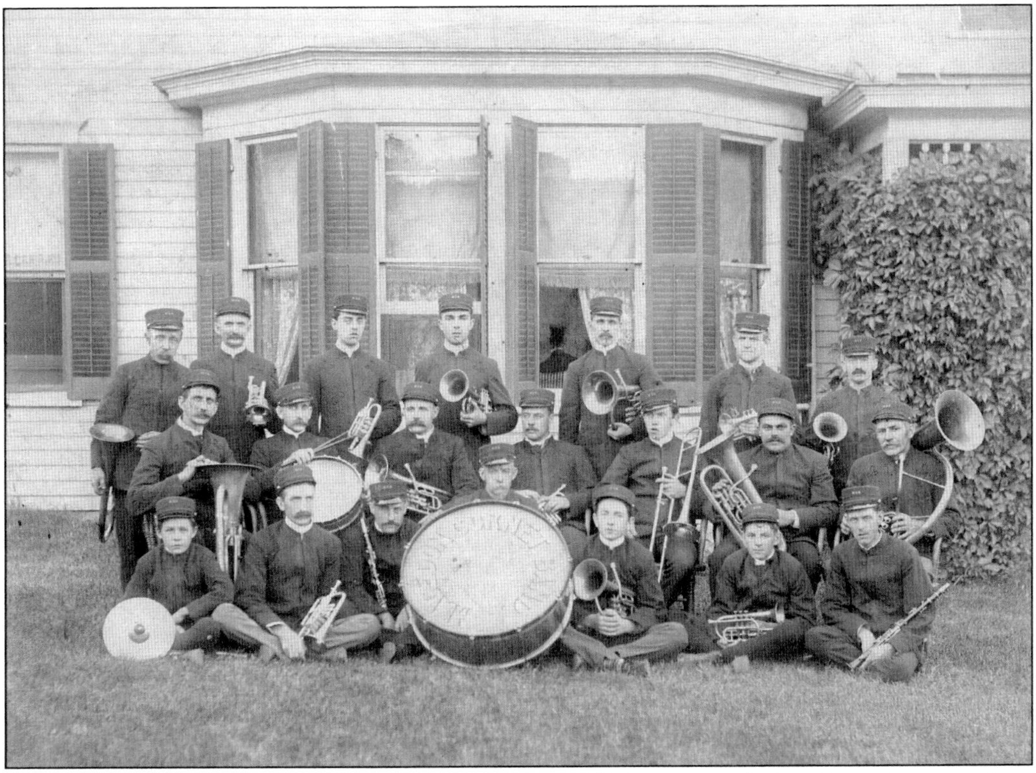

The Macedon Cornet Band was established in August 1884. Some of the band members seen here are John Hughes, Peter Gratton, John O'Keefe, James Burns, Emmett Gratton, Thomas Wesley, and Phillip Gratton, who was 13 years old in 1904 when this photograph was taken. Uniformed musical bands were very popular community activities in the early 20th century and were an important source of civic pride. (Courtesy of Macedon Town Historian.)

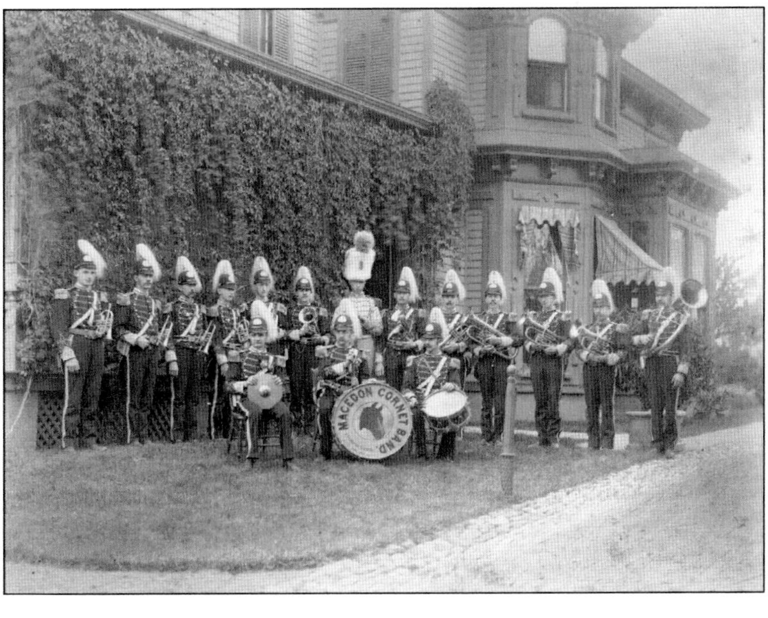

The Macedon Cornet Band appears here in full parade regalia. These uniforms are much more elaborate than those in the previous photograph. The inscription identifies the leader, in the white plumed hat, as Wayne Gallup. He was a commercial traveler, or salesman, for Bickford & Huffman. (Courtesy of Macedon Town Historian.)

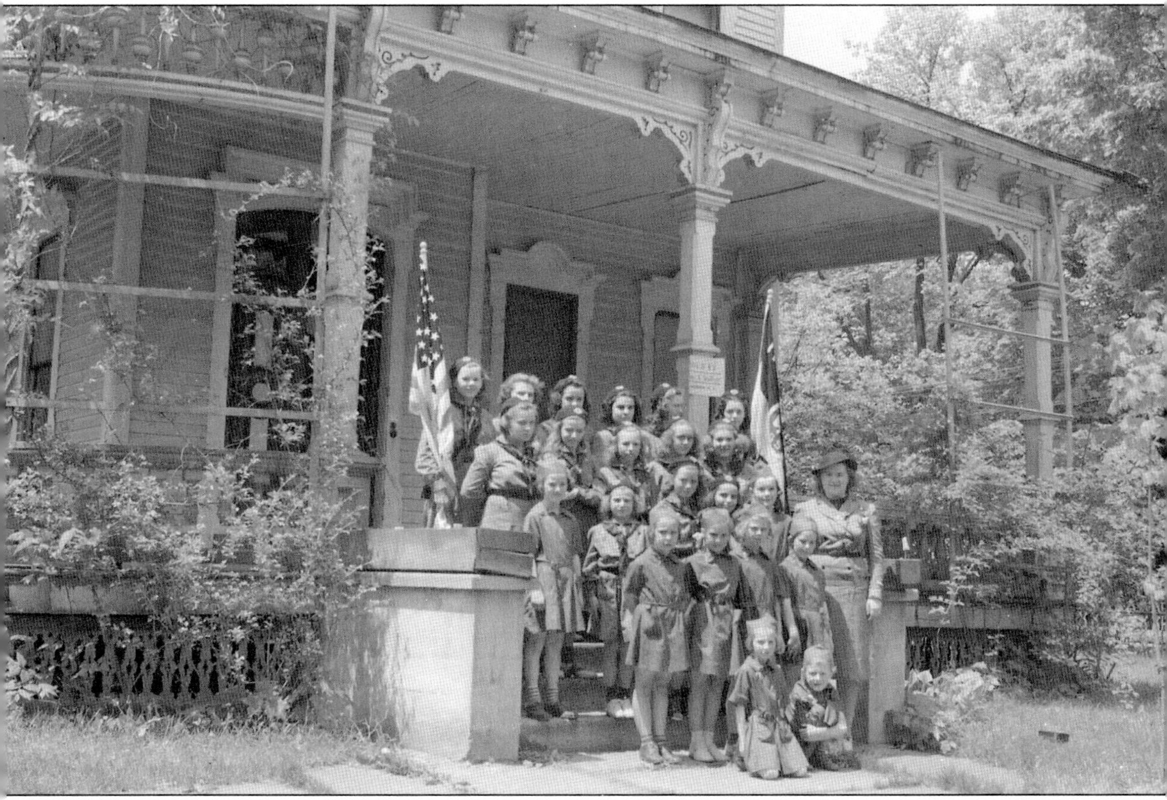

A troop of Macedon Girl Scouts poses with its leader around 1940. Some of these girls may be great-grandmothers today. The notice on the column of the porch behind the girls is a realtor's Sold sign. (Courtesy of Macedon Historical Society.)

This 1940s Memorial Day fell on a beautiful, sunny day. Here, the drum majorette wields a baton as she leads the band down West Main Street toward the center of the village. The Macedon High School band traditionally dressed in green-and-white uniforms. (Courtesy of Macedon Historical Society.)

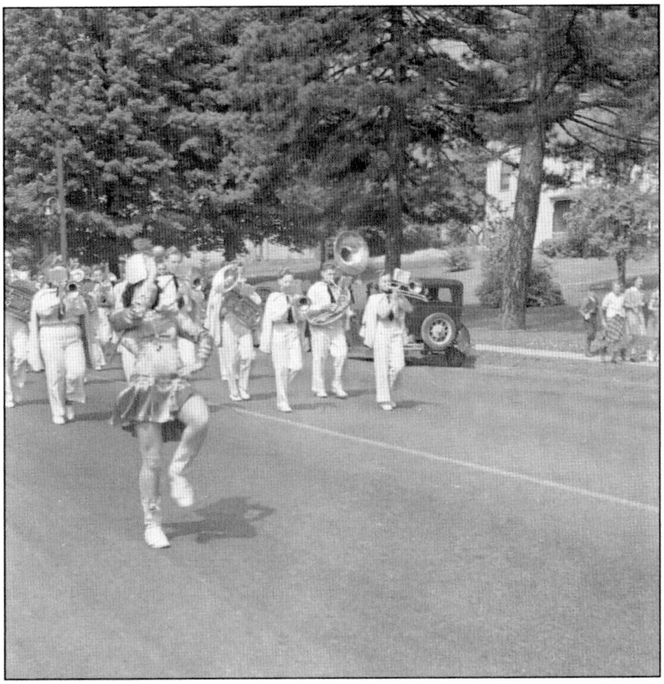

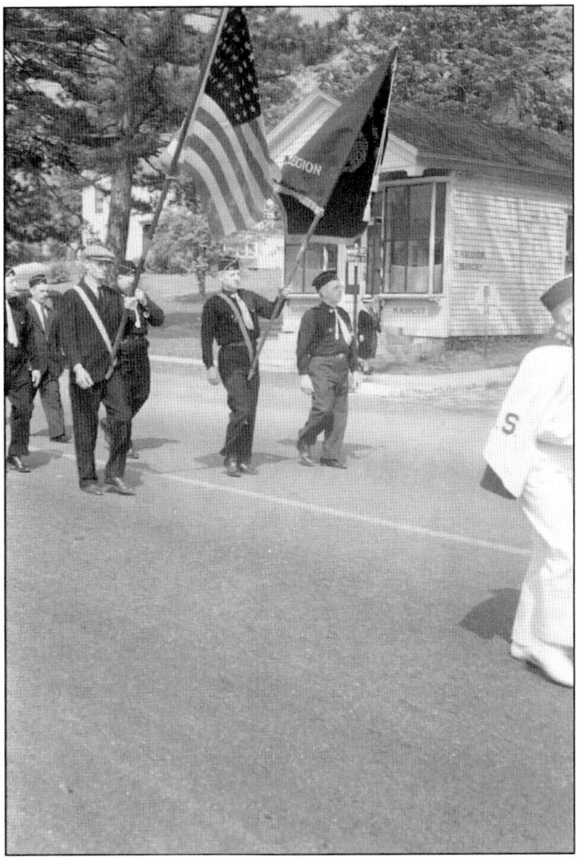

The American Legion Honor Guard carries the colors past the barbershop/antique shop at the west corner of Main and Center Streets in the Memorial Day parade. (Courtesy of Macedon Historical Society.)

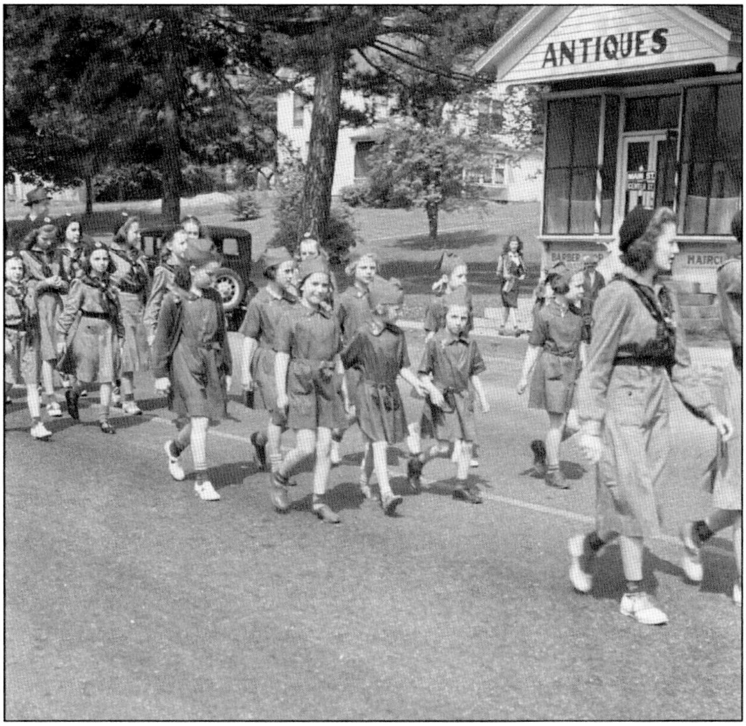

Macedon's Girl Scout troop marches down Main Street in a Memorial Day parade. The building behind the Scouts, on the west corner of Center and Main Streets, is the present-day home of Chapman Insurance. (Courtesy of Macedon Historical Society.)

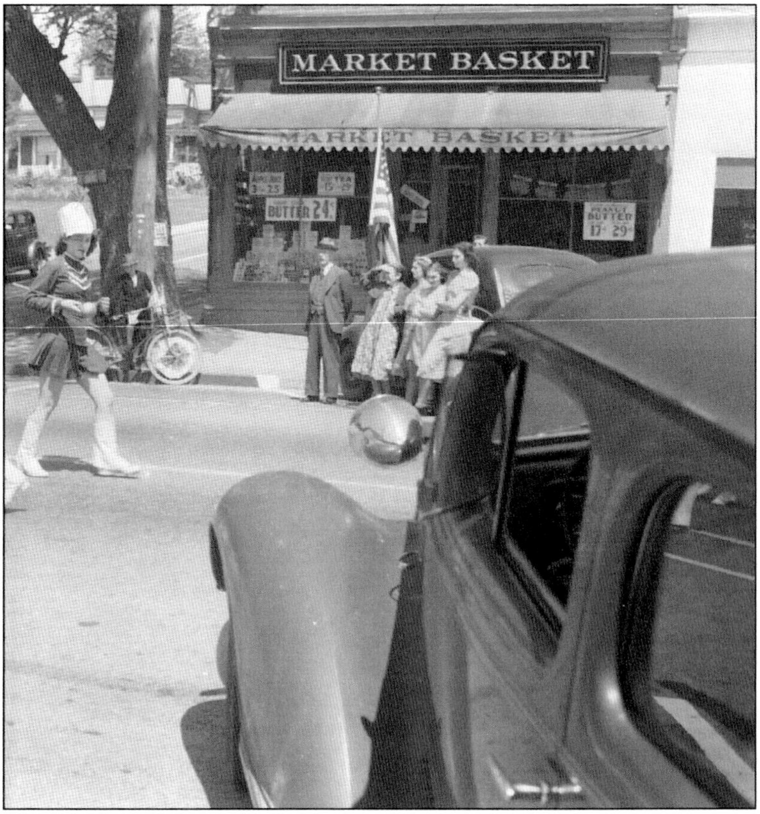

On this 1940s Memorial Day, the drum majorette is leading the parade in front of the Market Basket store, on the east corner of Center and Main Streets. The store was operated by Harriet Carne Fluker. At the turn of the century, it was the Purdy Grocery and Dry Goods store. Today, it is the site of a parking lot. (Courtesy of Macedon Historical Society.)

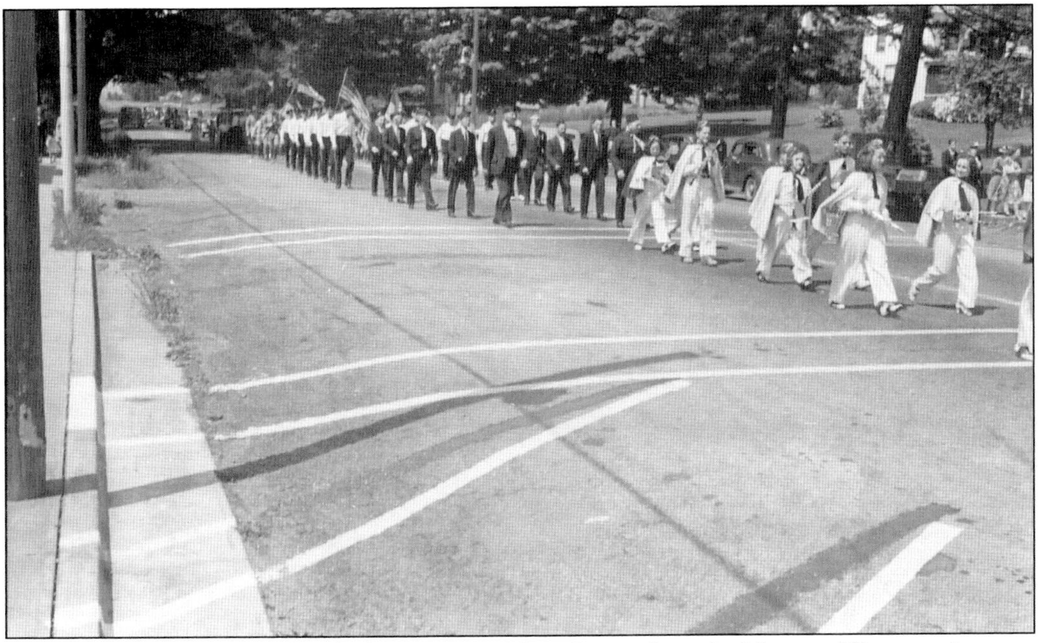

The view in this photograph is looking west up Main Street along the Memorial Day parade route. Members of the band are visible on the right, followed by volunteer firemen and, in the distance, the end of the Memorial Day parade. (Courtesy of Macedon Historical Society.)

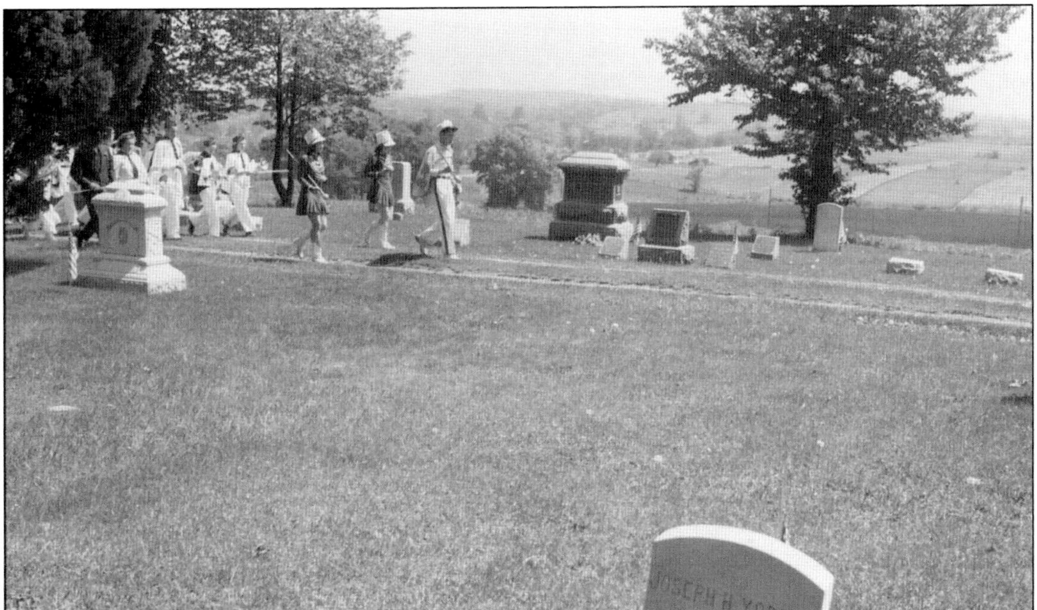

The band arrives on top of Cemetery Hill for the Memorial Day ceremonies. These 1940s parade photographs were taken by W. Charles Jennings, second son of Dr. Cyrus Packard Jennings of Macedon. (Courtesy of Macedon Historical Society.)

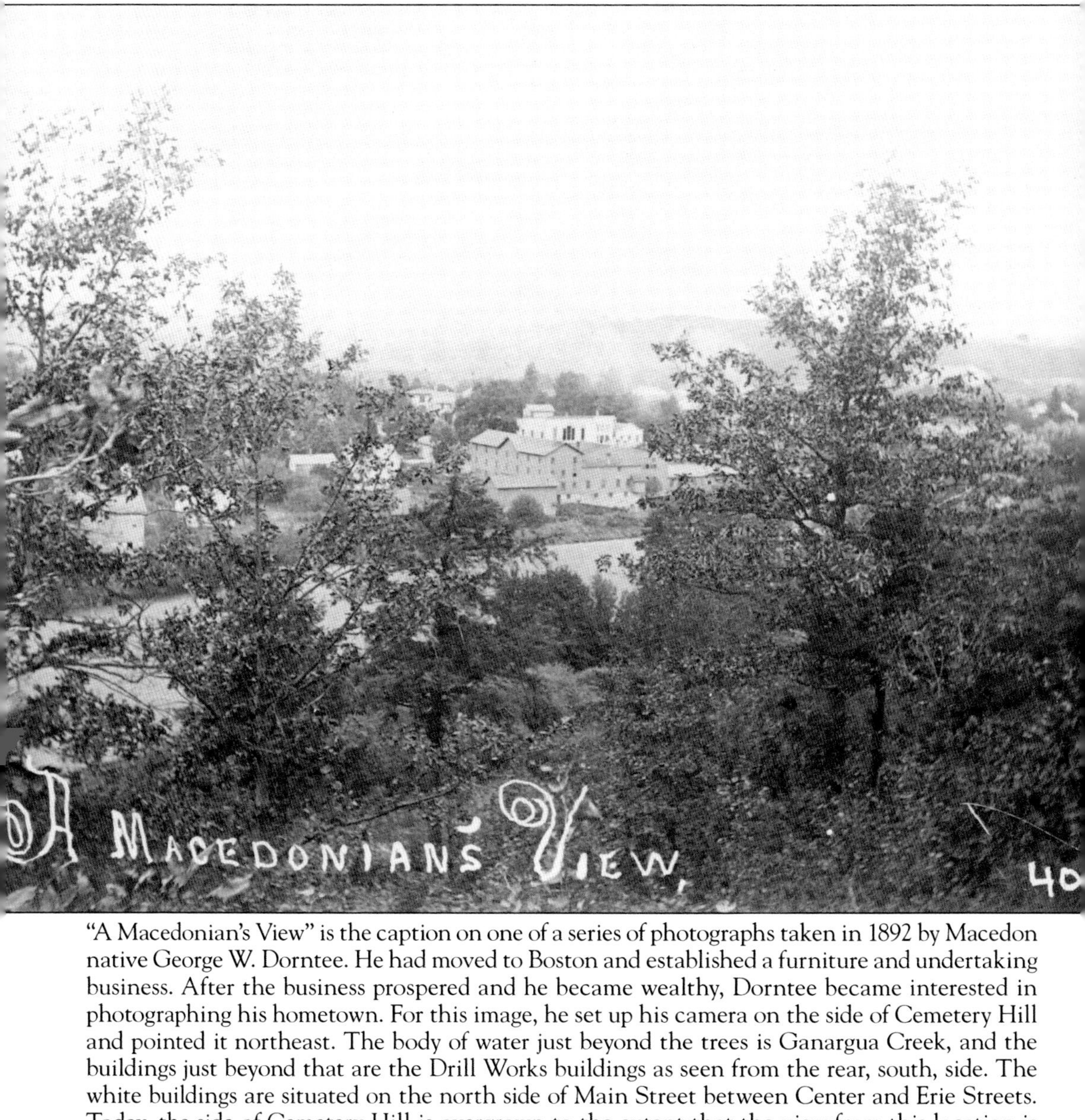

"A Macedonian's View" is the caption on one of a series of photographs taken in 1892 by Macedon native George W. Dorntee. He had moved to Boston and established a furniture and undertaking business. After the business prospered and he became wealthy, Dorntee became interested in photographing his hometown. For this image, he set up his camera on the side of Cemetery Hill and pointed it northeast. The body of water just beyond the trees is Ganargua Creek, and the buildings just beyond that are the Drill Works buildings as seen from the rear, south, side. The white buildings are situated on the north side of Main Street between Center and Erie Streets. Today, the side of Cemetery Hill is overgrown to the extent that the view from this location is almost completely obstructed. Dorntee is buried in St. Patrick's Cemetery, on the east side of the village. (Courtesy of Macedon Historical Society.)

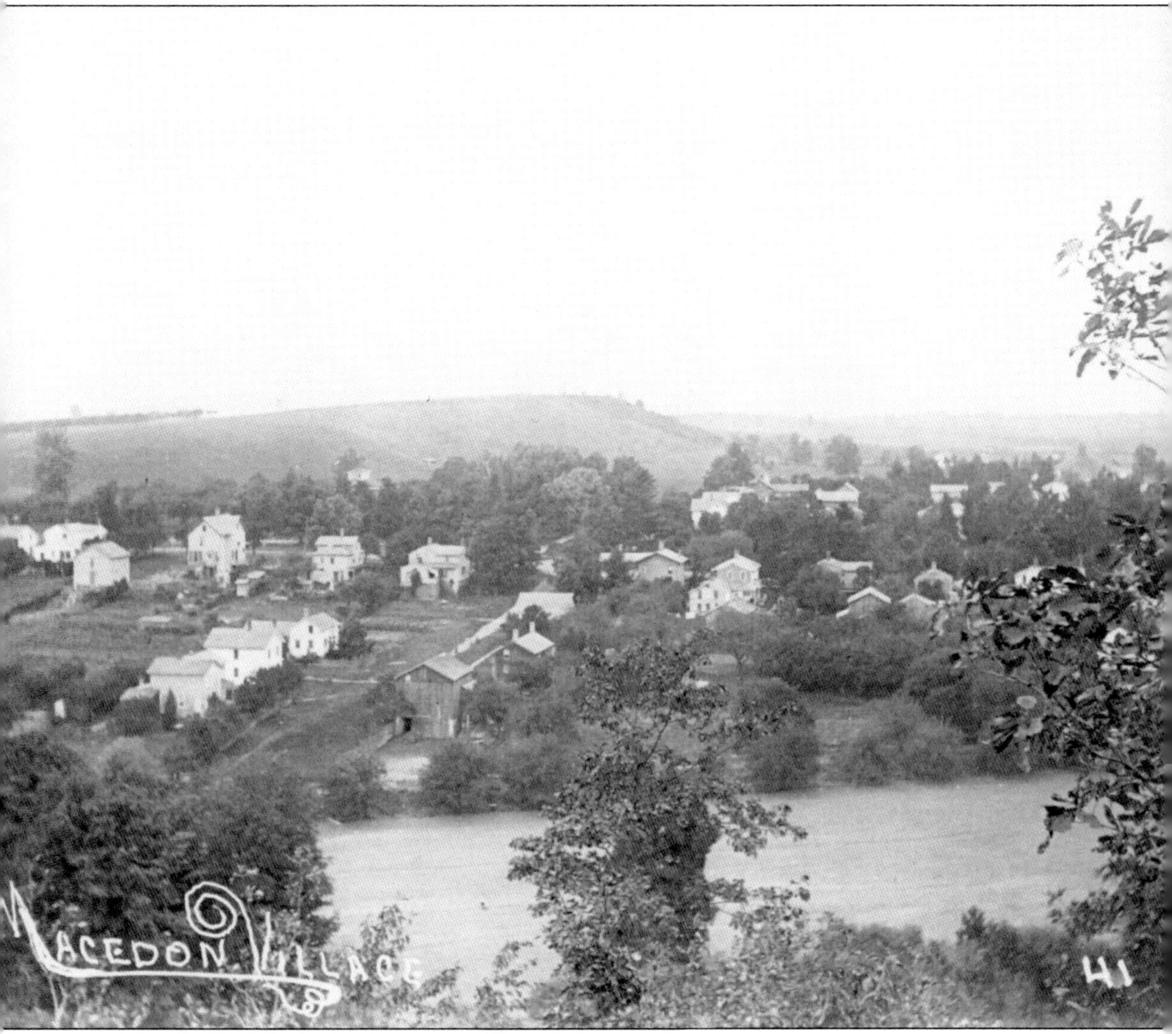

This photograph by George W. Dorntee was taken from a little further west on the north flank of Cemetery Hill. The creek is in the foreground. Part of the raceway is visible through a break in the trees at left center. Houses and buildings on Race Street are clearly visible on the left, and beyond them, houses on West Main. At the time of this photograph, glass plate negatives were still the main photographic technology. An inscription was added to an image by being written directly on the developed glass negative. The inscription was written backwards so that it would appear correctly when the negative was printed. (Courtesy of Macedon Historical Society.)

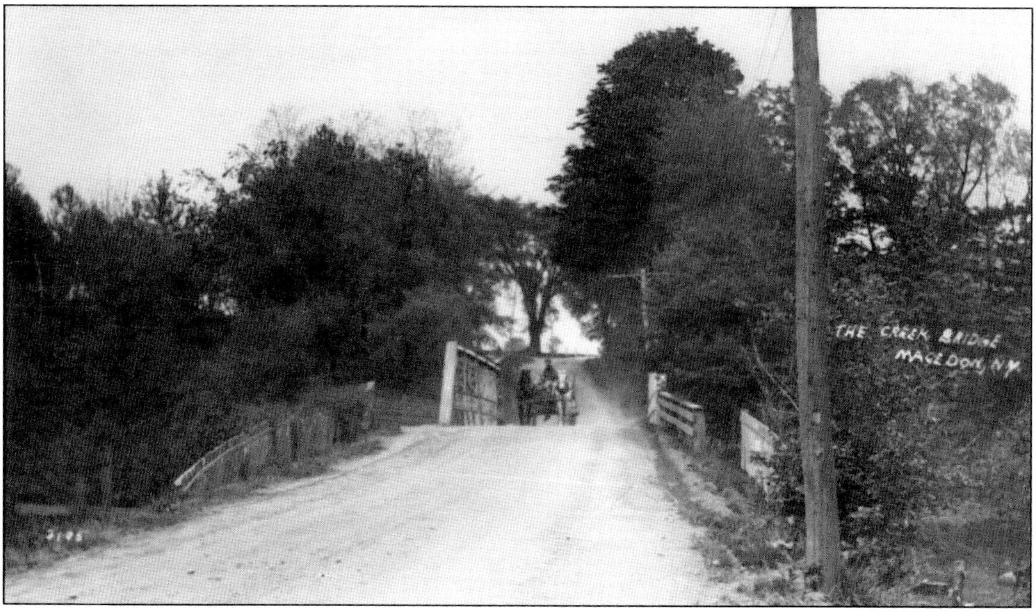

A horse-drawn wagon heads south from downtown Macedon across the old Erie Street Bridge. At the time of this photograph, the road was not yet paved. This thoroughfare, formerly South Erie Street, still exists, but its north end terminates at a parking lot on the south side of Main Street. (Courtesy of Hod Conant.)

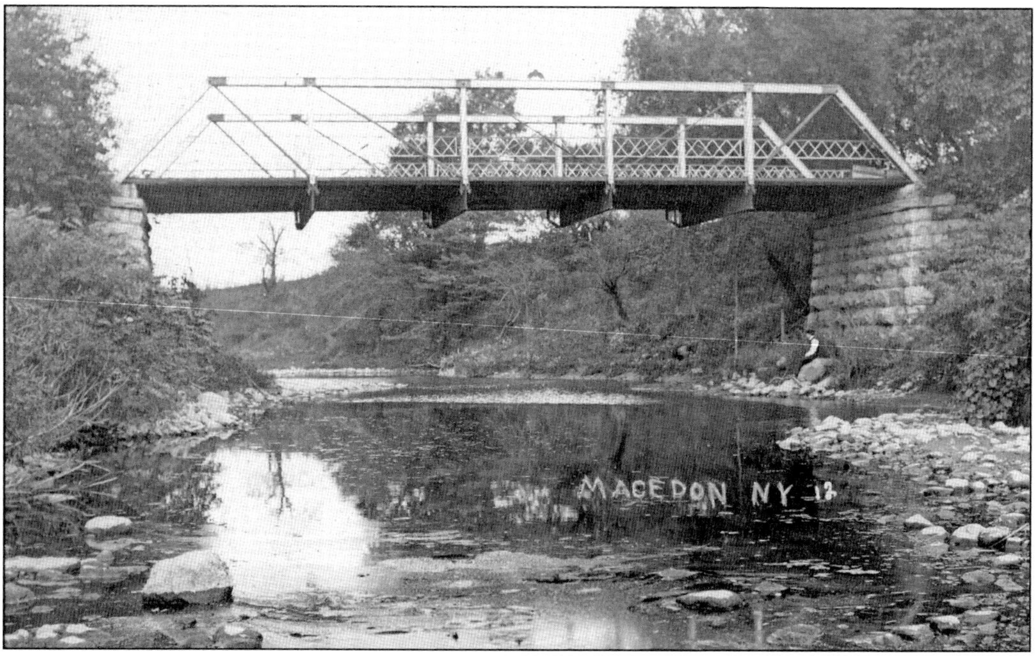

A solitary man sits on a rock underneath the old Erie Street Bridge, contemplating the placid water. This bridge has been replaced by a modern structure a little further east, where it links old Erie Street with a new Erie Street extension that begins at the Route 31/350 stoplight. (Courtesy of Hod Conant.)

This photograph of Macedon's Universalist church was taken around 1900. The church was organized by Rev. Harvey Boughton in 1874. The building still stands on the east side of Center Street. Services were discontinued in 1959, and in 1961, the Town of Macedon bought the building to use as town offices. It was later converted into apartments. The house next door at 5 Center Street was originally the Universalist parsonage. (Courtesy of Hod Conant.)

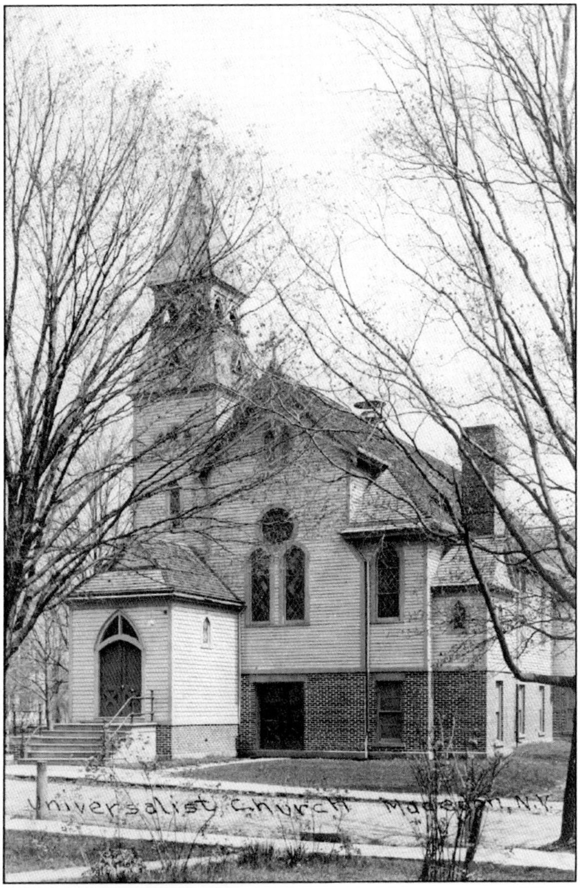

The interior of the Universalist church is seen here at a time when it was still a functioning church. When the congregation dwindled during the 20th century, the building was used as offices for the Town of Macedon and as a public reading room. (Courtesy of Macedon Town Historian.)

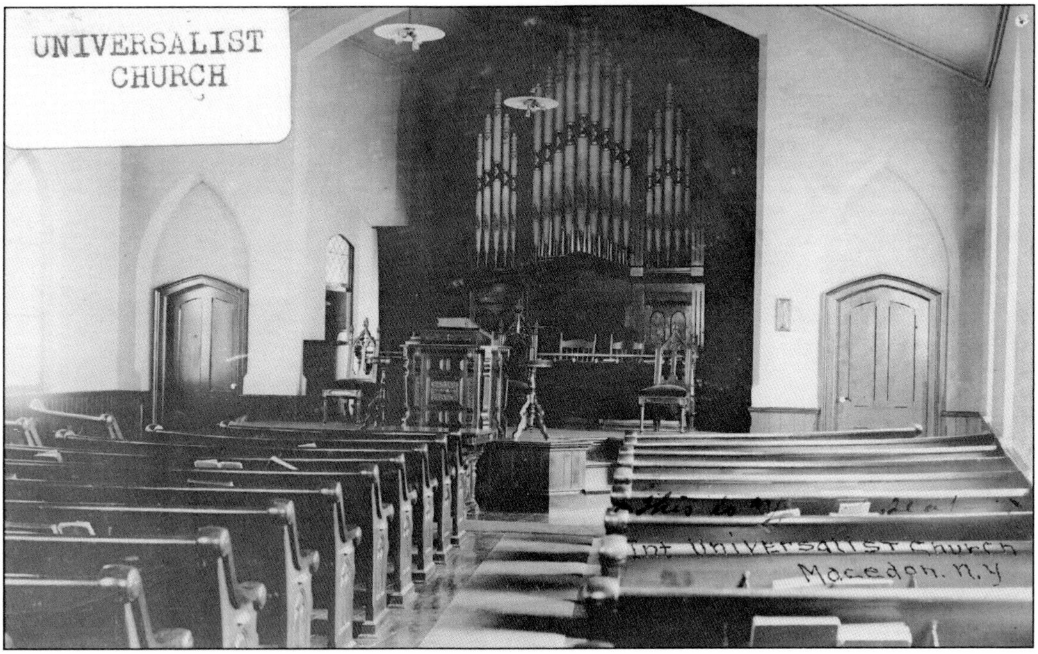

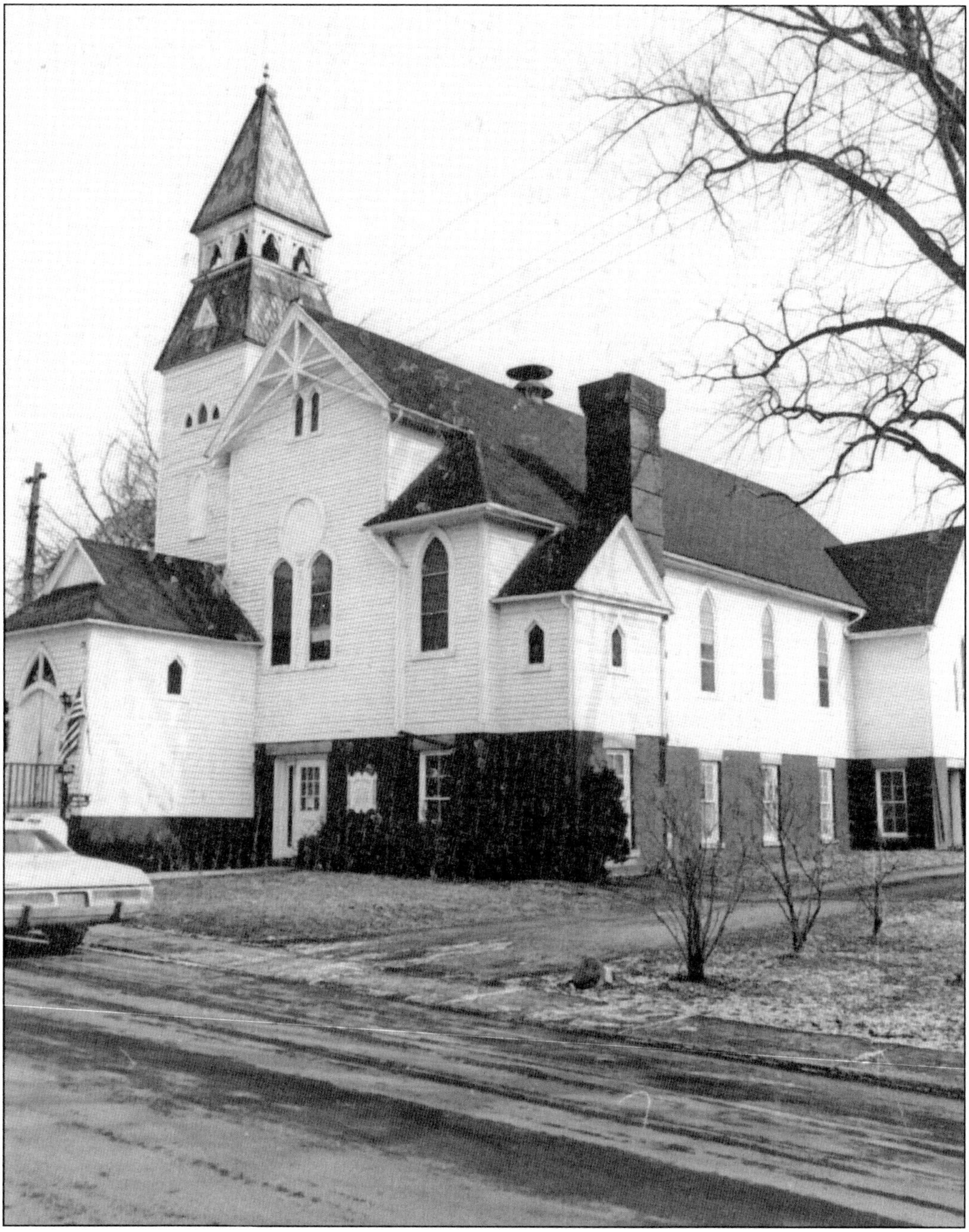

This photograph of the former Universalist church was taken in the 1960s, when it was briefly owned by the Town of Macedon and was used as town offices. It was also home to the Macedon Reading Center, which ultimately became the Macedon Library. When these services outgrew the former church, both functions had to be relocated. Some residents wanted to build a new town office at a city-owned site on O'Neill Road. Eventually, offices were established in the former Alles home at 30 West Main Street. When that facility was destroyed by fire in 2001, the present Town Complex was built, with separate buildings for the library and the town offices. (Courtesy of Macedon Town Historian.)

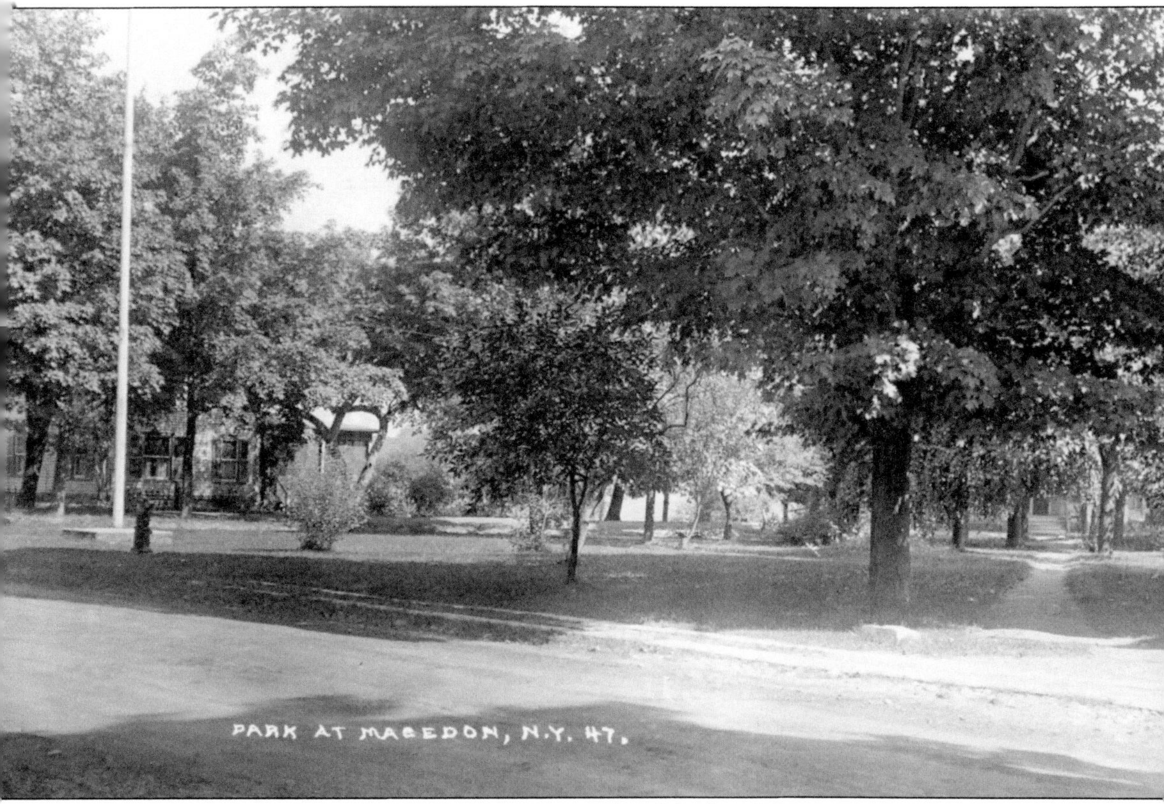

Bickford Park, on the east side of the intersection of Bickford and Center Streets, is seen in this photograph, probably taken in the early 1900s. Lyman Bickford donated the land for the park, which is across Center Street from his former residence and next to the former Universalist church. (Courtesy of Hod Conant.)

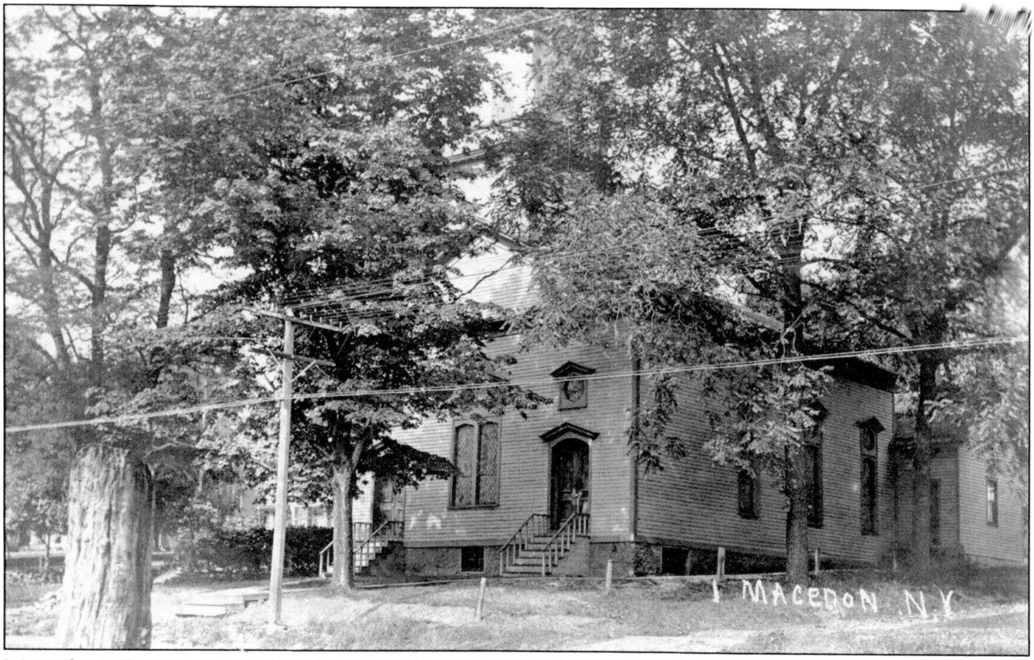

Macedon's First Baptist Church is the oldest church of record in the town of Macedon. The church was organized at the home of settler Lemuel Spear on May 29, 1800. In 1995, a New York State Historic Marker was placed near that spot. In 1820, early settlers built a church at the corner of Quaker and Walworth Roads. The church in these photographs, at 56 West Main Street, replaced that earlier church. Both photographs are from early in the 20th century. The above, earlier photograph shows wooden steps and railings. In the below photograph, some mature trees have been removed. The steps are now concrete, and the railings are metal. (Both, courtesy of Hod Conant.)

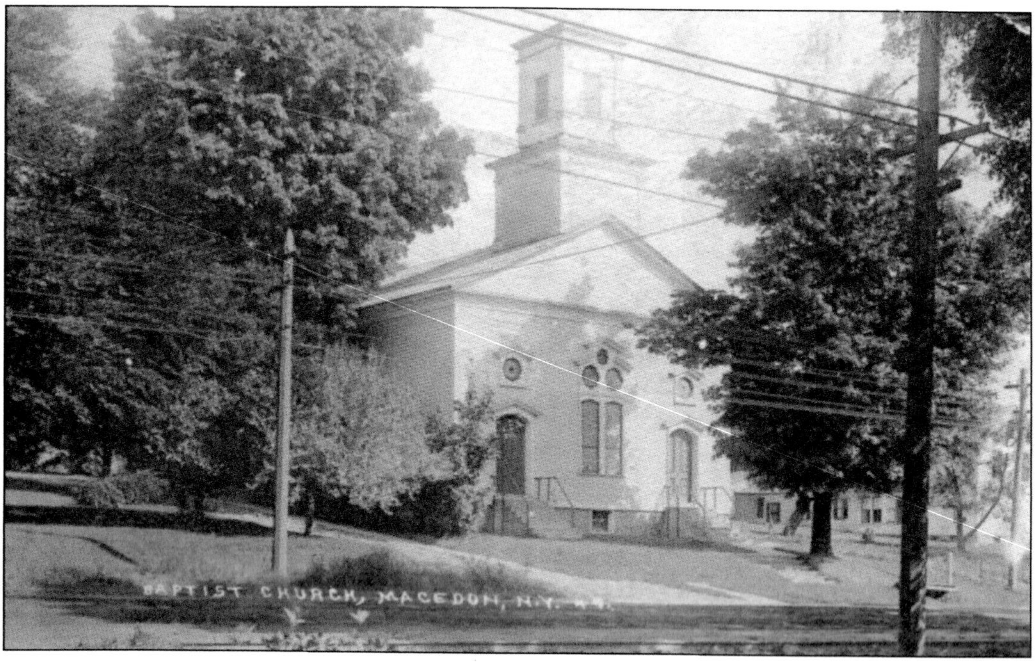

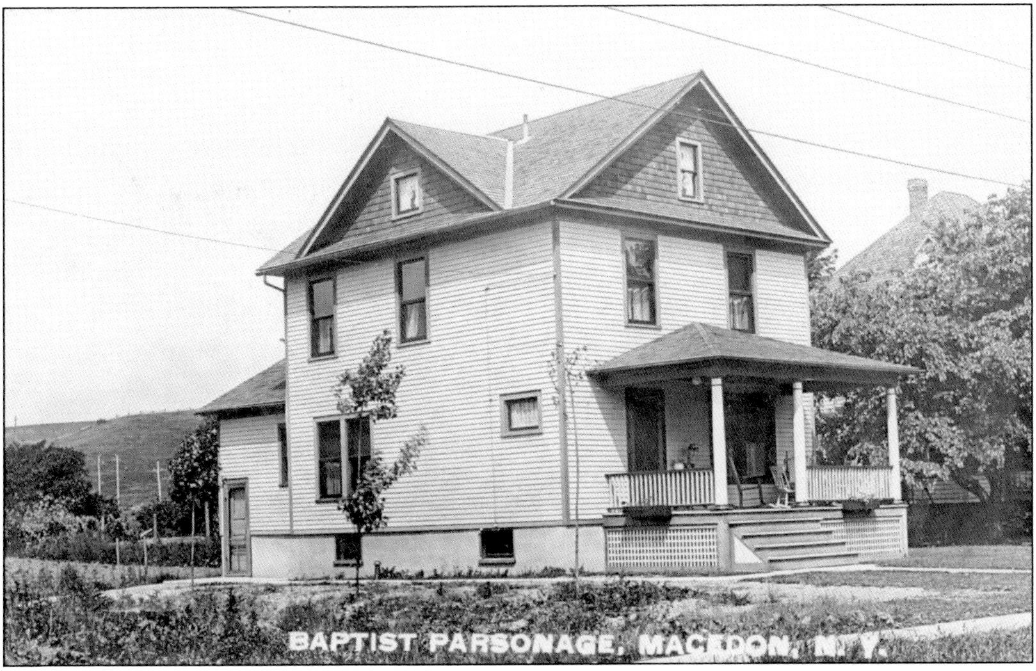

In the early 1900s, this house on School Street (later called Lapham Street) served as a parsonage for the pastor of Macedon's First Baptist Church. In 1974, the congregation bought a house on the south side of the village, on Crest Avenue, and the house pictured here became a private residence. (Courtesy of Hod Conant.)

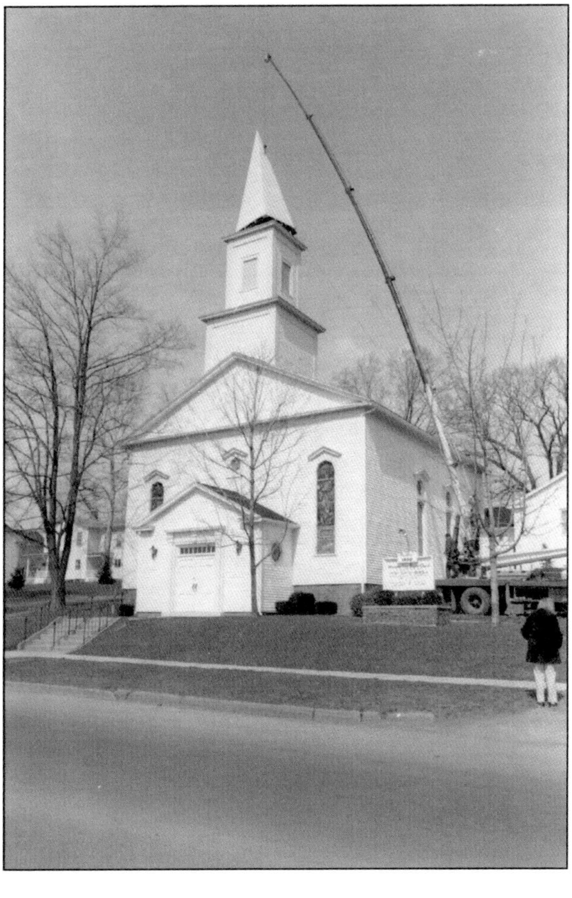

Several decades after the photographs on page 120 were taken, the Macedon First Baptist Church acquired a new front entryway. Here, contractors are placing a spire on top of the steeple. The new spire was dedicated in 1978. (Courtesy of Macedon Town Historian.)

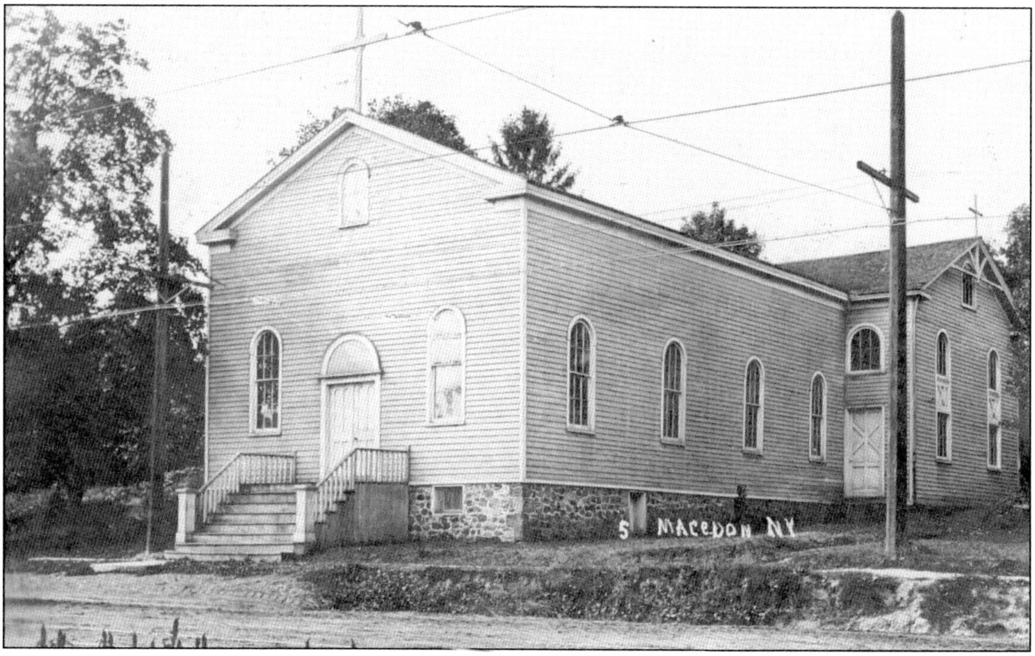

This photo postcard is postmarked 1908. It shows the old St. Patrick's Catholic Church, at 110 Main Street. The church, along with two neighboring houses, was demolished in the 1950s to allow the creation of a new intersection at State Routes 31, 31F, and 350. This building was replaced by the current St. Patrick's Church at 52 Main Street, west of the old location. (Courtesy of Hod Conant.)

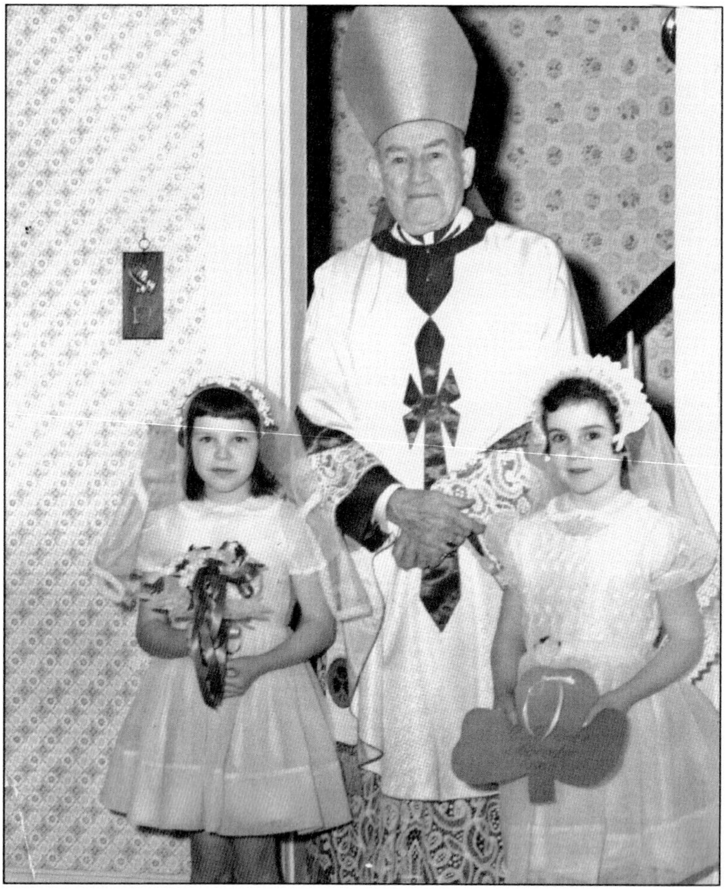

Tina Galens (left) and Mary Murphy pose with Bishop James Kearney of the Rochester Diocese. This photograph was taken sometime in the 1960s. (Courtesy of Macedon Town Historian.)

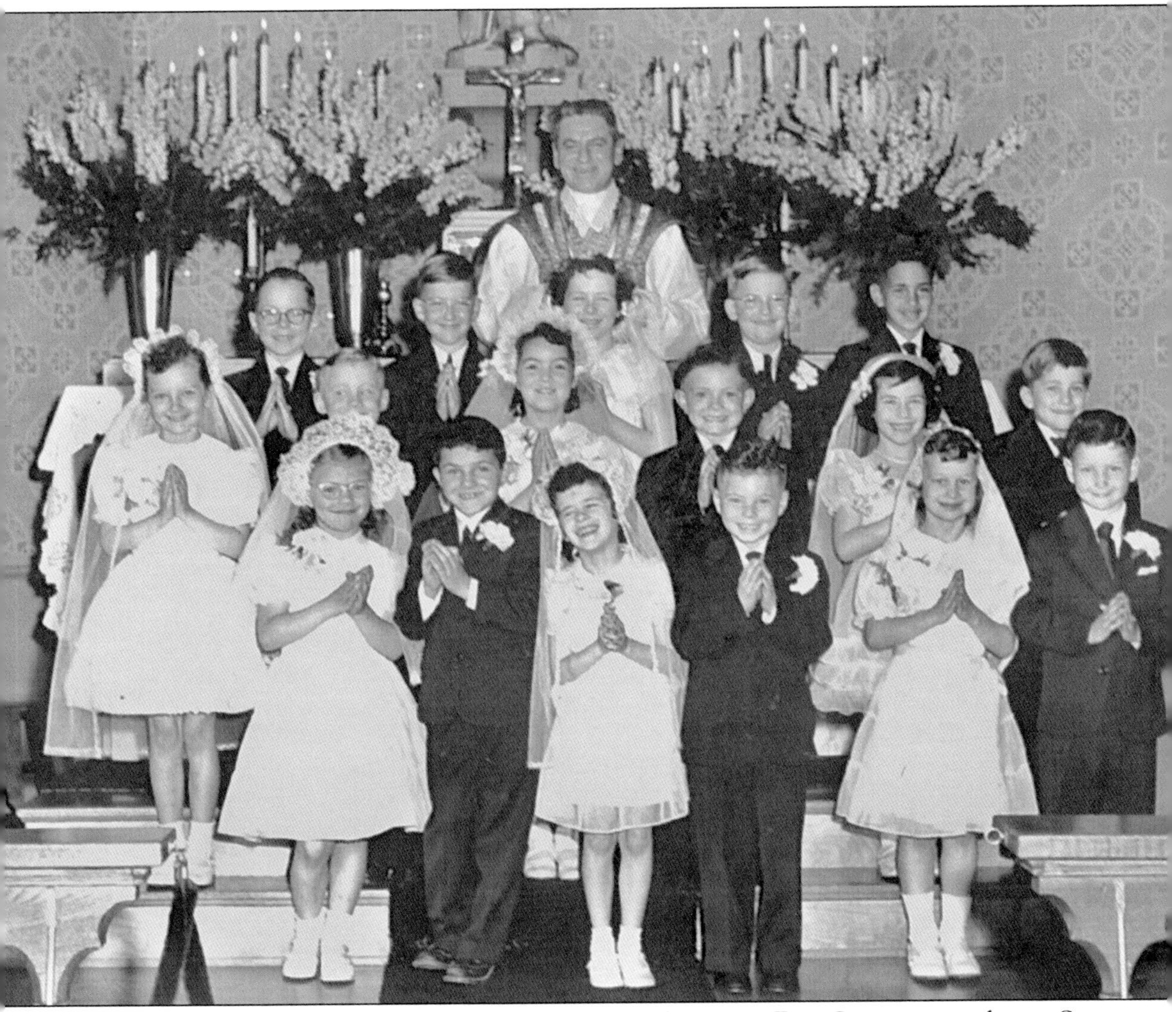

These smiling boys and girls are members of Fr. Bernard Hanna's First Communion class at St. Patrick's Church in 1954. The inscription identifies only one child, Tom Gagliano, who is in the first row, second from the left. (Courtesy of Macedon Town Historian.)

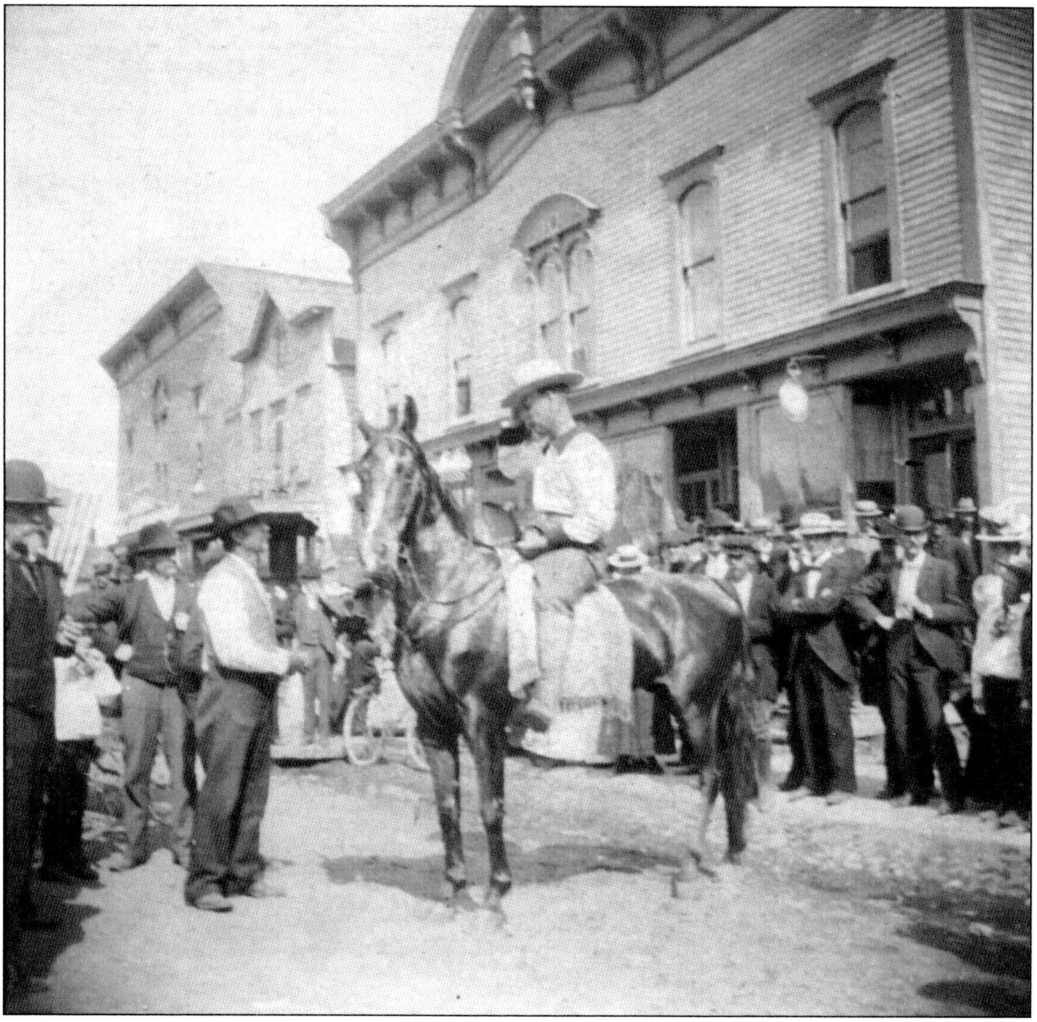

An unidentified man on horseback poses for a crowd of onlookers during the 1898 Macedon Fourth of July celebration. The crowd is gathered in front of 99 Main Street, on the south side of the street. Many of the parade participants rode horses or traveled on horse-drawn vehicles. At the turn of the century, Independence Day was observed as a major holiday by the entire community, with parades, fireworks, picnics, and reenactments of historic events. (Courtesy of Macedon Town Historian.)

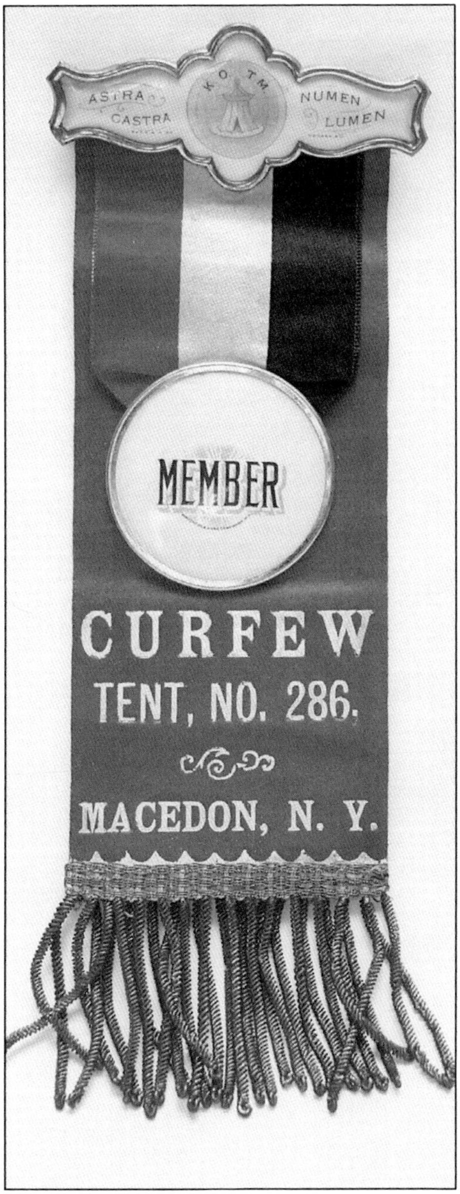

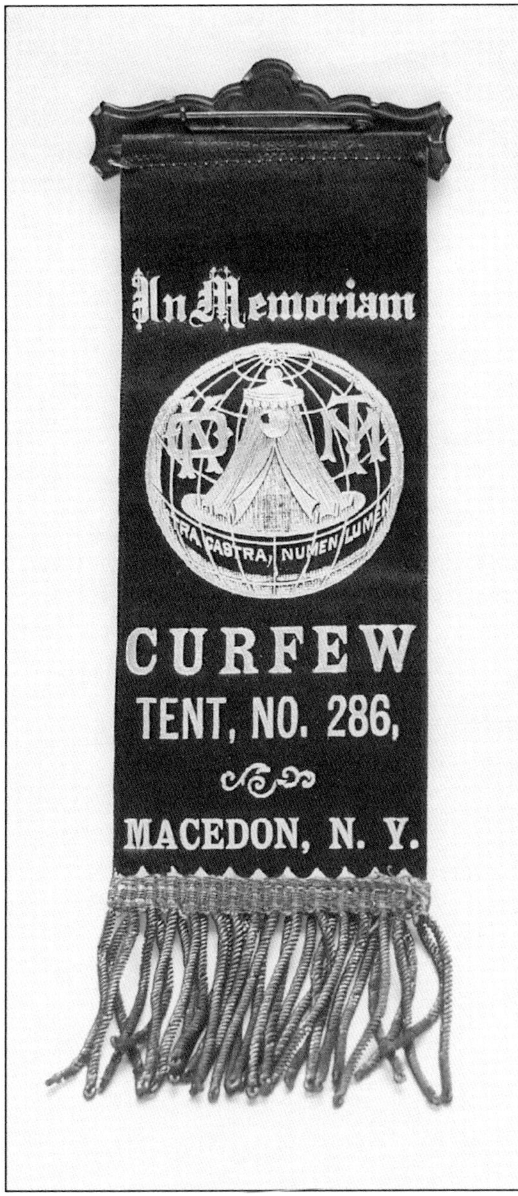

Pictured here are the front and rear views of a Macedon fraternal badge. The organization is the Knights of the Maccabees, a national fraternal lodge founded in 1878. By 1896, there were more than 200,000 members. The fraternity was said to have been inspired by a historic account of a Jewish rebellion that reconsecrated the Temple of Jerusalem. The Maccabees lodges were called "tents," a reference to the biblical Maccabees' belief that their members should not live in houses. The Latin motto on the enameled clasp at the top of the badge is *Astra castra, Numen lumen*, which translates to "the stars my camp, the deity my light." On the front of the badge, the enameled "Member" medallion is centered on a tricolor ribbon. The reverse side features an embroidered lodge insignia. The badge is about eight inches long and has a gilt fringe at the bottom. In the days before radio, television, or computers, fraternal organizations were an important component of civic activity. Villages like Macedon often had several lodges, each with extensive social calendars. (Both, courtesy of Macedon Town Historian.)

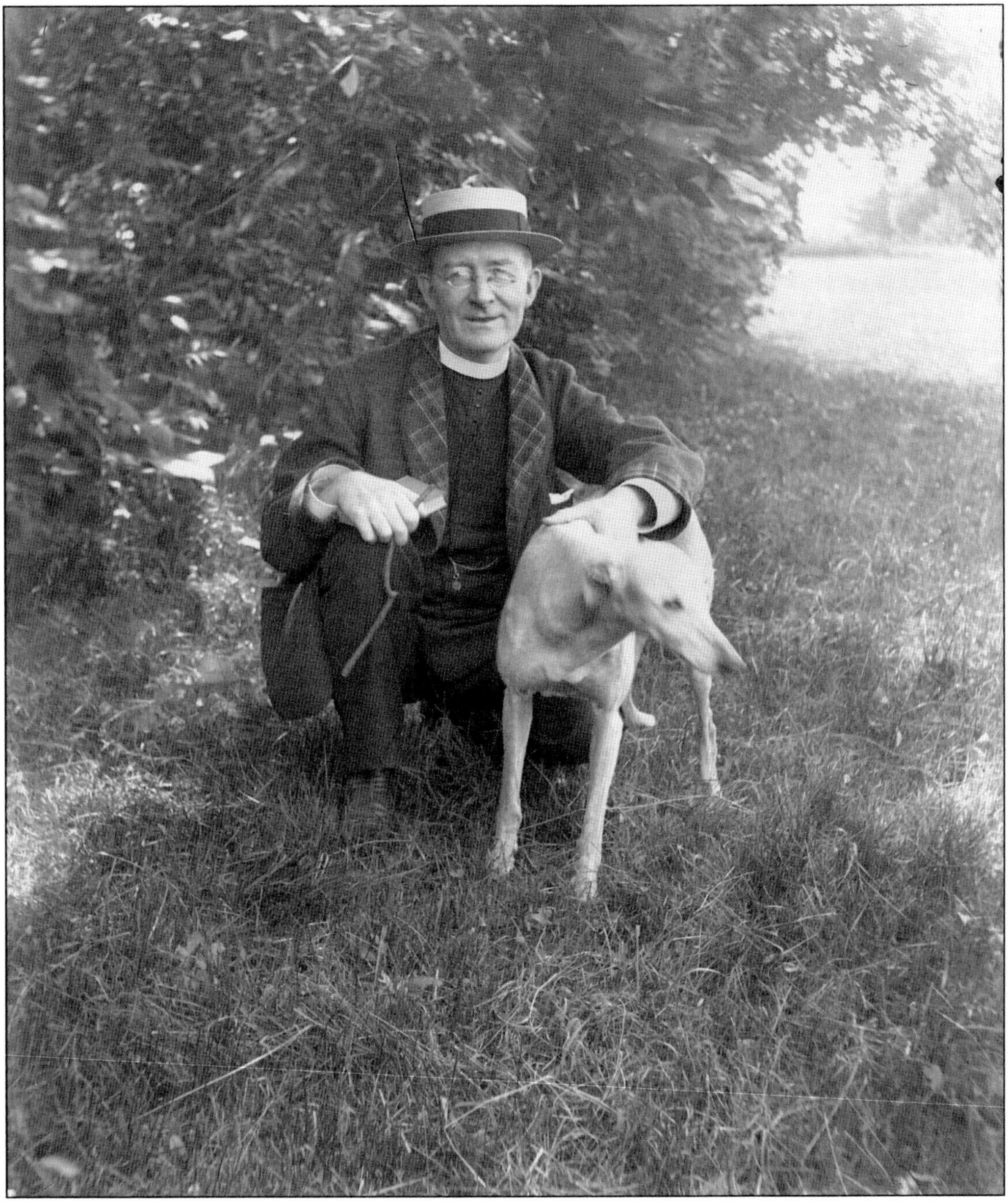

Fr. Michael A.F. Holmes, the first resident pastor of Macedon's St. Patrick's Church, poses with his dog. Father Holmes was born in 1857, ordained in 1880, and served in Macedon for 45 years. At the time of this photograph, the church was at 110 Main Street. Holmes's residence, at 25 Main Street, is now a private home. (Courtesy of Marlene Zimmer LeMoyne.)

Preserving Macedon's Heritage

The following statement acknowledging local organizations that help preserve Macedon's unique heritage was provided by June Hamell, Macedon's town historian: "Macedon has dedicated citizens who recognize the importance of their history. Some of those citizens have their own historic collections, which they willingly shared for this book. Others are members of organizations that collect items and study history. The Macedon Historical Society, located in the Macedon Academy Building in Macedon Center, is one such organization. There, you will find not only a historic building but a collection of items, ledgers, books, scrapbooks, and papers that shows the path that Macedon has traveled to this day. The Macedon Public Library houses the Town of Macedon Historian's Office and the Bullis Collection, a Victorian-era collection of thousands of books placed in the library's care by the last descendant of a local family. The library also is the meeting place of the Macedon Memory Keepers, who record interviews of local citizenry, transcribe portions of those interviews, and create a recording with written notes and photographs that can be circulated in the Pioneer Library System. The village historian works from her home and provides walking tours of the village and talks on historic figures from Macedon. The Macedon Trails group maintains the local trails, provides signage, and promotes the canal trails as a community resource. All of these people and organizations collaborate and work together to promote our history in the town of Macedon."